Studying the
Historical Jesus

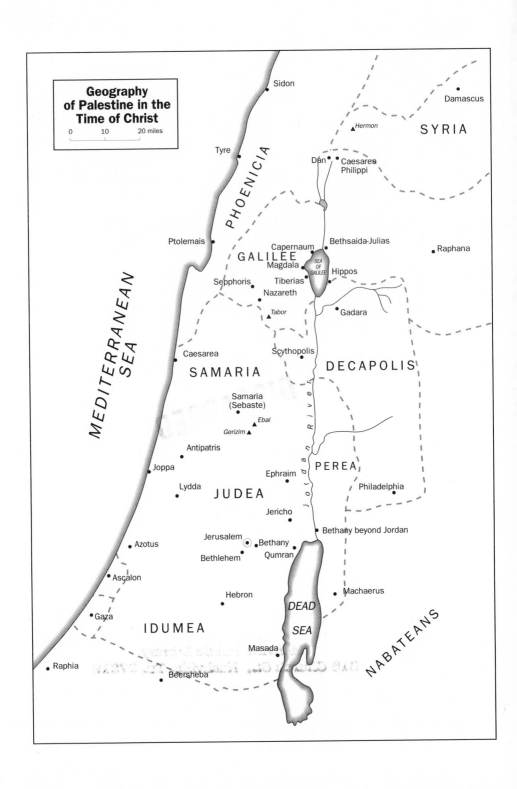

**Geography
of Palestine in the
Time of Christ**

0   10   20 miles

MEDITERRANEAN SEA

Sidon

Damascus

Hermon

SYRIA

Tyre

Dan

Caesarea
Philippi

PHOENICIA

Ptolemais

Capernaum

Bethsaida-Julias

Raphana

GALILEE

Magdala

SEA
OF
GALILEE

Hippos

Sepphoris

Tiberias

Nazareth

Tabor

Gadara

Caesarea

Scythopolis

DECAPOLIS

SAMARIA

Samaria
(Sebaste)

Ebal

Gerizim

Jordan River

Antipatris

Joppa

Ephraim

PEREA

Lydda

JUDEA

Philadelphia

Jericho

Jerusalem

Bethany

Bethany beyond Jordan

Bethlehem

Qumran

Azotus

Ascalon

Machaerus

Hebron

DEAD
SEA

Gaza

NABATEANS

IDUMEA

Masada

Raphia

Beersheba

Studying the Historical Jesus

A Guide to Sources and Methods

Darrell L. Bock

Baker Academic
A Division of Baker Book House Co
Grand Rapids, Michigan 49516

APOLLOS

©2002 by Darrell L. Bock

Published by Baker Academic
a division of Baker Book House Company
P.O. Box 6287, Grand Rapids, MI 49516-6287

and

Apollos (an imprint of Inter-Varsity Press)
38 De Montfort Street
Leicester LE1 7GP England
email: ivp@uccf.org.uk
web site: www.ivpbooks.com

Printed in the United States of America

Library of Congress Cataloging-in-Publication Data

Bock, Darrell L.
　　Studying the historical Jesus : a guide to sources and methods / Darrell L. Bock.
　　　　p.　　cm.
　　Includes bibliographical references and indexes.
　　ISBN 0-8010-2451-X (pbk.)
　　1. Jesus Christ—Historicity—Study and teaching. 2. Jesus Christ—Biography—Study and teaching. I. Title.
　　BT303.2 .B53　　2002
　　232.9′08′071—dc21　　　　　　　　　　　　　　　　　　　2002001510

British Library Cataloguing in Publication Data
A catalogue record for this book is available from the British Library.
Apollos ISBN 0-85111-273-0

For information about Baker Academic, visit our web site:
www.bakeracademic.com

Contents

Illustrations

Maps

Tables and Graphs

Preface

As a student of the Gospels who has long appreciated what detailed study of Jesus can yield, I have yearned to write such a book for my students. What I have desired is a work that briefly goes over the background to the Gospels and the critical study of the Gospels that reflects both the value and limitations of these elements. I wanted to supply a basic introduction to these areas that was brief enough for students to digest and that had enough guidance for students to encourage further independent study. Only time will tell if I have succeeded. Much of the material here has been used in one form or another in classes on New Testament Introduction and on Jesus, as well as in a class I teach with my colleague W. Hall Harris on introduction to exegesis in Gospel narrative. I submit the material knowing that it has helped many students get an initial grasp on many controversial themes associated with the study of the Gospels. They have urged me to make it more widely available. This work is intentionally not technical. It is a primer. My audience is the beginning student of the Gospels who desires to start to dig deeper into its depths.

Special thanks go to Baker Book House: to Jim Weaver, who originally pursued the development of the work; to Jim Kinney, who shepherded it through to its current configuration; and to Wells Turner, who edited it with care and patience. In addition, thanks go particularly to three students who read the manuscript with care, making comments on how it would be received: Greg Herrick, Carol Kahil, and especially Jim Samra, who read through it all and commented in detail. Thanks to Katie Gay, my administrative assistant, for deciphering my handwriting and turning it into typescript. Finally, I would like to thank my daughter, Elisa Bock, who is training at Northwestern's Me-

9

dill School of Journalism to become an editor. She also read through the whole with an editor's eye, helping me immensely with expression. To my wife, Sally, and my other children, Lara and Stephen, goes gratitude for understanding why another "few" hours were required at my Mac.

I dedicate this work to students at Dallas Theological Seminary and Talbot Theological Seminary, whose need created the desire to write this work and whose response has been so gracious. To all of them go my wishes for a fruitful walk with the Lord and refreshing times of study and growth gained from a careful interaction with the Gospels.

Darrell L. Bock

Abbreviations

Bibliographic

Ag. Apion	Josephus, *Against Apion*
Ant.	Josephus, *Jewish Antiquities*
BECNT	Baker Exegetical Commentary on the New Testament
Ber.	tractate *Berakot*
ConBNT	Coniectanea biblica, New Testament
CD	Damascus Document
DJG	*Dictionary of Jesus and the Gospels,* ed. Joel B. Green et al. (Downers Grove, Ill.: InterVarsity, 1992)
Eccl. Hist.	Eusebius, *Ecclesiastical History*
Embassy	Philo, *On the Embassy to Gaius*
Good Person	Philo, *That Every Good Person Is Free*
JB	Jerusalem Bible
JETS	*Journal of the Evangelical Theological Society*
JSNT	*Journal for the Study of the New Testament*
JSNTSup	Journal for the Study of the New Testament: Supplement Series
NICNT	New International Commentary on the New Testament
NIV	New International Version
NRSV	New Revised Standard Version
Sanh.	tractate *Sanhedrin*
SBL	Society of Biblical Literature
War	Josephus, *Jewish War*
WUNT	Wissenschaftliche Untersuchungen zum Neuen Testament
ZNW	*Zeitschrift für die neutestamentliche Wissenschaft und die Kunde der älteren Kirche*

Scripture

Old Testament

Gen.	Genesis	Neh.	Nehemiah	Hos.	Hosea
Exod.	Exodus	Esth.	Esther	Joel	Joel
Lev.	Leviticus	Job	Job	Amos	Amos
Num.	Numbers	Ps.	Psalms	Obad.	Obadiah
Deut.	Deuteronomy	Prov.	Proverbs	Jon.	Jonah
Josh.	Joshua	Eccles.	Ecclesiastes	Mic.	Micah
Judg.	Judges	Song	Song of Songs	Nah.	Nahum
Ruth	Ruth	Isa.	Isaiah	Hab.	Habakkuk
1–2 Sam.	1–2 Samuel	Jer.	Jeremiah	Zeph.	Zephaniah
1–2 Kings	1–2 Kings	Lam.	Lamentations	Hag.	Haggai
1–2 Chron.	1–2 Chronicles	Ezek.	Ezekiel	Zech.	Zechariah
Ezra	Ezra	Dan.	Daniel	Mal.	Malachi

Old Testament Apocrypha

1–4 Macc.	1–4 Maccabees
Sirach	Wisdom of Jesus Son of Sirach
Wisdom	Wisdom of Solomon

New Testament

Matt.	Matthew	Gal.	Galatians	Philem.	Philemon
Mark	Mark	Eph.	Ephesians	Heb.	Hebrews
Luke	Luke	Phil.	Philippians	James	James
John	John	Col.	Colossians	1–2 Pet.	1–2 Peter
Acts	Acts	1–2 Thess.	1–2 Thessalonians	1–3 John	1–3 John
Rom.	Romans	1–2 Tim.	1–2 Timothy	Jude	Jude
1–2 Cor.	1–2 Corinthians	Titus	Titus	Rev.	Revelation

Introduction

Sources of Our Knowledge

The evangelists, I have argued, did not write for specific churches they knew or knew about, not even for a very large number of such churches. Rather drawing on their experience and knowledge of several or many specific churches, they wrote *for any and every church* to which their Gospels might circulate. No more than almost any other author, at their time or at most other periods, could they know which specific readers and hearers their work would reach. Thus, to ask, for example, if Luke knew whether there were any Christian churches in Gaul at the time when he wrote, and, supposing he knew there were, if he intended to address them in his Gospel, is to ask altogether the wrong sort of question. His intended audience was an *open category*—any and every church to which his Gospel might circulate—not a specified audience in which he had consciously either to include churches in Gaul or not.[1]

Appreciating the Cultural Context of the Gospels

It is hard to know if the Gospel writers themselves were aware of the ultimate impact their writings about Jesus would produce. If they had known the impact their works would come to have, they would likely have been amazed at how God has used their writings. Their goal was to witness to Jesus and strengthen the new communities formed around him. They wrote about the Jesus they knew, the Jesus they preached, and the Jesus others needed to know. They succeeded far be-

1. Richard Bauckham, "For Whom Were Gospels Written," in *The Gospels for All Christians: Rethinking the Gospel Audiences*, ed. Richard Bauckham (Grand Rapids: Eerdmans, 1998), 46.

yond what they likely intended. This is why studying Jesus as presented in these four Gospels is so profitable. The impact these Gospels have had on the world can hardly be exaggerated. Whatever skeptical criticism of the Bible has tried to do with these Gospels, there is no denying the importance of these four treatments of Jesus in the history of thought. It is a fact of history that whoever were the original recipients of these Gospels, the eventual audience has extended far beyond those limits, making these Gospels "classic" texts in every sense of that term.

Many details about the original audiences of the Gospels are unclear. A consensus, which the opening citation challenges, is the idea that the Gospels were written for one community or set of local communities with the stories told in such a way that the account would be relevant to that specific community. That view is slowly being rejected. Rather, the Gospel writers wrote for the church at large and ultimately the world at large to which these churches would witness. Although their work might have begun in a given community, the point of the exercise was to get the word out about Jesus and spread it far and wide through what one author called "the holy Internet."[2]

The implication of their intention to address the church at large is that what we do not know about the specifics of each Gospel's original setting has little impact on our appreciation of the message of these Gospels. Intimate knowledge of the original community to which each Gospel was addressed is not a requirement for understanding the key elements of a Gospel's message, though where such can be determined, they help us to grasp a Gospel's message more precisely. What we do need to appreciate is the general culture in which these works were written, as well as the culture in which Jesus lived. This will help to explain why the focus of this book and the scriptural volume to follow will be on Jewish backgrounds.[3] For Jesus was culturally, religiously, and ethnically a Jew. Such cultural appreciation requires that one become aware of the sources that illumine the study of Jesus, as well as the history and cultural makeup of the first-century society in which Jesus lived and moved. Thus this introductory chapter has two goals: (1) to provide an overview of the most basic elements of what we know about the four Gospels and (2) to trace the sources—biblical and extrabiblical—that give us insight into what the Gospels say about Jesus. Subsequent chapters in part 1 treat issues of the extrabiblical evidence for Jesus' existence, dating the basic outline of his ministry, as well as

2. Michael B. Thompson, "The Holy Internet: Communication between Churches in the First Christian Generation," in ibid., 49–70.

3. Darrell L. Bock, *Jesus according to Scripture* (Grand Rapids: Baker Academic, forthcoming).

the political and sociocultural history that informs his message and ministry. Then part 2 discusses the various methods scholars use to read and evaluate the Gospels and their message. In this section we will see a constant tension between those who have read the Gospels skeptically to assess their "true" historical validity (often excluding huge portions of the material in the process) and those who have read them carefully to see if the portrait of Jesus in the Gospels can be unified (debating here and there how those details best hold together). The perspective of these volumes is that the second approach is a more fruitful way to read the text, for reasons I hope to make clear. Regardless of the view taken, however, no one can debate the significance these four Gospels have had for major segments of Western society, as well as large portions of the world.

We turn first to the sources that inform our study of Jesus and the Gospels, especially the Old Testament and the Gospels themselves. Appreciating the movement of the Old Testament toward a hope of deliverance and the structure of each Gospel, as well as understanding what we know and do not know about their origin, enhance our ability to interact with each Gospel's message. We first examine the sources that predate his ministry or fall in a time contemporary with it. Then we survey the structure, themes, authorship, date, and setting of each of the four Gospels. In a subsequent volume, I fill out the details of this overview and of the Gospels' contents. At the end of this chapter, I consider the extrabiblical resources that fall after the time of Jesus but that may also help us understand the immediate world of the Gospels.

Sources Predating or Contemporary with Jesus' Ministry

Numerous sources contribute to our understanding of the first-century world of Judaism, and numerous other materials trace the history of Judaism in the period following the life of Jesus.[4] These sources tell us what we know about the world of Jesus, the history of Judaism, Jew-

4. Craig A. Evans (*Noncanonical Writings and New Testament Interpretation* [Peabody, Mass.: Hendrickson, 1992]) gives a full survey of the nature of these sources. My notes about these sources cite volumes that are translated into English and readily accessible. More scholarly sources can be found by consulting the bibliography in Evans's work. A solid, more complete introductory overview to this literature and to the Judaism of this period is found in James C. VanderKam, *An Introduction to Early Judaism* (Grand Rapids: Eerdmans, 2000). For a concise bibliography of key Jewish intertestamental and rabbinic literature, see David W. Chapman and Andreas J. Köstenberger, "Jewish Intertestamental and Early Rabbinic Literature: An Annotated Bibliographic Resource," *JETS* 43 (2000): 577–618.

ish religious practice, the customs of everyday Jewish life, and the impact on Israel of Roman occupation and that of other nations before them. It is important to divide these sources into various periods to avoid anachronism in their study and use. Thus I group together those sources that predominantly predate or are contemporary with the arrival of Jesus and those that follow him. I save the sources that follow Jesus for after the summary of the Gospel material itself. My goal is simply to note what these sources are, where they can be located and referenced, and what they contribute to our study of Jesus and his world.

The Old Testament, or the Hebrew Scriptures

The major elements of Israel's story and history emerge from what would have been known in Jesus' time simply as the Scriptures, what we call today the *Old Testament*, or the Hebrew Scriptures.[5] This sacred text for both Judaism and Christianity traces the formation of the nation, their sense of vocation, and the instruction of practices for their worship offered in faithfulness to God. This body of material was known as "the law of Moses, the Prophets and the Psalms" (Luke 24:44 NIV) or "the Law, the Prophecies, and the rest of the books" (Sirach, prologue, lines 8–10 NRSV), or "the book of Moses [and the words of the] prophets and of David [and the annals] [of eac]h generation" (4QMMT, lines 95–96, also known as 4Q397, frags. 7–8, lines 10–11).[6] Central to the Old Testament are themes of hope and promise that look to a day when God's justice will be fully realized through an age, a central figure of peace, and a deliverance he will one day bring. Much of Jesus' story has rich roots

5. The best critical version of the Masoretic text is *Biblia Hebraica Stuttgartensia*, ed. K. Elliger and W. Rudolph (Stuttgart: Deutsche Bibelgesellschaft, 1977). For standard abbreviations of the Old Testament books, see *The SBL Handbook of Style for Ancient Near Eastern, Biblical, and Early Christian Studies*, ed. Patrick H. Alexander et al. (Peabody, Mass.: Hendrickson, 1999), 73. One should also mention here the targums, which are for the most part later Aramaic translations of these Old Testament texts. Access to this material is more difficult than the other sources cited in this chapter. Various ancient editions of the targums exist. For details one can check the bibliographies in Evans, *Noncanonical Writings*, 97–113. Such works are usually cited by name, either that of the book translated (like *Targum Job*) or its technical rabbinic name (like *Pseudo-Jonathan* or *Onkelos*, which became the official targum of the rabbis centuries later). For widely used abbreviations of some of the more common texts, see *SBL Handbook*, 80. For introductory details on these targumic texts, see Ernst Würthwein, *The Text of the Old Testament*, trans. Erroll F. Rhodes (Grand Rapids: Eerdmans, 1979), 75–79.

6. Florentino García Martínez, *The Dead Sea Scrolls Translated: The Qumran Texts in English*, trans. Wilfred G. E. Watson, 2d ed. (Grand Rapids: Eerdmans, 1996), 84.

in this hope. Thus one of the most important themes to trace through his ministry is how Jesus appeals to the teaching, imagery, and symbolism of such hope. These themes are what make Jesus' message so Jewish in its character. For as Jesus claims to fulfill the calling of Israel, he also is fulfilling God's call to bless the world by his work through this nation and the promised hope expressed for them (Gen. 12:1–3).

Not to be forgotten in this category of texts is the *Septuagint* (LXX), the Greek translation of the Old Testament, which dates from c. 250–100 B.C.[7] This form of the Old Testament, which itself has various versions, is often the form cited in the New Testament.

The sources that come after these foundational texts attempt to reflect upon and understand the Hebrew Scriptures' promises and teaching.

The Apocrypha, or Deuterocanonical Books

Another major source is the *Apocrypha*, or the *deuterocanonical* books, a collection of fifteen works.[8] These texts cover the period of history between the Testaments. They contain wisdom literature (Sirach, Wisdom) as well as the history that leads directly into the first century A.D. They cover the crucial period of the Maccabean War, when Judaism faced one of the greatest challenges to its existence. Most important for our study are 1 and 2 Maccabees, which cover this key period in some detail. To understand first-century Judaism, one must appreciate the impact of events that this material describes.

I shall cite numerous materials from this collection as we look at the Gospel texts. These sources are important because they show us how Jews of the Greek and Hasmonean eras tried to make sense of their faith and how they attempted to express the importance of the role of the Law and the nature of Israel's hope in a period just preceding Jesus.

7. Handbook versions of this text are available in the *Septuaginta,* ed. Alfred Rahlfs (Stuttgart: Deutsche Bibelgesellschaft, 1935). But key work should be done in the critical Göttingen and Cambridge versions of these texts. For details see Würthwein, *Text of the Old Testament,* 49–74. See also Karen H. Jobes and Moisés Silva, *Invitation to the Septuagint* (Grand Rapids: Baker Academic, 2000).

8. Some translations of the Bible (NRSV, JB) contain these books. A good translation is *The Oxford Annotated Apocrypha,* ed. Bruce M. Metzger (New York: Oxford University Press, 1977). Standard abbreviations for these books can be found in *SBL Handbook of Style,* 74. Roman Catholics accept this material as part of the canonical Old Testament. This is the reason for the name *deuterocanonical.* Citations are like those of biblical books with chapter and verse. Josephus gives an ancient Jewish view that no Scripture was written after Artaxerxes (*Ag. Apion* 1.8.40–41). Though these works were often included in important Jewish manuscript collections and were respected Jewish literature, they did not emerge within Judaism as part of the recognized Jewish canon.

Thus these texts give us a window into how certain strands within Judaism tried to make sense of their faith, especially in a context where Israel was under pressure from other national groups.

The Old Testament Pseudepigrapha

A third source of Jewish material is known as the *Old Testament Pseudepigrapha*.[9] It contains a variety of texts reflecting an array of genres: apocalyptic, wisdom, testaments, prayers, hymns, and texts expanding on the Old Testament. These texts span a period from about the sixth century B.C. to the ninth century A.D. Yet the bulk of the important material comes from the second century B.C. to the second century A.D. Many of the concepts and customs mentioned only briefly in the Old Testament are elaborated upon in these texts, showing Jewish views in various areas that the Gospels also discuss. This literature was not always widely circulated, but it does reflect what various Jewish groups were thinking at various times about important religious issues. This material helps us to appreciate the complexity and concerns of Judaism at this time. In fact, this literature shows that Judaism was not monolithic in this period but had many substreams and strands. Particularly important here are the apocalyptic or eschatologically oriented works like 1 Enoch, 4 Ezra, and the Psalms of Solomon. Other texts, such as Jubilees, show how important legal concerns were. Still another type of text tried to show that Jews and Gentiles could get along, best exemplified in The Letter to Aristeas, which also describes the traditional view of the origin of the Septuagint, the Greek translation of the Old Testament.

The Dead Sea, or Qumran, Scrolls

Perhaps the most dramatic archaeological discovery of the twentieth century was the texts found in caves at Qumran overlooking the Dead Sea. These texts probably belonged to a community of Essene Jewish separatists who had become disenchanted with temple practices in the second century B.C. The texts became known as the

---

9. The standard edition now is James H. Charlesworth, ed., *The Old Testament Pseudepigrapha*, 2 vols. (New York: Doubleday, 1983–85). Pseudepigrapha means "falsely inscribed," indicating their pseudonymous and noncanonical character. However, the works are still of value as historical sources and a reflection of thinking at the time, operating as key historical resources in much the same way as the previous category of sources. Citations are like biblical references, by chapter and verse. For book abbreviations see *SBL Handbook of Style*, 74–75.

Dead Sea Scrolls.[10] These works are the remains of the library of this separatist community, which came into existence as a result of the Maccabean War and lasted up to A.D. 68. These texts contain not only copies of ancient Old Testament manuscripts but also various religious texts, including some of the Pseudepigrapha. Many of these texts describe the practices of this unique community, which had chosen not to risk any compromise with Hellenism or official Judaism, which was tainted by Hellenism in their view. They went to the desert to be a pure community and wait for God to deliver and vindicate their stand as God's true people. The importance of ritual and religious calendars is also evident from this material, revealing an approach to religious practice that is far different from much religious expression today but that shares concerns that existed within first-century Judaism. Much literature exists about these texts and how they have revolutionized New Testament study in particular.[11]

Philo

Another contemporary Jewish source, Philo of Alexandria (c. 20 B.C.–A.D. 50), is more important for informing us about how Jews in the Diaspora viewed their faith than about those in Israel-Palestine. Nevertheless, Philo is still significant for revealing how some intellectually oriented Jews thought.[12] He gives us a glimpse of how some Jews took from the world of Hellenism and yet still vigorously defended their faith and people. Many of Philo's expositions attempt to make sense of key narratives of Hebrew Scripture and relate them to the cultural-philosophical environment of the Greco-Roman context as found in

10. See García Martínez, *Dead Sea Scrolls Translated.* It is usually easy to spot a reference to a Dead Sea Scroll text, as its sigla normally has a number (of the cave), the designation Q for Qumran, and a manuscript number (e.g., 4Q175). A few texts are known by other names as well. A diglot version of these texts exists in Hebrew/Aramaic and English: Florentino García Martínez and Eibert J. C. Tigchelaar, *The Dead Sea Scrolls Study Edition,* 2 vols. (Grand Rapids: Eerdmans, 2000). Standard abbreviations and identifications can be found in these works and in *SBL Handbook of Style,* 75–77.

11. For a good initial reading list, see García Martínez, *Dead Sea Scrolls Translated,* lvii.

12. For an English translation see *The Works of Philo: Complete and Unabridged,* trans. C. D. Yonge, new updated ed. (Peabody, Mass.: Hendrickson, 1993). The Greek texts with English translations can be found in F. H. Colson et al., eds., *Philo,* Loeb Classical Library, 10 vols. plus 2 supplemental vols. (Cambridge: Harvard University Press, 1929–53). Latin names for these books are noted in the contents of this volume. Standard names, both English and Latin, appear in the Hendrickson edition, while names and abbreviations can be found in *SBL Handbook of Style,* 78.

Egypt at this time. As such, his work is of limited importance to our study.

Josephus

When we think about the history of Judaism as seen in the first century A.D. and about the first century in general, pride of place must go to the pro-Roman, Jewish general and historian Josephus (A.D. 37–c. 100).[13] Without him, we would know far less about this period. His four works cover from Genesis through to the fall of Jerusalem in A.D. 70 and the political fallout that resulted. *Antiquities* surveys Israel's history from Genesis to the time of Josephus's writing in c. A.D. 90. *The Wars of the Jews* (also called *The Jewish War*) covers the period from the Maccabean War and the controversial Syrian ruler Antiochus Epiphanes to the period current with the writing. *Against Apion* is a work defending Judaism against Greek critics. Finally, *The Life of Flavius Josephus* is an autobiography extolling the merits of his life. These texts are crucial because they give us insight into how a major figure living in this time viewed Israel's history and key political events. His discussions are full of treatments of everyday life and give examples of how terms were regularly used. The study of Josephus is a branch of Jewish studies all its own; one must consider and weigh the testimony and varying perspectives his works reflect.[14] At one time in the West's educational system, Josephus was the most read text after the Bible. Josephus is usually fairly reliable as a source, but his perspective needs critical assessment.

After Josephus we cross a major boundary in our sources. Most sources mentioned up to this point come from the period of the first century or earlier (some pseudepigrapha are later). All the sources after this point postdate the time of Jesus. Material coming from these sources needs to be used with caution to avoid the danger of projecting concepts back into an earlier period, because we cannot be sure that

13. For an English translation, see *The Works of Josephus: Complete and Unabridged*, trans. William Whiston, new updated ed. (Peabody, Mass.: Hendrickson, 1987). The technical edition of Josephus is H. St. J. Thackeray et al., eds., *Josephus*, Loeb Classical Library, 10 vols. (Cambridge: Harvard University Press, 1926–65). Here one can find the Greek text with English translation. It is important that a translation of Josephus have full sentence versification, as these resources do (e.g., *Ant.* 12.1.3 is inadequate, but 12.1.3 §§119–53 or 12.119–53 is sufficient). The numbers identify book, chapter, paragraph, and sentence. Often the titles of Josephus's works appear in Latin. The Hendrickson edition lists the Latin titles in its contents. For names and abbreviations of Josephus's works, see *SBL Handbook of Style*, 79.

14. The study of Josephus and his reliability is not controversy free. For discussion and more detail, see Evans, *Noncanonical Writings*, 86–96.

ideas from the later period were also present in the earlier period. On the other hand, because Judaism is a conservative religious tradition, ideas and especially practices were fairly stable, depending on the group in question. Thus this later material can still have value for us, especially when it comes to describing religious practice and custom.

I shall return to these remaining Jewish sources after I give an overview of the Gospels themselves. Before I leave this discussion, however, it is good to remember that Greco-Roman sources also abound for this period. An example of a collection of such texts that are often related to New Testament study is edited by M. Eugene Boring, Klaus Berger, and Carsten Colpe.[15] This collection has both Jewish and Hellenistic sources in it, but many references cite Greco-Roman literature, Hermetica texts,[16] inscriptions, papyri, and letters.[17]

Greek Biblical Sources on the Life of Jesus: The Four Gospels

The canonical Greek New Testament contains four accounts of the life of Jesus: Matthew, Mark, Luke, and John.[18] Since the 1980s much attention has been given to other sources for Jesus' life and ministry, such as the *Gospel of Thomas*. These works do have a role to play in the study of Jesus, but their role has been exaggerated in many popular circles.[19] For now my goal is to survey briefly the basic themes, outline, and probable origins of these Gospels to the extent of our current knowledge.[20]

15. *Hellenistic Commentary on the New Testament* (Nashville: Abingdon, 1995).

16. The Corpus Hermeticum is a collection of seventeen tractates written in Greek and dating from the mid–first to the mid–third centuries A.D. The texts reflect religious and philosophical teachings present in mystical forms of Gnosticism. For some discussion and introductory bibliography, see Everett Ferguson, *Backgrounds of Early Christianity*, 2d ed. (Grand Rapids: Eerdmans, 1993).

17. In the index, seven pages refer to Greco-Roman background while four pages refer to Jewish texts. While both contexts are important to the history and culture of the region, the Jewish sources are in general more important and are the focus of my volumes.

18. The most widely used version of the Greek New Testament is the Nestle-Aland 27th edition of *Novum Testamentum Graece* (Stuttgart: Deutsche Bibelgesellschaft, 1994). A diglot version with the 2d edition RSV also is published as the *Greek-English New Testament*, 8th ed. (Stuttgart: Deutsche Bibelgesellschaft, 1994).

19. For details of this debate, see the later discussion on the quests for the historical Jesus and the various methods of criticism, chaps. 5–11.

20. In the sister volume, *Jesus according to Scripture*, I cover the same ground in more detail. Here I wish only to cover the most salient features of each Gospel and introduce the debates.

Matthew

Overview of Content and Themes. Matthew's Gospel is the one most focused on Jewish issues and concerns. Also important to his Gospel is the key role that Jesus' discourses play in the development of the argument. Although it is often said there are five discourse units, the last unit is particularly large and combines two distinct discourses, the condemnation of the leadership followed by the eschatological discourse (Matt. 23–25). The reason Matthew 23 is often excluded from the count of five discourses is that it lacks the literary marker that ends the other five discourses. Other discourse units cover blessing, law, righteousness, and the walk with God (Matt. 5–7); instructions for mission (Matt. 10); the kingdom (Matt. 13); and remarks about community—accountability and forgiveness (Matt. 18).

A look at a working outline of Matthew reveals much about its concerns:

I. Prologue: "God with Us," "King of the Jews," "Born of God" according to Promise in Midst of Conflict; Israel and Gentile Adoration (1:1–2:23)
II. Introduction: John the Baptist Prepares Way for Beloved Son, Who Overcomes Temptation (3:1–4:11)
III. Messiah Confronts Israel in Galilee and Meets Rejection (4:12–12:58)
IV. Responses: Kingdom, Provision-Acceptance-Call for Disciples, and Rejection by Israel (13:1–20:34)
V. Messiah Inaugurates Kingdom through Rejection and Vindication (21:1–28:20)

For Matthew, Jesus' relationship to Israel and explaining Israel's rejection of Jesus are major concerns. Matthew points out that those who are Christian do not seek a break with Judaism but have been forced to be distinct because the nation rejected the completion of the divine and scriptural promise Jesus brought and offered. However, that rejection did not stop God's promise. Rather, that rejection raised the stakes of discipleship and led to the creation of a new entity, the church. The message concerning Jesus continued to appeal not only to Israel but to the whole world. As with all the Gospels, there is an interaction and interchange between Jesus' words and deeds. What Jesus does supports what he preaches. Jesus' death was an act of the divine plan that led to his vindication and mission. Disciples are those who come to him and set upon the task of reflecting the righteousness God so graciously offers.

A brief listing of major Matthean themes shows the variety of his interests. Italics identify the key themes, which in some cases overlap with other Gospels and in other cases are unique. Matthew's Christology presents fundamentally a *royal, messianic understanding of Jesus,* who as *Son of God* comes to be seen as the revealer of God's will and the bearer of divine authority. As the promised King of the Jews, Jesus heals, teaches *the real meaning of Torah in all its dimensions,* calls for a *practical righteousness,* inaugurates the *kingdom,* and teaches about the *mystery* elements of God's promise. This mystery includes both Israel's hard-heartedness and God's unfolding kingdom program, which starts small and ends up comprehensive, including the final judgment of all humanity. This is all part of a program that involves what Matthew calls the *kingdom of heaven.*[21] This kingdom is both present and future (12:28; 13:1–52; 24:1–25:46). John the Baptist announces the approach of this kingdom. Jesus proclaims its hope throughout the nation to the lost sheep of *Israel.* He *calls on them to repent, challenges their current practices, expresses his authority over sin and Sabbath, and calls them to read the law with mercy.* Most of Israel rejects the message, but a key element of the mystery is that the promise comes despite that rejection. One day that kingdom will encompass the entire world (see the parables of Matt. 13). At the consummation, the authority of Jesus in that kingdom will be evident to all in a *judgment* rendered on the entire creation (Matt. 24–25). Thus the kingdom program, eschatology, and salvation history are bound together for Matthew.

God is seen as the *Father* who has a *sovereign and abiding presence* in the world. That presence is seen in the way his program is a realization of his promises. His presence is also seen in the way he exercises judgment over Israel in the promise of the judgment of the temple. God's sovereignty over the world emerges through the Messiah, who bears responsibility at the final judgment. Disciples have the benefit of calling on God as Father through the work of the Promised One.

Most of Matthew's claims to *scriptural fulfillment* help us understand who Jesus is and how he is realizing God's plan. Scripture is fulfilled as Jesus (1) is conceived of a virgin, (2) born in Bethlehem, (3) emerges from Egypt, (4) comes to life in a period of suffering for the nation, (5) is called a "Nazarene" (Matt 1:23), (6) goes to Galilee of the Gentiles, (7) bears our sicknesses, (8) is a shepherd sent to a shepherdless people, and (9) is the *servant who brings justice to Gentiles* (4:14–16; 9:36; 12:18–21). All of these promises underscore the deliverance and mission Jesus brings for Israel. The Promised One has been sent to Israel

---

21. In all but 4 of 36 references to the "kingdom," Matthew uses the phrase "kingdom of heaven" instead of "kingdom of God" (12:28; 19:24; 21:31, 43 are the exceptions).

to bring them back to God, just as the prophets had earlier tried to do. Yet now and then there are hints that the story circulates beyond Israel. A centurion and a Syro-Phoenician woman have exemplary faith (8:5–13; 15:21–28). Gentiles as well as Jews hear the Sermon on the Mount. As Israel's rejection becomes more intense, Jesus is sent as a servant who brings justice and hope to the nations.

The final *commission* sends disciples into the entire world (28:16–20). All of this takes place through a new community to be called the *church*, which Jesus will build (16:16–20; 18:15–20). Matthew is the only Gospel to speak directly of the church. Those disciples who compose the church are called to a *demanding discipleship* that puts following Jesus first; is grounded in *spiritual accountability, mercy,* and *forgiveness;* pursues righteousness as a calling; and goes out into the world to make more disciples (16:24–28; chap. 18).

Introductory Issues. The issues of authorship, date, and setting are debated. The association of the Gospel with the apostle Matthew dates back to a remark from the early church father Papias (c. A.D. 140) about Matthew having collected sayings of Jesus in a Hebrew dialect (Eusebius, *Eccl. Hist.* 3.39.16). Much about this citation is disputed.[22] Is Papias referring to the Gospel or to something else? If something else, what is the relationship between our Greek Gospel and what Papias describes? The answer to both of these questions is not clear.[23] On the other hand, the superscripts (ancient titles) that accompany manuscripts of the Gospel uniformly refer to Matthew as the author of this Gospel.[24] In addition, this Gospel was widely accepted and the most popular in the early period, judging by how frequently the fathers quote from it. The likelihood is excellent that its roots were well known to the early church, or it would never have received such early and widespread acceptance. If this is the case, the traditional argument for Matthew the apostle is stronger than it might first appear.

22. Details of this debate await the sister volume, *Jesus according to Scripture.* The debate over whether the apostle Matthew is the author of this Gospel is also treated there. Those who reject Matthew as author usually see the author as a Jewish Christian, argue that the date of Mark as the first Gospel makes it less than likely that the apostle Matthew wrote this later Gospel, and point to some matters of internal style as arguing against Matthew as author. For these arguments see W. D. Davies and Dale C. Allison, *The Gospel according to Saint Matthew,* International Critical Commentary, 3 vols. (Edinburgh: Clark, 1988–97), 1:33, 58.

23. See Scot McKnight, "Matthew," *DJG,* 527–28, although his explanation that the passage is merely about Hebrew style is less likely than that Papias is describing a Hebrew work that preceded the Gospel we now have.

24. Martin Hengel, *Studies in the Gospel of Mark,* trans. John Bowden (Philadelphia: Fortress, 1985), 65–67. He notes that this process was earlier and distinct from that which led to the recognition of the four Gospels as canonical.

As one can see, the arguments surrounding authorship are a matter of tradition versus judgments about internal evidence. This will often be the case as we consider these issues for each Gospel. The weight of the argument, especially given the quick and widespread acceptance of the Gospel, is that its roots do go back to the apostle. That conclusion best explains its rapid and wide use in the early church.

Determining the book's date is also difficult. The earliest citations of the Gospel come in the early second century with Ignatius, who died about A.D. 107 (*To the Smyrneans* 1.1; *To Polycarp* 2.2). Some of the instruction is given in a form that makes it look as if the temple is still in service when the Gospel is read (Matt. 5:23–24; 17:24–27). The problem is that this teaching also reaches back into the life of Jesus when the temple was present. The argument is that retaining such instruction about sacrificial practice and the temple tax makes more sense if a temple still existed to make the examples practical. Irenaeus claimed that the Gospel was written while Paul and Peter were still in Rome founding that church, placing it in the mid-60s at the latest and suggesting it was even earlier (*Against Heresies* 3.1.1; Eusebius, *Eccl. Hist.* 5.8). The picture of intense conflict with Judaism could fit any period in the mid–first century, especially that tied to Nero in the mid-60s, because he pressured the Christians in a way that distinguished them from Jews. In A.D. 62 the Jews stoned James, Jesus' brother, an incident that caused some Jews to worry about Roman reaction, because they did not have authority to execute (Josephus, *Ant.* 20.197–203).[25] All of this evidence appears to point to a date in the 60s.

Those who prefer an earlier date argue again that the Gospel of Matthew preceded Mark or that an apostle would not rely on a nonapostolic Gospel.

Those who argue for a date after the 60s contend that texts like the prediction of Jerusalem's destruction (Matt. 24:1–2) and the burying of "their" city (Matt. 22:6–7), indicate a Gospel written after A.D. 70. Here is someone who has separated himself from a Jewish perspective, as the pronoun *their* indicates. Most who see some merit in these arguments place Matthew after A.D. 70, usually somewhere in the 80s.[26]

Determining the setting for this Gospel is the most uncertain exercise of all, involving only inference. The heavy Jewish concerns of the Gospel point to either a setting in Israel or to a locale with a major Jewish population. The use of Greek points to a racially mixed setting. The

---

25. Everett F. Harrison, *Introduction to the New Testament*, rev. ed. (Grand Rapids: Eerdmans, 1971), 176.

26. For example, Davies and Allison, *Matthew*, 138. Harrison opts for anywhere between the 70s and 80s.

best candidate for a community outside Israel is Antioch of Syria. But no one really knows. As already noted, this determination is not so crucial to appreciating the message, because the Gospel was certainly intended to circulate beyond this one community.

It is also worth noting why the Gospels appear in our canon in the order they do. Matthew is first because when the church solidified recognition of the canon in the fourth century, Matthew was believed to be the first Gospel written and the one with the most developed connection to the Old Testament. In the early centuries of the church, it was the most popular Gospel among the Synoptics because it had a direct tie to the apostles in a way that Mark and Luke did not, given that the second and third Gospels were written by nonapostles. John assumed the fourth position because his story differed from the first three Gospels and was probably the last written of the four as well.

Mark

Overview of Content and Themes. This Gospel is today generally regarded as the first one to have been written, as the forthcoming discussion on the Synoptic problem will note. Thus its outline of Jesus' ministry has become the basic structure through which his life has been traced, even though sections of it are probably given not in chronological order but in topical arrangement (e.g., the conflicts of Mark 2–3).

Here is a basic working outline:

    I. Prologue on Beginning of Gospel (1:1–15)
   II. Jesus' Public Ministry (1:16–8:26)
 III. To Jerusalem: Passion and Vindication (8:27–16:8)

After the introduction, the second section of this Gospel cycles through a consistent structure in each of its three parts. There is a story about disciples at the start (1:16–20; 3:13–19; 6:7–13) and a note about rejection or a summary at the end (3:7–12; 6:1–6; 8:22–26).[27] The turning point of the Gospel is the confession in 8:27–29 that Jesus is the Christ. Before this confession, a miracle occurs that pictures Jesus giving sight to a blind man. After the confession, Jesus repeatedly tells the disciples that the Son of Man will suffer. Half of the Gospel treats the movement toward the final week of Jesus' ministry, while a full quarter of it is on the last week alone. For Mark, the events of the final week are central to the story.

27. R. A. Guelich, "Mark," *DJG*, 516.

The key themes are also evident in how the account proceeds. It begins with a note that what is being told is *the gospel*. Though to a lesser degree than Matthew or Luke, Mark also traces the *kingdom of God* as a theme. For Mark, it has elements that indicate its initial presence, while the bulk of the emphasis is that the kingdom will come in fullness one day. Kingdom entry, available now, requires one to be like a child. The parables look to a day when it will be a place where birds nest. The *mystery of the kingdom* is that it starts out small but still will accomplish all that God has called it to be. It will grow into a full harvest. Another theme that is present but less developed than in Matthew or Luke is that *the time of fulfillment has come*. Mark opens with this theme (1:15), and it appears here and there.

Mark is more a gospel of action than teaching, although Jesus is often called "teacher" in Mark. Things happen *immediately,* one of Mark's favorite expressions. Mark has only two discourses, one involving the parables of the kingdom (4:1–33) and the eschatological discourse (13:1–37). Miracles abound. Mark has twenty *miracle accounts.* Combined with healing summaries, these units comprise one-third of the Gospel and nearly one-half of the first ten chapters.[28] These pictures of Jesus' authority are important to Mark, as this Gospel presents Jesus as one who teaches with authority. However, a key part of that authority involves Jesus' activity, not just his pronouncements. The authority underscores that Jesus is the *Christ, the Son of God* (1:1; 8:29; 14:39). Mark's Christology presents Jesus as this promised figure. His claims of authority over sin, relationship, practices tied to purity, Sabbath, and temple get him into trouble with the Jewish leaders, who determine early on that they must stop him. The *conflict* emerging from Jesus' claims also constitutes a central feature of the Gospel.

However, Jesus' authority is not one of raw power. In terms of proportion, Mark highlights Jesus as *the suffering Son of Man and Servant* more than the other Gospels. In fact, nine of thirteen uses of "Son of Man" look to Jesus' suffering. Although Isaiah 53 is not cited, the descriptions of Jesus clearly parallel the portrait of this figure, especially the claim that his mission is to come and give his life as "a ransom for many" (10:45). The importance of understanding the suffering role probably explains the *commands to silence* given in Mark to those, including demons, who confess Jesus as Messiah (1:44; 5:43; 9:9). Without an appreciation of his suffering, one cannot understand Jesus' messianic calling. Some have labeled this call to silence Mark's messianic

28. Graham H. Twelftree, *Jesus the Miracle Worker: A Historical and Theological Study* (Downers Grove, Ill.: InterVarsity, 1999), 57.

secret, but it is not that Jesus' messiahship is to be kept secret indefinitely but that it is not to be shared until it is more fully understood. Only as the cross draws near does the full scope of divine promise and calling emerge. The disciples are not in a position to preach Jesus until they appreciate this aspect of his mission, as the subsequent mission of the church makes clear.

The servant Jesus is an example of how to walk with God in a world that rejects those sent by God. It is here that the pastoral *demands of discipleship* appear as well (10:35–45). Mark is like Matthew here. After the suffering comes glory and vindication. The same Son of Man will return one day to render judgment, as the eschatological discourse reveals. The need for discipleship and listening carefully to Jesus is clear as Mark notes without hesitation *the failures of the disciples*. Their instincts will not take them in the right direction. Trust in God and in his ways is required. Alongside this Mark notes *the emotions of Jesus and the disciples* more than any of the other Gospels.

In sum, Mark addresses the church under duress, suffering a rejection like that of their deliverer-teacher. Yet the call to serve, to rest in God's plan, and to look to Jesus as the example serve as the antidote for their stressful situation.

Introductory Issues. As with the other Gospels, discussions about authorship, date, and setting revolve around external testimony and inferences from internal features of the Gospel. As with the other Gospels, the author does not name himself in his work. The association of the Gospel with Mark comes to us through early church testimony.[29] Papias describes Mark as Peter's interpreter (Eusebius, *Eccl. Hist.* 3.39.15).[30] The Anti-Marcionite Prologue (c. A.D. 180), Irenaeus (*Against Heresies* 3.1.1–2), and Clement of Alexandria, as reported in *Eccl. Hist.* 6.14, confirm this identification.[31] There is no external evidence for any other author. For many, Mark is John Mark, known as an assistant to Peter, Paul, and Barnabas (Acts 12:12, 25; 13:13; 15:37–39; 1 Pet. 5:13; Philem.

29. Vincent Taylor, *The Gospel according to St. Mark,* 2d ed. (New York: Macmillan, 1966), 1–8.

30. Papias notes that his remark goes back to John the Elder, reaching back another generation. The identity of John the Elder is disputed. Some regard him as the apostle John, but more likely he is a key elder of Papias's day. Even Eusebius is aware of the dispute (*Eccl. Hist.* 3.39.4, 33). Either way, the testimony pushes the evidence back at least one generation. For arguments identifying the apostle John as the Elder, see D. A. Carson, *The Gospel according to John,* Pillar New Testament Commentary (Grand Rapids: Eerdmans, 1991), 69–70. For arguments distinguishing the two, see C. K. Barrett, *The Gospel according to St. John* (London: SPCK, 1955), 88–92.

31. The prologue contains the now famous reference to Mark as "stump fingered." In *Jesus according to Scripture,* I present more detail on the consistency of this tradition.

24; Col. 4:10; 2 Tim. 4:11).[32] It is this Gospel's close connection to Peter that explains its acceptance and circulation in the church. It must have had apostolic links for the church to welcome it into the basic fourfold Gospel collection, even though the church readily acknowledged that a nonapostle wrote it.

Determining Mark's date is slightly more difficult, because the external witnesses disagree. Irenaeus (*Against Heresies* 3.1.1) places the composition after the death of Peter and Paul in the late 60s, while Clement of Alexandria looks to a date during Peter and Paul's time in Rome, which could push the date back into the 50s. Most modern commentators opt for a date in the A.D. 65–70 range, while others place Mark just after A.D. 70. If one accepts the testimony of Clement of Alexandria reported by Eusebius that Peter ratified Mark's work (*Eccl. Hist.* 2.15.2), however, then a date in the late 50s to mid-60s is necessary.[33] As is the case for each Gospel, the discussion turns around what part of the external testimony one accepts as well as one's view of the order of composition among the Gospels.

The same text from Clement gives the Gospel's setting as Rome. Later tradition claims a setting as far away as Egypt (John Chrysostom, *Homilies on Matthew* 1.3). However, the evidence of Latinisms in the book suggests that the traditional association with Rome is best. That this community had to experience pressure both from Rome and from Jews may well explain the Gospel's emphasis on suffering.

Luke

Overview of Content and Themes. The third Gospel is the longest. It has a mix of teaching, miracle, and parable, with more parables than any other Gospel. Where Matthew presents teaching in discourse blocks, Luke scatters his teaching throughout his Gospel, usually in smaller units. Many key discourses happen in meal scenes (Luke 7:36–50; 11:37–52; 14:1–24; 22:1–38; 24:36–49), which recall Greek symposia, where "wisdom" was presented.

A working outline of Luke shows his concern for geographic progression:

   I. Preface and Introduction of John the Baptist and Jesus (1:1–2:52)

---

32. Taylor, *Mark*, 26: "There can be no doubt that the author of the Gospel was Mark, the attendant of Peter." He argues that the conclusion that this was John Mark "may be accepted as sound."

33. A mid- to late-60s date assumes that although Mark got his material from Peter, he took some time to compile and compose his Gospel.

The Gospel proceeds from Galilee to Jerusalem. The first half of the Gospel is structured much like Mark. The key distinctive section appears in Luke 9–19, which covers the journey of divine destiny Jesus takes as he draws near Jerusalem. This section juxtaposes two key themes, the rejection by the leadership and the preparation of disciples for ministry without Jesus. Like Mark and Matthew, the disciples must learn that Jesus suffers as Messiah, but here the scope of discipleship in relationships and values is given much more development. In the final week, Jesus dies unjustly as an innocent, but it is all according to a divine plan (Luke 23). Luke also shows how Jesus goes to great lengths to prepare the disciples for his departure, as the journey section of the Gospel and the discourse at the final meal show. John's Gospel does a similar thing with his upper room discourse (John 13–17).

Key themes center in the activity of *God's plan*. Things *"must be"* (δεῖ, *dei*) in Luke (2:49; 4:43; 9:22; 24:7, 26, 44–47). God has designed a plan by which he will reach and deliver *the poor, the oppressed, and those caught in Satan's oppressive grip* (4:16–18; 11:14–23). The plan reflects a *promise-and-fulfillment* structure, where scriptural realization of the plan is expressed through the words of key figures (7:28; 16:16). The opening infancy section does this through hymns using scriptural language, underscoring the note of *joy* that works through the Gospel. Events also happen with an immediacy: many texts speak of what is happening *"today"* (2:11; 4:21; 5:26; 19:9; 22:34; 23:43). The Gospel marches forward, as is indicated by *the geographic progression* in the story.

Jesus appears as the *Messiah-Servant-Lord*. The basic category is Messiah (1:31–35; 3:21–22; 4:16–30; 9:18–20), but as the story proceeds it is clear that this role is one of great authority that can be summarized by the image of *the judging Son of Man* or by the concept of *Lord* (5:24; 20:41–44; 21:27; 22:69). All of these connections reflect what Scripture has said about the plan. Jesus also functions as a *prophet*, one promised like Moses, one who is to be heard (4:20–30; 9:35). Jesus brings the *kingdom*, with the miracles evidencing its inaugurated presence and the ultimate *defeat of Satan* (11:14–23; 17:20–21). Yet the future of that kingdom will see Jesus return to reign over both Israel and the nations,

visibly expressing the sovereignty he now claims (chap. 21). Thus Jesus'
deliverance looks to the realization of covenantal promises made to
Abraham, David, and the nation (1:45–54).

The national leadership is steadfast in its rejection. The plan proceeds nonetheless. *Israel* will experience judgment for their unfaithfulness (13:6–9, 34–35; 19:41–44; 21:20–24). Their city will be destroyed to
picture what final judgment is like and to assure that God's program is
taking place. Efforts to call Israel to faithfulness continue despite their
refusal to embrace God's care and the Promised One.

In the meantime, Jesus forms a *new community*, which in the Book
of Acts is called "the Way." This community is made up of those who
turn to embrace Jesus' message and *follow in faith.* Luke likes to speak
of this response in terms of *repentance*, looking back to the change of
direction faith brings (5:32). Surprisingly it is *tax collectors and sinners*
who are most responsive, while the *Jewish leadership* is steadfast in its
refusal (7:29–30; 18:9–14). *Women* also abound in Luke as examples of
spiritual responsiveness (2:38–39; 7:36–50; 8:1–3). Jesus wants the
community to take the initiative in reaching out to all these fringe
groups, including the *poor, suffering, and oppressed* (4:16–18; 6:20–23;
7:22–23; 14:12–14).

Jesus' work brings intense rejection and will lead to *persecution* one
day. This means that disciples must *persevere* in their walk in the face
of great pressure (21:7–19). However, enemies should be loved, God
should be trusted, *prayer* should abound, and *watchfulness* for God's remaining work should continue (6:27–36; 11:1–13; 12:22–31; 18:1–8).
The two great obstacles to discipleship are the pressure this persecution produces and excessive attachment to the world, especially
through *possessions* (8:11–15; 12:15–21; 16:19–31; 18:1–8). Thus Luke
challenges the wealthy with regard to their stewardship of what God
gives to them.

Luke seeks to reassure his readers that rejection by the world is not
a sign of the Gospel's inauthenticity. Such rejection has been at the
heart of the plan all along. Thus readers can be assured of the truth
concerning the things they have heard about Jesus (1:1–4). It is *reassur-
ance* that is the key motif for this Gospel.

As part of the two-volume book of Luke-Acts, Luke's Gospel defends
the heritage of this new movement. In the ancient world, something old
was of value. Thus Luke argues that although the faith appears new, his
readers can be assured that it has emerged in conjunction with God's
promises of old.

What Jesus gives through his work is *deliverance, forgiveness,* and ultimately *enablement.* For this evangelist, the "power from on high" of

the *Spirit* is given now that Jesus is raised (3:15–16; 24:49). Jesus' *ascension* will allow disciples to accomplish all God has for them. For Luke this hope stands at the core of the gospel alongside the *eternal life* God gives.

Introductory Issues. Issues tied to authorship, date, and setting involve the usual mix of evidence from tradition and from within the Gospel itself. As with the other Gospels, the author of the third Gospel does not name himself in the work. However, external evidence again is consistent in naming Luke as the author (Justin Martyr, *Dialogues with Trypho* 103.19, who notes that this "memoir of Jesus" was written by a follower of the apostles).[34] Allusions to the Gospel appear as early as 1 and 2 Clement (c. A.D. 95 and 100, respectively). The Muratorian Canon also attributes the Gospel to Luke, a doctor. What makes this evidence impressive is that there is a large list of possible companions of Paul who might have filled in the blank of the "we" sections, had the author not been known. The unanimity of the tradition on authorship is important.[35] If Luke is the figure described in Colossians 4:10–14, which is likely given that there are no other prominent persons by that name in the tradition, then he was a non-Jew and a doctor.

The date of the volumes is related in part to three issues: the relationship to Mark's date, the ending of Acts, and whether allusions to Jerusalem's destruction in A.D. 70 occur in Luke 21. Those who see the ending of Acts as key argue that the events narrated there take us to about A.D. 62. The Gospel would have to be written before Acts, making a date in the late 50s and early 60s plausible.[36] Those who see allusions to Jerusalem's destruction in Luke 21 argue that a date sometime after that event is required. The allusions to Acts in 1 and 2 Clement make the 90s the latest possible date. Some also argue that time would be needed for Paul to emerge as a hero and that the developed theology of church structure points to the 80s.

Evidence for a late date in the 80s or 90s is thin. Those who prefer a date in the mid-60s to 70s rely in part on Luke's relationship to Mark. It seems likely that Luke knew Mark's Gospel. Luke's Gospel follows Mark's basic structure, and the most prominent solution to the synoptic problem proposes that Mark's Gospel was written first and Luke

34. Darrell L. Bock, *Luke 1:1–9:50*, BECNT (Grand Rapids: Baker, 1994), 5–6.

35. Joseph A. Fitzmyer, *The Gospel according to Luke (i–ix)*, Anchor Bible (Garden City, N.Y.: Doubleday, 1981), 40. For more detail see my *Jesus according to Scripture*.

36. Such arguments assume the writer of Luke also wrote Acts, which is a common view in light of how the end of Luke and the beginning of Acts connect thematically, as well as the recognition of a narrative thematic unity extending through the two volumes.

used it as a source. What is impossible to know is how long Mark must have been circulating for Luke to make use of him.

A date in the 60s seems likely. For Luke the outcome of the trial of Paul was not as important as that the Gospel was shared openly in Rome. Favoring a 60s date are factors that emerge mostly from Acts. There is next to nothing about the Roman community, which is against a later date, for the Roman community became increasingly prominent as the first century progressed. Neither is there an explicit reference to the destruction of Jerusalem in A.D. 70, even where it could have been inserted as a narrative note (as would have been possible in presenting Stephen's speech about the temple). The degree of uncertainty about Jew-Gentile relations is also more likely for an earlier period. As the church became more Gentile and less Jewish in its orientation in the later first century, issues pertaining to Jew-Gentile relations lessened in importance (as Acts 11–15 shows). By the later decades of the first century, the question of how Gentiles should function as part of an originally Jewish community had been settled.

The setting is not known. Candidates abound, including the traditions for Antioch, those for Achaia in Greece, and suggestions for Rome in light of the ending of Acts. However, the Gentile concerns in the book could fit a host of settings. Issues dominate that involve a mixed Jewish Christian and Gentile Christian community. Beyond that we can say little.

John

Overview of Content and Themes. The Fourth Gospel's account emphasizes Jesus as the unique one sent from God, who acts in unity with the Father. They work so closely together that Jesus is presented as God taking up flesh. From the declaration of the incarnation through a narration of seven signs and multiple discourses that resemble dialogues, John highlights Jesus' uniqueness. This Gospel's explicit christological portrayal of Jesus gives it its literary power. It is in John that Jesus speaks most directly about who he is in relation to the Father.

A working outline of John goes as follows:

    I. Prologue (1:1–18)
   II. Book of Seven Signs and Key Discourses: Before the Hour (1:19–12:50)
 III. Book of Glory: Farewell Discourse and Johannine Passion: The Hour Has Come (13:1–20:31)
 IV. Epilogue: Miraculous Catch Picturing Mission, and Discussion with Peter (21:1–25)

John's themes focus on *Christology*. Unlike the Synoptics, he speaks little of the kingdom. Rather it is *eternal life* that is the key theme to express what in the Synoptics is the kingdom promise. The emphasis on the term *eternal life* is not only about the duration of the life (eternal) but its quality (i.e., real, unending life). Thus to know the Father and Jesus Christ whom the Father sent is eternal life (17:3). This life is available now (5:24–26). This opportunity also brings the prospect of judgment for those who refuse it (3:16–21, 36). John speaks little of future eschatology, preferring to highlight what God has already given and done.

It is the *Word/Logos* sent from God in the form of human flesh that brings this promise. The various ways in which Jesus represents the way of God are also developed in the *"I Am" sayings*. He is the truth (14:6), the light of the world (8:12), the resurrection and the life (11:25), the good shepherd (10:11), the bread of life (6:48), and the true vine (15:1). Each image specifies some central role that belongs to Jesus. As *Son*, Jesus does only that which the *Father* shows him. It is the *unity with the Father* in mission that John highlights. Jesus is the hoped-for *Messiah*. Jesus is also the *Son of Man* who ascends and descends between earth and heaven. In this role, he will judge (5:27), be lifted up (3:14), and serve in mediating salvation (3:13; 6:27). Even when Jesus is seen as a *prophet*, it is as a *leader*-prophet like Moses (6:14; 7:40).

Obviously, the role of *signs* for John is crucial. Seven signs dominate the first two-thirds of the Gospel. The response to them covers the range from rejection (12:37–39) to openness (9:25). Interestingly, unlike the Synoptics, there are *no exorcisms* in John. He focuses on acts of healing, restoration, and provision. What these signs highlight the most is *Jesus' superiority to Jewish institutions* (1:17; 2:19–21; 7:37–39; 9:38; 10:1–18). Most of the miracles take place in a setting of Jewish celebrations and underscore how Jesus provides what the feasts celebrate. At the end of the Gospel, blessing comes to those who have faith without the need for signs (20:29).

Jesus is seen as the *revelator* of God. Jesus makes the Father and his way known (1:14–18). This is part of Jesus' function as light. Jesus' death shows the love of the Father for his own people and is an example to the disciples of how they should love (13:1, 11–17). Jesus' death also serves to gather God's people together (10:1–18) and is a means by which the Son and Father are glorified, as life is made available through him (3:14–16). His ministry takes place in both Judea and Galilee.

Also of great importance to John is the *Spirit*, also called the *Paraclete*. This encourager-enabler will come after Jesus' death as one sent by the Son to lead the disciples into the truth, empower them for ministry and mission, and convict the world of sin, righteousness, and judgment (14:25–31; 16:8–11). Here is the one who sustains life (4:8–10; 7:37–39).

The new community Jesus forms is to be characterized by *love and unity*, which have their model in Jesus' offering of himself and in the Son's relationship to the Father (13:31–35; 17:1–25). To function effectively, the community must stay rooted in their relationship to Jesus, who is the vine (15:1–6). Such unity will testify to the world about their relationship to God.

John declares that his *purpose* is to write a Gospel so that the reader might believe and in doing so have life in Jesus' name (20:30–31). John supports the point by continuously showing how central one's relationship to Jesus is for establishing eternal life and for maintaining its quality in a hostile world. In this fundamental goal, John is like the other three Gospels.

Introductory Issues. When it comes to authorship, date, and setting, once again we encounter internal and external evidence. As with the other Gospels, the fourth evangelist does not name himself. To start with external evidence, the earliest indications of authorship come from the Anti-Marcionite Prologue to John and the Muratorian Canon in the second part of the second century. The prologue indicates that the Gospel was for the churches in Asia. The Canon speaks of the input of other apostles, a detail most scholars today reject as an elaboration on the tradition. Irenaeus, Tertullian, and Clement of Alexandria agree that John the apostle is the author. Irenaeus is important because he stood in a line that was only one generation away from John. In his *Epistle to Florinus*, Ireneaus has John writing his Gospel after the other Gospels, while he lived in Ephesus (*Eccl. Hist.* 5.20.6). In *Against Heresies* 3.1.2, he states that the author was John, the one who leaned on Jesus' breast, and that the Gospel was written in Ephesus.

Some scholars challenge this external testimony but without solid rationale.[37] Some efforts to undercut the tie to John involve an examination of internal evidence. These claims often have to do with what John lacks: the parables, the transfiguration, the Lord's Table, and other such accounts. It appears, however, that John has chosen to write a Gospel that concentrates on what the traditions of the other Gospels

---

37. Harrison (*Introduction to the New Testament*, 218–25) has a solid overview of the discussion as does George R. Beasley-Murray, *John*, Word Biblical Commentary (Waco: Word, 1987), lxvi–lxx, though he distinguishes John the evangelist from John the prophet, who wrote Revelation.

have not already covered.[38] At the least, he knows what has been in broad circulation for some time. John is consciously undertaking a fresh angle on things, so a lack of repetition is not surprising.

The well-known argument from internal evidence seeks to identify the author by working into increasingly narrow points.[39] The author was (1) a Jew, (2) of Palestine, (3) an eyewitness of what he describes, (4) an apostle, and (5) John. The linking of the argument with the "beloved disciple" (13:23; 19:26; 20:2; 21:7, 20) is key and shows up in Irenaeus's remark about the one who leaned on Jesus' breast. The best candidate for this identification is John, son of Zebedee.[40]

The setting of this Gospel seems more solidly established than the other Gospels, given the strong association with Ephesus. The generally recognized view, following the external evidence, is that John is writing after the other Gospels. Some, however, make a case for dating this Gospel in the 60s or 70s, since it does not mention Jerusalem's destruction in A.D. 70 and does not use the Synoptics.[41] The external evidence, however, would seem to suggest a date in the 80s or 90s, near the end of the apostle's life.[42] Older efforts to date the Gospel in the second century were refuted when a fragment containing John 18:31–33, 37–38 was found that indicated that the Gospel circulated in Egypt in the early second century.[43] The tie of the Gospel to Ephesus is rooted in

38. There is a finely balanced debate over whether the Fourth Gospel knows the other Gospels directly. C. K. Barrett argues for a knowledge (*The Gospel according to St. John* [London: SPCK, 1955], 34–45), while R. E. Brown often argues that John is working with independent but overlapping tradition (*The Gospel according to John*, 2 vols., Anchor Bible [Garden City, N.Y.: Doubleday, 1966–70). For a treatment of this debate, see D. Moody Smith, *John among the Gospels: The Relationship in Twentieth-Century Research* (Minneapolis: Fortress, 1992).

39. The argument goes back to B. F. Westcott in 1881 and reappears with more detail in his commentary on John (*The Gospel according to St. John* [London: Murray, 1908], x–lii). See also Leon Morris, *Studies in the Fourth Gospel* (Grand Rapids: Eerdmans, 1969), 139–292.

40. See Gary Burge, *Interpreting the Gospel of John* (Grand Rapids: Baker, 1992), 37–54.

41. Leon Morris (*The Gospel according to John*, rev. ed., NICNT [Grand Rapids: Eerdmans, 1995], 25–30) favors an early date but concedes that the later date "cannot be ruled out." For a comprehensive introduction to John, see D. A. Carson, *The Gospel according to John*, Pillar New Testament Commentary (Grand Rapids: Eerdmans, 1991), 21–104.

42. Tradition suggests that John lived to the time of Trajan (A.D. 98–117; Irenaeus, *Against Heresies* 2.22.5; 3.3.4; Eusebius, *Eccl. Hist.* 3.39.3–4). That John was the last Gospel written is indicated by Irenaeus (*Against Heresies* 3.1.1) and a quote from Clement by Eusebius (*Eccl. Hist.* 6.14.7). For discussion about the quality of this and other traditions, some suggesting an earlier date for John's death, see Barrett, *John*, 86–87.

43. The fragment is designated $\mathfrak{P}^{52}$, part of the John Rylands papyri collection and the oldest portion we have of any New Testament book.

church tradition (Irenaeus, *Against Heresies* 3.1.2). However, this later Asian origin does not preclude the use of respected and circulating traditions whose origins go back to Palestine, not to mention the Jewish roots of the author.[44]

Jewish Sources That Postdate the Time of Jesus

We now return to Jewish sources that reveal the character of Judaism, especially as it developed after the time of Jesus. Such sources have to be used with some care; since they postdate the time of Jesus, the problem of anachronism is real.[45] Still, it is important to appreciate that Judaism was a conservative tradition and that practices, especially those relating to the temple, would have little reason to be altered since the temple no longer existed when these works were written. It is unlikely that the tradition would significantly alter practices that could no longer be observed. Hence, it is likely that the descriptions of temple practices would be preserved rather than changed.

Midrashim

A key source for Jewish understanding of Scripture is the collection of *midrashim*. These texts, most of which postdate our period, give the rab-

44. See Beasley-Murray, *John*, lxxv–lxxxi, for the plausible option of the account having connections with Palestine or Antioch as well as Ephesus. John would not be averse to using circulating tradition with roots in the apostolic circle.

45. For a consideration of the difficulties in deriving reliable historical data from these sources as well as from Josephus, see John P. Meier, *A Marginal Jew: Rethinking the Historical Jesus*, vol. 3: *Companions and Competitors*, Anchor Bible Reference Library (New York: Doubleday, 2001), 299–310. Meier makes the point that information that is attested in multiple ancient Jewish sources is more likely to be historically accurate. This is the same principle of multiple attestation that we shall discuss later in tradition criticism of the Gospels (chap. 10). Meier is a little too skeptical of the New Testament Gospels' ability to reach back to the time of Jesus—rather than reflecting merely an early church perspective—when they address issues tied to the Pharisees. That the New Testament perspective reflects a polemical situation does not remove the fact that these writers were closer to the events than we are as we attempt to reconstruct the historical details. Many of these conflicts best explain the opposition Jesus ran into within official Judaism. Such perspectives may not require a choice between a Jesus setting or an early church setting. Still Meier's point that these later sources need to be handled carefully is well taken, and his rationale needs to be appreciated. Despite these difficulties, the wealth of Jewish material and the Jewish setting of Jesus' ministry requires that these Jewish sources be carefully examined and appreciated for their contribution to our understanding of Jesus' life and times. Despite his cautions about their use, Meier makes the point that using Jewish materials with care provides a needed corrective to reading Jesus' life exclusively through Greco-Roman sources and in only a Greco-Roman light.

binic collection of interpretation of individual texts. The *Midrash Rabbah* is the most important, covering the Pentateuch plus Song of Songs, Esther, Ecclesiastes, Ruth, and Lamentations. It was compiled from A.D. 450 to 1110. Such material also exists for the Psalms from A.D. 750 to 800. Earlier collections of *midrashim* exist for Exodus (*Mekilta*), Leviticus (*Sipra* [*Sifra*]), Numbers (*Sipre* [*Sifre*]), and Deuteronomy (*Sipre* [*Sifre*]).[46] These works date from the second century in the case of *Mekilta* to the fourth century for the others. We gain insight here into how later Jews read their Scripture and how tradition talked about it.[47] However, the use of the *midrashim* for Gospel study requires caution because of their later date and because the likelihood of later reflection embellishing scriptural interpretations increases over time. Thus, we cannot be certain that ideas expressed in the *midrashim* really go back to Jesus' time. When readings in this material are similar to material found in earlier sources, then these readings can be treated with more confidence. However, one should always note when later extrabiblical material is being cited.

Mishnah

A major source of Jewish religious practice and rabbinic legal reflection is the *Mishnah*.[48] This work contains a series of legal discussions covering the whole of Jewish religious practice. It represents an official codification of the oral law. Major topics make up the six divisions (also called orders or volumes) of the work. The volumes cover discus-

46. The bracketed items reflect alternate spellings of these books.

47. I have noted only the more prominent sources, which as a whole comprise volumes of material. The name *midrashim* is the plural form of *midrash*, which means "searching out." Citations come in various forms, though usually the name of the specific midrashic work is included. These works are variously divided and cited. For details and bibliography with regard to individual texts and translations, see Evans's discussion of the *midrashim* in *Noncanonical Writings*, 128–39. For abbreviations, see *SBL Handbook of Style*, 81.

48. Two capable translations of this material are Herbert Danby, *The Mishnah: Translated from the Hebrew and with Introduction and Brief Explanatory Notes* (Oxford: Oxford University Press, 1933); and Jacob Neusner, *The Mishnah: A New Translation* (New Haven: Yale University Press, 1988). A solid bilingual source is Philip Blackman, *Mishnayoth*, 6 vols. plus supplement (reprint, Gateshead: Judaica, 1977). The word *mishnah* means "repetition," indicating that this work is a codifying of oral tradition, which was learned by being repeated. Some additional tractates and remarks were added later and constitute the *Tosepta* (*Tosefta*), which means "addition." The standard method of citing the Mishnah begins with *m.*, followed by the tractate name (often abbreviated), and the chapter and paragraph number (e.g., *m. Sanh.* 7.2). Citations from the Tosepta are similar in form to those of the Mishnah, but *t.* instead of *m.* precedes the tractate name (e.g., *t. Ber.* 5.18). For details, see Evans, *Noncanonical Writings*, 118–25. For abbreviations, see *SBL Handbook of Style*, 79–80.

sions of seeds (*Zeraʿim*), feasts (*Moʿed*), women (*Našim*), damages (*Neziqin*), holy things (*Qodašim*), and cleannesses (*Ṭeharot*, i.e., purity). Subdivisions of these orders are called tractates, which have chapters and paragraphs. Two types of material are present: *halakah*, which are the texts presenting the legal rulings, and *haggadah*, which is edifying and illustrative material that is not legal in character. Though we must be careful how we use this later material (it was codified c. A.D. 170 under the leadership of Rabbi Judah Ha-Nasi), there is often much insight into Jewish attitudes and practices in a faith that was concerned to preserve its traditions and pass on its practices. This source is often the most helpful when it comes to ancient Jewish practices. Its roots lie in the Pharisees, however, while the period of Jesus' ministry was controlled by the Sadducees, who rejected oral tradition. Thus the practices described here would not be agreed upon or practiced by all Jews in Jesus' time.

Talmud

The final major Jewish source comes from the fifth and sixth centuries A.D., the *Talmud*.[49] There are two major versions of the Talmud, a Palestinian edition (fifth century, also called the Jerusalem Talmud) and the official rabbinic edition known as the Babylonian Talmud (sixth century). The Talmud is a legal rabbinic text that includes the Mishnah and the *Gemara*, a rabbinic commentary (*gemara* means "completion") on the Mishnah and an anthology of competing rabbinic views on specific matters. If care needs to be exercised in using the Mishnah, even more care is called for in appealing to the Talmud because of the late date of these sources.[50] These texts can still help us appreciate Jewish sensitivities and the history of later discussion on various points.

49. The Talmud consists of many volumes of material. For the Palestinian Talmud, see Jacob Neusner, ed., *The Talmud of the Land of Israel*, 35 vols. (Chicago: University of Chicago Press, 1982–94); for the Babylonian Talmud, see Israel Epstein, ed., *The Babylonian Talmud*, 35 vols. (London: Soncino, 1935–48). The word *talmud* means "studying." The form of the talmudic citation varies depending on which talmud is being cited. The Palestinian Talmud does not come with a uniform citation method. It is introduced with either *y.* or *j.* for Yerushalmi/Jerusalem. Often the numeration parallels the Mishnah, though Neusner's edition uses its own system. Citations from the Babylonian Talmud have a prefixed *b.* followed by the tractate name and folio number, which consists of a numeral and a letter (the letter indicating which side of the page is intended), making it easy to spot as a Babylonian talmudic reference (e.g., *b. Sanh.* 22ᵃ).

50. This is one of the failings of the old classic by Alfred Edersheim, *The Life and Times of Jesus the Messiah*, 2 vols. (1883; reprint, Grand Rapids: Eerdmans, 1953). He depended heavily on talmudic material. His work reflected the best that scholarship could offer in his time. Our knowledge of sources has grown in the century since he wrote.

Non-Jewish Sources

In addition, there are some significant non-Jewish sources. Most of these texts are by major Roman historians, giving us a sense of Greco-Roman life, ideas, expressions, and attitudes as well as literary genres.[51] However, Roman sources spend little time on Judea. It was too small a part of the empire to be considered significant from their perspective. Nonetheless, details about Greco-Roman culture abound in these sources, so they give us a glimpse into Hellenistic perspectives. Given the mix of Jewish and Greco-Roman elements in first-century Israel, both sets of sources are significant. The impact of a foreign presence in Israel and the impact of Hellenism was an important issue for Jews surrounded by it. These Jews wanted to be faithful to God and had distinct practices to mark out their uniqueness. The Jewish history leading to the time of Jesus reflects a constant struggle over how to be unique and faithful to God in the midst of a seeming divine judgment that had brought the nations into their land. It is this important story that we will trace when we review the political history of the nation from exile to the time of Jesus.

Conclusion

Sources relevant to the study of Jesus are largely Jewish in nature. Fortunately, these sources have become the object of renewed study and interest since the mid–twentieth century and the discovery of the Dead Sea Scrolls. This renewed study of Judaism has marked out a fresh and potentially fruitful path for the study of Jesus. Most students have little familiarity with such sources; many are unaware that they even exist. This chapter has sought to orient students to such sources so that they become more accessible. The background they provide is important to the study of Jesus and will be a key element of my own survey of Jesus in Scripture. The value of these extrabiblical sources is not in any claim to canonical authority but as a barometer of cultural feelings and expectations concerning God's promise. Every culture has its "cultural script" that is assumed in its communication. These sources help us get a reading on the cultural script at work in the time

51. For solid introductions to the Greco-Roman background, see Everett Ferguson, *Backgrounds of Early Christianity* (Grand Rapids: Eerdmans, 1987), 1–312; and James S. Jeffers, *The Greco-Roman World of the New Testament Era* (Downers Grove, Ill.: InterVarsity, 1999). For sources see David Aune, *Greco-Roman Literature and the New Testament: Selected Forms and Genres,* SBL Sources for Biblical Study 21 (Atlanta: Scholars Press, 1988); as well as the bibliography in Boring, Berger, and Colpe, eds., *Hellenistic Commentary,* 594–601.

of Jesus. They help us to understand the reaction to Jesus and his ministry. They also deepen our own perception of Jesus' claims.

My survey of the roots of the four Gospels shows two with apostolic origins (Matthew and John) and two with apostolic connections (Mark with Peter; Luke with Paul and others). They are four different works. While Matthew is concerned with Jewish response and rejection, Mark treats the issue of persecution and suffering. Luke reassures by making clear how the message went from Jew to Gentile through divine direction, although the completion of this theme required a second volume, Acts. John goes his own way, highlighting the unique sending of the only Son, who brings full blessing and life now. All of them present Jesus as a messianic claimant and uniquely sent Son of God who challenged the Jewish leadership while offering deliverance to any who would embrace him and his message.

Part 1

Jesus in His Cultural Context

Background considerations are necessary if the student is to uncover elements in the text that were simply assumed by the first-century writer and his audience in order to understand the intention of the author as made known in the text. By the original author and his readers, this knowledge was shared; due to historical distance, this information is arcane to us. And there is much the gospel traveler will need to know in order to be a perceptive visitor in that world.[1]

The non-Christian evidence uniformly treats Jesus as a historical person. Most non-Christian authors were not interested in the details of his life and teaching, and they saw him through the Christianity they knew. They provide a small but certain corroboration of certain New Testament historical traditions on the family background, time of life, ministry, and death of Jesus. They also provide evidence for the content of Christian preaching that is independent of the New Testament.[2]

These two citations summarize the first part of this book. On the one hand is the cultural background of Jesus, namely, the history and cul-

1. Scot McKnight, *Interpreting the Synoptic Gospels* (Grand Rapids: Baker, 1988), 27.
2. Robert E. Van Voorst, *Jesus outside the New Testament: An Introduction to Ancient Evidence* (Grand Rapids: Eerdmans, 2000), 217.

ture of second temple Judaism, ruled by Rome and surrounded by a Greco-Roman presence. On the other hand is the need to survey the nonbiblical evidence for Jesus' existence and to discuss the general outline of the dates of Jesus' birth and death. This second discussion reveals how historical method works and the judgments it calls the student to make. This entire unit places Jesus in his proper cultural-religious setting. Part 2 then takes up the methods that students of the Gospels have used to study Jesus, assessing the strengths and weaknesses of these approaches and tracing carefully the judgments these methods assume, argue for, or ask students to make.

chapter 1

Nonbiblical Literary Evidence for Jesus

Several years ago I received a letter propounding a question of a kind which I am frequently asked to answer. The writer was a Christian, to whom the question had been put by an agnostic friend in the course of a lengthy discussion, and it had caused him, he said, "great concern and some little upset in my spiritual life."

Here is the question, as framed by my correspondent:

What collateral proof is there in existence of the historical fact of the life of Jesus Christ? If the Bible account of his life is accurate, he should have caused sufficient interest to gain considerable comment in other histories and records of the time; but in fact (I am told), apart from obscure references in Josephus and the like, no mention is made.[1]

Evidence for Jesus in Nonbiblical Texts: An Interesting Question to Ponder

The question Professor Bruce's friend raised is an interesting one to consider. The first time I heard about this issue, it came not as a query but as a claim. I was a student at the University of Texas, where debate took place between a Texas Baptist pastor and the prominent atheist, Madalyn Murray O'Hair. The debate was broadcast on the radio. As I

1. F. F. Bruce, *Jesus and Christian Origins outside the New Testament* (Grand Rapids: Eerdmans, 1974), 13.

listened, she stated that there is *no* credible evidence outside the Bible that Jesus even existed. I have since heard variations of this statement many times. Sometimes it shows up in documentaries or publications. The pastor tried to challenge the claim, but when pressed, he did not know the details of the evidence. He knew only that the Jewish historian Josephus had said something about Jesus. So he lost an opportunity to make an important point about the evidence for Jesus' existence from sources outside the Bible.

In fact, it is amazing and significant that Jesus shows up at all in the sources we have. Even a seemingly important "middle management" figure like Pontius Pilate, the decade-long governor of Judea, is mentioned by only a single pagan source, the Roman historian Tacitus. What we know of Pilate from first-century documents comes through the Jewish sources of Josephus and Philo as well as from the Gospels. After all, only the educated members of ancient society were literate, and those who wrote came from the upper classes. Historical works tended to focus on the major figures and events of interest to the upper class. Three reasons make the mention of Jesus in extrabiblical material surprising:

First, we lack records from numerous major figures of the ancient world. What has survived to our time is extremely limited, though important and enlightening. For example, we do not have a single official record of any report that "Pontius Pilate, or any other Roman governor of Judaea, sent to Rome about anything."[2] Thus we have only a small amount of the material that was surely produced.

Second, we possess few of the potential sources from first-century Judea and its environs. In fact, we possess only three major Jewish sources. (1) We have one Jewish historian, Josephus, who lived c. A.D. 36–100. (2) There is one Jewish philosopher, Philo, who lived in Alexandria, Egypt. He only rarely mentions contemporary events in Judea. (3) The Dead Sea Scrolls of Qumran is a collection of documents from a separatist Jewish movement living in the Judean wilderness. Most of the Qumranian material, when it covers history, is not dedicated to a historical description but treats history with largely descriptive and symbolic imagery that is more allusive in character. Moving beyond Jewish sources, we have a selection of works from various writers on the history of the Roman Empire (of whom only Suetonius, Tacitus, and Pliny the Younger mention Jesus or "one called Christ"). The final

---

2. Bruce, *Jesus and Christian Origins*, 19. This work is still an excellent survey of the material for this chapter. Another full discussion of much of the material, especially the key examples from Josephus, appears in John Meier, *A Marginal Jew: Rethinking the Historical Jesus*, vol. 1: *The Roots of the Problem and the Person* (New York: Doubleday, 1991), 56–111.

major source for first-century Judea is the New Testament, but these texts are excluded from consideration in this chapter except for how they relate to what the other sources bring to our attention.

Third, from a Roman perspective, Jesus was a seemingly minor figure. He was a religious leader from an ethnic minority tucked away in a small, distant corner of a massive empire. He lived in a time when communication was not nearly as easy as today. Not only that, but the bulk of his ministry took place not in the central city of the minor province but further north in Galilee. Thus he lived and worked on the outskirts of this region. It would be like someone working in the countryside within a distant territory of the United States, say on one of the Pacific territorial islands. For the Romans, there would have been dozens of more important historical figures in the region from the early portion of the first century. Even to the Jewish leadership, Jesus was seen originally as a troublemaker, one who had been successfully removed. Why would one expect anything to be written about a figure Rome regarded as insignificant and the Jewish leadership had rejected as one who made false claims?

Yet the traces of his existence in the documents we have are significant, given these three factors. What we see is evidence of the unusual effects his ministry produced in those who came to follow him. The remarks come with a clear recognition that the growing movement's origins went back to Jesus. In addition, there are statements, both neutral and against Jesus, that confirm his existence. They reveal the issues of debate we will come to see in much more detail in the Gospel record. This element of the record is fascinating and serves as an introduction to the Gospels themselves. What is the extrabiblical evidence for the existence of Jesus? What does it tell us about him?

Evidence from Roman Sources

Bruce characterizes the evidence from Roman historians as "police news." They are reports that indicate aspects of the Christian movement that troubled the Roman authorities.[3] There is no prejudice in these reports; they are descriptive, given almost in passing as the writer reviews the record concerning key figures.

Suetonius, Claudius 25.4

The first evidence of turmoil associated with Christians shows up in a report by a Roman historian who wrote on the lives of twelve emper-

3. Bruce, *Jesus and Christian Origins*, 18.

ors of Rome (*De Vita Caesarum*, Lives of the Twelve Caesars). C. Suetonius Tranquillus was a member of the equite class and worked as a law-
yer for Pliny the Younger until he found administrative positions under
the emperors Trajan and Hadrian.[4] This role gave him access to the
Roman archives, a rich deposit of historical sources. His work comes
from c. A.D. 120 and covers the emperors from Julius Caesar to Domi-
tian. The citation appears in a section explaining how Claudius dealt
with various ethnic groups. In A.D. 49 riots broke out in the large Jewish
community in Rome. Acts 18:2 alludes to the same event when it notes
that Aquila and Priscilla were in Corinth, where they became acquainted with Paul, "because Claudius had commanded all the Jews to
leave Rome."

In a short sentence, Suetonius explains Claudius's reaction to the
riots: "He expelled the Jews from Rome, on account of the riots in
which they were constantly indulging, at the instigation of Chrestus."[5]
The problem with the citation is that "Chrestus" is not "Christ." Yet
there are good reasons to suggest that "Christ" is meant. First, Latin
style would suggest that a *quodam* would introduce a new or unknown figure, but that is lacking here. Second, though several hundred names of Roman Jews have been found in the Roman cata-
combs, none of them is "Chrestus," which suggests a mistake in the
reference. The confusion may come from the name *Chrestiani*, a vul-
gar form of the name for "Christians." This name then probably produced a derivation that saw its founder as Chrestus.[6] Suetonius's report apparently regards Chrestus as the cause of the riots and leaves
the impression that the instigator of the riots was in Rome. The historian's source is not a Christian, nor is Suetonius himself a Christian. His hostile perspective emerges in his reference to Christians
holding to "a novel and mischievous superstition" (*Life of Nero* 16.2).

---

4. An equite is a landowner and military man who was worth at least 100,000 denarii.
The name described one who could outfit his own horse. This was often called the eques-
trian class. They were socially just below the elite senatorial class.

5. The Latin reads, "Judaeos impulsore Chresto assidue tumultuantes Roma expulit."
A good brief discussion of this text appears in Gerd Theissen and Annette Merz, *The Historical Jesus: A Comprehensive Guide* (Minneapolis: Fortress, 1998), 83–84.

6. This suggestion is in ibid., 82 n. 57, 84 n. 62. It should be noted that these writers
are often skeptical about historical detail, so their making this point is significant. Meier
(*Marginal Jew*, 1:92) suggests merely a pronunciation confusion in the record. It is Meier
(102 n. 16) who notes the reasons one should think that Christ is meant in this passage.
Bruce (*Jesus and Christian Origins*, 21) suggests that *Chrestus* is a common slave name.
The absence of the common name *Chrestus* from catacomb inscriptions, however, shows
that the name made no imprint on Christian circles, although it is clear that Suetonius
is describing Christian activity. The lack of catacomb evidence shows that *Chrestus* is an
error on Suetonius's part.

Suetonius's description comes as he portrays the persecution of Christians under Nero (an example of which follows in the next passage from Tacitus).

The Suetonian text is significant if the allusion is to Jesus, because it shows that (1) within a few decades the movement he spawned had reached from Jerusalem to Rome; (2) his followers had grown to be a source of commotion in the city; and (3) though the text does not make a direct reference to Jesus, the historical effect of his presence surfaces here, because it points to the close connection between the earliest church and Judaism, so much so that the Romans saw them as one group.

Tacitus, Annals *15.44*

In A.D. 64, fifteen years after Claudius's expulsion of the Jews from Rome, a great fire broke out in the city. The Roman historian and member of the senatorial aristocracy P. Cornelius Tacitus discusses the event in his final work, *Annals*. The treatise covers Roman history from A.D. 14 to 68. The work dates from c. A.D. 115–117.

It was popularly believed that Nero had ordered this devastating fire, and he attempted to shift the blame to the Christians. He burned many at the stake (a sentence that was said to fit the crime) and fed others to wild animals. Tacitus's explanation gives us one of the longer texts about Christians in the extrabiblical material:

> Therefore, to squelch the rumor, Nero created scapegoats and subjected to the most refined tortures those whom the common people called "Christians," [a group] hated for their abominable crimes. The author of this name, Christ, during the reign of Tiberius, had been executed by the procurator Pontius Pilate. Suppressed for the moment, the deadly superstition broke out again, not only in Judea, the land which originated this evil, but also in the city of Rome, where all sorts of horrendous and shameful practices from every part of the world converge and are fervently cultivated.[7]

Once again the citation is important for a number of reasons. (1) It is the one reference to Pilate in a non-Jewish and non-Christian docu-

---

7. This translation mostly follows Meier's rendering in *Marginal Jew*, 1:89–90. The Latin reads: "Ergo abolendo rumori Nero subdidit reos et quaesitissimis poenis adfecit quos per flagitia invisos vulgus Christianos appellabat. Auctor nominis eius Christus Tiberio imperitante per procuratorem Pontium Pilatum supplicio adfectus erat; repressaque in prasens exitiabilis superstitio rursum erumpebat, non modo per Iudaeam, originem eius mali, sed per urbem etiam quo cuncta undique atrocia aut pudenda confluunt celebranturque."

ment.[8] (2) Christ is described as a Jew slain in Judea under the authority of Pilate, a point made in the biblical material as well. (3) The use of the name *Christ*, which means "anointed one," indicates that the claim of being *anointed* is the key to this figure. (4) This Christ is the founder of a movement that made its way from Judea to Rome, a point Suetonius's citation also made. That this movement never died out but remained, grew, and spread after Christ's execution makes it noteworthy. Jesus' death failed to produce the movement's extinction. (5) Tacitus makes clear that the Romans viewed the Christians with some hostility. In a later text, he accuses Christians of "hatred against the human race" (*Annals* 15.44.4). This charge probably stems from the Christians' hesitancy to engage in acts of reverence for the emperor, acts the rest of the empire performed (see the citation from Pliny below for details about this dispute). Yet Tacitus's sense of injustice surfaces when he reports, "Hence, even for criminals who deserve extreme and exemplary punishment, there arose a feeling of compassion; for it was not, as it seemed, for the public good, but to glut one man's cruelty, that they were being destroyed."

We do not know the source of Tacitus's information. It appears to have come from archival reports or some later Roman sources. The perspective is clearly not Christian. Strictly speaking, the one error in his report is that Tacitus cites Pilate as procurator (not prefect). However, the difference may only reflect that Tacitus refers to the equivalent office of his time.[9]

Pliny the Younger, Epistles 10.96–97

C. Plinius Caecilius Secundus, better known as Pliny the Younger,[10] gives us the chance to listen in on the development of civic policy in respect to Christians located in Pontus and Bithynia (in what is now northern Turkey). A Roman noble and senator, he was governor in that region from about A.D. 111 to 112. He assumed the office during the rule of Trajan (A.D. 98–117).

Pliny was a prolific letter writer. The tenth and final volume of his letters contains one epistle to Trajan asking how he should treat Christians.[11] Pliny explains, "In investigations of Christians I have never

8. Another reference to Pilate appears in an inscription found at Caesarea Maritima in 1961 that refers to him as "prefect." See C. K. Barrett, *The New Testament Background*, 2d ed. (San Francisco: Harper & Row, 1989), 155–56.

9. Meier, *Marginal Jew*, 1:100 n. 8; and Barbara Levick, *Claudius* (New Haven: Yale University Press, 1990), 48–49.

10. He was the nephew and adopted son of Pliny the Elder.

11. A full presentation of the letter and Trajan's reply appears in Bruce, *Jesus and Christian Origins*, 25–27.

taken part; hence I do not know what is the crime usually punished or investigated, or what allowances are made." Most of the letter concerns his procedure in questioning Christians. It involves a request for advice about whether his approach is a good one. Trajan's reply, which we also possess, assures Pliny that he has "acted with perfect correctness." The key to that policy is getting Christians to declare reverence toward the gods and to the emperor and to be willing to curse Christ (*Christo male dicere*). According to Pliny's informants, these acts were something real Christians would not do. Pliny released those who agreed to worship the gods or the emperor. He also set free those who confessed to giving up the faith.

Those interrogated had described the elements of their faith and worship. Here is Pliny's description of their experience:

> That it was their habit on a fixed day to assemble before daylight and recite by turns a form of words to Christ as a god (*carmenque Christo quasi deo dicere*); and that they bound themselves with an oath, not for any crime, but not to commit theft or robbery or adultery, nor to break their word, and not to deny a deposit when demanded. After this, they went on, it was their custom to separate, and then meet again to partake of food, but food of an ordinary and innocent kind.

The citation notes that Christians gathered twice on what we know as Sunday, first to worship Christ and then to partake in the *agape* meal, the Lord's Supper.

The citation is significant. (1) Despite not telling us anything about Jesus' life, it does show that just as the movement had spread to Rome, it also was growing and becoming an issue in still another part of the empire (northern Turkey). (2) It gives us our first outside description of their worship and notes the reverence in which Christ was held in the early second century. (3) Their reverence was so focused that they refused to worship another god, even when the state threatened them with severe punishment. Christians were thus seen as despising other humans by not being part of the faithful members of the empire. They followed a "perverse and extravagant superstition," as Pliny says later in this letter. (4) There was no set policy on how to deal with them, so Pliny had to seek the emperor's guidance. In sum, Pliny reports that Christ is the cultic deity of the movement. This belief is so strong that the Christians see the Roman gods, including the emperor, as anti-God. As we shall see, there was no separation of church and state in this culture; religion and loyalty to the authorities who ruled were often tightly linked.

Two Brief Notes: Thallus and Peregrinus

Two more Roman references come to us indirectly. The Christian chronographer Julius Africanus (A.D. 170–240) writes about the crucifixion. He reports the remarks of Thallus, a Roman or Syrian who wrote about the history of the eastern Mediterranean c. A.D. 52.[12] The work is now lost, but Africanus tells us about Thallus's third volume. There he comments on the crucifixion of Jesus and the accompanying earthquakes and darkness. Thallus simply explained that this darkness was an eclipse of the sun (ἔκλειψιν τοῦ ἡλίου, *ekleipsin tou hēliou*). This explanation Africanus took as irrational (ἀλόγως, *alogōs*) because if the crucifixion occurred at Passover there would have been a full moon, which would prevent such an eclipse. Even if coming from Christian sources, Thallus's remark is significant because it shows that details about the crucifixion were widespread enough that a non-Christian writer wanted to refute them.

Lucian of Samosata (c. A.D. 115–200) wrote a satire of a Christian convert who later defects from the faith. The work is known as *The Passing of Peregrinus*. The character is a foil for the worship of Jesus. Lucian argues in chapter 11 that Christians are so enamored with Peregrinus that they revere him as a god "next after the other, to be sure, whom they still worship, the man who was impaled (ἀνασκολοπισθέντα, *anaskolopisthenta*) in Palestine because he introduced this new cult into the world." The reference to impaling is a mocking allusion to the origin of crucifixion, which developed from the older custom of impaling victims.[13] This text does not name Jesus but surely alludes to him and corroborates the facts cited above. It shows that knowledge of Jesus circulated widely in the second century.

A Syrian Philosopher, Mara Bar Sarapion

We possess one sympathetic report from the first century. It is the letter of a Syrian Stoic philosopher just after the fall of Jerusalem. This event places the letter at c. A.D. 73.[14] The incident that gives rise to his remarks appears to be the expulsion of King Antiochus IV of Commagene (whose governing city was Samosata), a moment described in Jo-

---

12. It is possible, but not certain, that this Thallus is the rich freedman of Tiberius that Josephus mentions in *Ant.* 18.167. Africanus's remarks are in his *Chronology*, fragment 18.

13. Meier, *Marginal Jew*, 1:102 n. 20.

14. Theissen and Merz, *Historical Jesus*, 76–79.

sephus, *War* 7.219–43. Mara suggests that persecuting the wise is common in a world of violence, but it never pays.

> What good did it do the Athenians to kill Socrates, for which deed they were punished with famine and pestilence? What did it avail the Samians to burn Pythagoras, since their country was entirely buried under sand in one moment? Or what did it avail the Jews to kill their wise king, since their kingdom was taken away from them from that time on?
> God justly avenged these three wise men. The Athenians died of famine, the Samians were flooded by the sea, the Jews were slaughtered and driven from their kingdom, everywhere living in the dispersion.
> Socrates is not dead, thanks to Plato; nor Pythagoras, because of Hera's statue. Nor is the wise king, because of the new law which he has given.

The remarks reflect reports he may have received from Christians, who viewed Jesus as the king of the Jews and as one who was unjustly slain for his wisdom. In addition, there is no note of Roman participation in the death, and the defeat of the Jews is seen as payment for this action.

Yet in another way Mara's view is that of an outsider, given that he equates Jesus with other wise men. He also gives no hint of resurrection. Jesus is one among many wise men, a typical secular view about Jesus that many adhere to today.

Josephus

The most important extrabiblical evidence for Jesus comes from the Jewish historian Joseph ben Matthias, better known as Flavius Josephus (c. A.D. 36–100). Josephus was the son of a priest and became a Pharisee. He came from a well-to-do family, had been a commander of Jewish Galilean forces against the Romans in the Jewish War, and became a prisoner of war in 67. Josephus predicted that Vespasian would rise to power, so Vespasian freed him when he became emperor in 69. Josephus lived under Roman protection with the approval of this ruler and wrote a series of works tracing Jewish history, in which he sought to defend the Jews to the Romans. The most comprehensive work was *Antiquities*, which traced Jewish history from creation through the aftermath of the fall of Jerusalem. In this work Josephus mentions Jesus, James, and John the Baptist. The *Testimonium Flavianum* is the most comprehensive first-century citation of Jesus outside the Bible. The citation about John does not mention Jesus but does discuss the significance of his ministry and baptism (*Ant.* 18.116–19). I will not treat it in this chapter, but I mention it in *Jesus according to Scripture* in the Synoptics section that discusses John the Baptist's ministry (§20).

On James the Just

Josephus mentions the execution of the Lord's brother during the transition of rule from Festus to Albinus in c. A.D. 62. In the three months during which a Roman ruler was absent from Judea, the Jewish leadership met under a new high priest, Annas the Younger. He was the son of the high priestly patriarch Annas, who is mentioned in Luke 3:2, John 18:13, and Acts 4:6. Annas the Younger took advantage of the lack of Roman supervision and acted to secure greater control. As Josephus says in *Antiquities* 20.200,

> He convened a judicial session of the Sanhedrin and brought before it the brother of Jesus the one called Christ (τὸν ἀδελφὸν Ἰησοῦ τοῦ λεγουμένου Χριστοῦ, *ton adelphon Iēsou tou legoumenou Christou*)—James by name —and some others, whom he charged with breaking the law (ὡς παρα- νομησάντων, *hōs paranomēsantōn*) and handed over to be stoned to death.

Some Jews protested this action. Since the Romans kept the authority to execute for themselves, Annas's act was a violation of civil power, and he was removed. The act was part of what had certainly been a long-standing feud between the family of Annas and the Christians. The conflict had extended back three decades to the life of Jesus. Caiaphas, who was high priest when Jesus was executed, was Annas the Younger's brother-in-law. Annas's charge that James broke the law recalls the charge against Stephen years earlier when Caiaphas was still high priest (Acts 6–7). James had been head of the church in Jerusalem for years, as Galatians 1:19 notes. Josephus's use of "the brother of Jesus the one called Christ" to identify James is significant because it suggests a well-known figure who needs no further description. Josephus mentions him in such an indirect manner that it lacks the look of a later insertion.[15] Christ's bare mention here suggests that this figure has already been discussed by Josephus earlier. Thus the reference here looks back to the earlier fuller treatment of the Christ. It supports the claim that the earlier passage about Jesus is an authentic part of Josephus's work.

15. The reference to the "one called Christ" could be rendered pejoratively as the "so-called Christ." This is the likely implication of the Greek and is not an expression a Christian interpolator would use. Thus, the language likely goes back to Josephus.

On Jesus

In *Antiquities* 18 Josephus outlines the various problems that the Judean people experienced under Pontius Pilate, Roman prefect from A.D. 26 to 36. The *Testimonium Flavianum* contains the most extensive, early extrabiblical description of Jesus that we currently possess. The text is cited below as it stands in all the extant manuscripts. However, I note in italics those portions whose authenticity has been challenged.[16] The text comes from *Antiquities* 18.63–64.

> Now, there was about this time Jesus, a wise man, *if it be lawful to call him a man,* for he was a doer of surprising works, a teacher of such men as receive the truth with pleasure. He drew over to him both many of the Jews, and many of the Gentiles. *He was the Christ.* And when Pilate, at the suggestion of principal men among us, had condemned him to the cross, those that loved him at the first did not forsake him; *for he appeared to them alive again the third day, as the divine prophets had foretold these and ten thousand other wonderful things concerning him.* And the tribe of Christians, so named for him, are not extinct to this day.[17]

Most scholars are confident that Josephus wrote something like this because the later mention of the Christ in the James citation from *Antiquities* 20.200 assumes a previous mention of this figure. In addition, Eusebius, the church historian, mentions this text in his *Ecclesiastical History* (1.1.7–8) and in his *Demonstration of the Gospel* (3.5.105–6). These writings show that the texts from Josephus were known by A.D. 325. Finally, four expressions sound more like Josephus than a Christian author, namely (1) "a wise man," (2) "a doer of surprising works," (3) "receive the truth with pleasure" (probably with an ironic, negative force as is often its sense in Greek), and (4) the designation of Christians with a probably derogatory reference to them as a "tribe."

Nonetheless, many have questioned whether the italicized portions of this citation go back to Josephus. They appear to be things a non-

---

16. For details see Meier, *Marginal Jew,* 1:62, 78 n. 37. The main Latin manuscripts come from the ninth century, while the earliest Greek manuscripts come from the eleventh century. As Meier notes (57), the Slavonic version of Josephus is unlikely to be authentic. Meier's treatment (56–88) is also an excellent summary of the debate.

17. The Greek reads: Γίνεται δὲ κατὰ τοῦτον τὸν χρόνον Ἰησοῦς σοφὸς ἀνήρ, εἴγε ἄνδρα αὐτὸν λέγειν χρή· ἦν γὰρ παραδόξων ἔργων ποιητής, διδάσκαλος ἀνθρώπων τῶν ἡδονῇ τἀληθῆ δεχομένων, καὶ πολλοὺς μὲν Ἰουδαίους, πολλοὺς δὲ καὶ τοῦ Ἑλληνικοῦ ἐπηγάγετο· ὁ χριστὸς οὗτος ἦν· καὶ αὐτὸν ἐνδείξει τῶν πρώτων ἀνδρῶν παρ' ἡμῖν σταυρῷ ἐπιτετιμηκότος Πιλάτου οὐκ ἐπαύσαντο οἱ τὸ πρῶτον ἀγαπήσαντες. ἐφάνη γὰρ αὐτοῖς τρίτην ἔχων ἡμέραν πάλιν ζῶν τῶν θείων προφητῶν ταῦτά τε καὶ ἄλλα μυρία περὶ αὐτοῦ θαυμάσια εἰρηκότων. εἰς ἔτι τε νῦν τῶν Χριστιανῶν ἀπὸ τοῦδε ὠνομασμένον οὐκ ἐπέλιπε τὸ φῦλον.

Christian would never say about Jesus. The discussion goes back into the sixteenth century. Even during that time, Lukas Osiander said, "Had Josephus been so inclined, . . . Josephus would have been Christian."[18] The confession of Jesus as more than a man, as the Christ, the recognition without qualification of the resurrection, and the acknowledgment that he did many things according to prophecy—these do not sound like the language of a Jewish loyalist.[19] These elements lead many to suggest that a Christian interpolator added the italicized portions or something very similar to them.

There are credible suggestions as to what the original wording may have been. An example that reflects a neutral rendering comes from F. F. Bruce.[20] The few differences from the above citation are an attempt to make this section read like the other "troubles" described in *Antiquities* and reflect the corresponding more negative tone.

> Now there arose about this time *a source of further trouble* in one Jesus, a wise man who performed surprising works, a teacher of men who gladly welcome *strange things*. He led away many Jews, and also many of the Gentiles. He was the *so-called* Christ. When Pilate, acting on information supplied by the chief men among us, condemned him to the cross, those who attached themselves to him at first did not cease *to cause trouble*, and the tribe of Christians, which has taken this name from him, is not extinct even today.

This translation emphasizes the trouble that surfaced as a result of the Christian movement. It turns the confession of Christ into a "so-called" confession. It renders the remark about those who responded to Jesus gladly with the ironic tone that the Greek likely indicates.

Another, even more neutral suggestion comes from John Meier.[21] He merely removes the three interpolations:

> At this time there appeared Jesus, a wise man. For he was a doer of startling deeds, a teacher of people who receive the truth with pleasure. And he gained a following among many Jews and among many of Greek origin. And when Pilate, because of an accusation made by the leading men among us, condemned him to the cross, those who had loved him previously did not cease to do so. And up until this very day the tribe of Christians (named after him) has not died out.

18. Theissen and Merz, *Historical Jesus*, 67. This work gives a fine summary of the discussion surrounding the text.

19. Origen tells us that Josephus was not a Christian in *Contra Celsus* 1.47 and in *Commentary on Matthew* 10.17.

20. *Jesus and Christian Origins*, 39.

21. *Marginal Jew*, 1:61.

However, this rendering lacks mention of "the Christ" in any form, which is the one feature that seems required by Josephus's later reference to James as the brother of the so-called Christ.

A final suggestion comes from Shlomo Pines.[22] He works with the Arabic tradition. His reconstruction treats a recension of Agapius, a tenth-century Christian historian:

> At this time there was a man who was called Jesus. His conduct was good, and he was known to be virtuous. And many people from among the Jews and other nations became his disciples. Pilate condemned him to be crucified, and he died. And those who had become his disciples did not abandon his discipleship. They reported that he had appeared to them three days after his crucifixion and that he was alive. Accordingly, he was thought to be the Messiah, concerning whom the prophets have related wonders. And the people of Christians, named after him, has not disappeared till [this] day.

The distinct feature of this reconstruction is that it includes an allusion to the dispute over Jesus being Messiah, but it has two problems. First, the text is late, though to its credit it seems to reflect a distinct strand of tradition about this passage. Second, it is already a translated text, which makes it uncertain how carefully Josephus has been rendered.

We cannot determine the sources Josephus used. Nor can we be positive which of the above suggestions is closest to Josephus's original text. Yet the Jewish historian's testimony is of great importance, regardless of which version one accepts. Josephus corroborates that (1) Jesus had a reputation as a wise man and a teacher of wisdom; (2) Jesus was a man with a reputation for performing unusual works; (3) Jesus' significant following led the Jewish leadership to respond against him; (4) Jesus was crucified in Judea under Pontius Pilate; and (5) the movement Jesus started was still alive and well at the end of the first century. This point matches what the Roman historians also indicated. This text removes any doubt about whether Jesus existed. It indicates that Jesus caused a stir that significantly affected history. If the version of either Bruce or Pines is correct, then the messianic claim of his ministry is also corroborated. However, of this last point we cannot be certain.

22. Shlomo Pines, *An Arabic Version of the Testimonium Flavianum and Its Implications*, Publications of the Israel Academy of Sciences and Humanities (Jerusalem: Israel Academy of Sciences and Humanities, 1971), esp. 33, 38–39 n. 145. My citation combines these two discussions, but Pines is not certain if the last sentence should be included.

One final set of texts remains. It is the testimony of the rabbinic tradition. These passages give evidence of the debate those views caused between Jews and the church fathers. How do they fit with what the other writers say?

Rabbinic Sources and Evidence of Debate with the Church Fathers

I treat the rabbinic testimony and that of the fathers together, but I limit the use of the fathers to those places where they are reacting to the Jewish position about Jesus. The discussion will not consider debates about the relationship of Jesus to prophecy and Scripture but only issues tied to the character of Jesus' life.

The difficulties in referring to the rabbinic material are the late date of this material and the seeming inaccuracies in the references. Of the many candidates often set forth from this material, only two texts from the Babylonian Talmud apparently refer to Jesus. In addition, another strand of tradition tied to Christian healing is mentioned in three distinct locations. The Babylonian Talmud is a key official rabbinic text finalized in the sixth century. The citations are not valuable for recording historical details about Jesus' life. Rather, the references may contain an important trace of a fundamental, official Jewish charge against Jesus.[23]

Two Rabbinic Texts (b. Sanhedrin 43^a and 107^b)

The first rabbinic text comes from *b. Sanhedrin* 43^a. This textual tradition is identified as a *baraita*, which means that it is an old tradition:

> On the eve of Passover Yeshu [Jesus] was hanged. For forty days before the execution took place, a herald went forth and cried, "He is going forth to be stoned because he has practised sorcery and enticed Israel to apostacy. Any one who can say anything in his favour, let him come forward and plead on his behalf." But since nothing was brought forward in his

---

23. The treatments of both Meier, *Marginal Jew*, 1:93–98, and Theissen and Merz, *Historical Jesus*, 74–76, discuss the genuine difficulties of drawing accurate, detailed information from this material. They are skeptical about its usability. Nonetheless, the correspondence between this material and the reports of Justin Martyr and Origen about Jewish views in the second century suggest that Jews did raise a charge against Jesus as a magician/deceiver. So argues Graham Stanton, "Jesus of Nazareth: A Magician and a False Prophet Who Deceived God's People?" in *Jesus of Nazareth: Lord and Christ: Essays on the Historical Jesus and New Testament Christology*, ed. Joel B. Green and Max Turner (Grand Rapids: Eerdmans, 1994), 164–80. Each of these treatments explains why other suggested texts are not likely to refer to Jesus or are too late to be of any value.

favour, he was hanged on the eve of the Passover. Ulla retorted: "Do you suppose that he was one for whom a defence could be made? Was he not a Mesith [enticer], concerning whom Scripture says [Deut. 13:8], "Neither shalt thou spare, neither shalt thou conceal him?" With Yeshu however it was different, for he was connected to government [kingship?].[24]

This text has several interesting points. (1) The clearly apologetic claim that a forty-day period was allowed for people to come to Jesus' defense contrasts with the Gospels' portrait of a rush to judgment. (2) The mention of hanging and stoning is the traditional way that Judaism referred to the death penalty. (3) The dating of the execution appears to correspond with John's chronology. (4) If the allusion to Jesus' connection to government is an allusion to his Davidic ancestry, then there is an implicit remark about his ancestral claim to kingship. Each of these points is debated, and the resolution of each detail is not clear.

But one other observation is of great potential significance. It is the claim that the leadership executed Jesus because he was for them a sorcerer-enticer and a deceiver of the nation. He led the people of Israel astray. The charge comes with a scriptural appeal to Deuteronomy 13:8, which covers how to treat false prophets. It is Jesus' teaching and powers that are attested as controversial. Here an ancient echo may exist of what we have in the fathers and in the Gospels.

The second rabbinic text, *b. Sanhedrin* 107[b], makes a similar claim, though it alludes to an event whose authenticity is questionable:

One day he [R. Joshua] was reciting the Shema when Jesus came before him. He intended to receive him and made a sign to him. He [Jesus] thinking it was to repel him, went, put up a brick, and worshipped it.

"Repent," said he [R. Joshua] to him. He replied, "I have thus learned from you: He who sins and causes others to sin is not afforded the means of repentance." And a Master [another major rabbi] has said, "Jesus the Nazarene practiced magic and led Israel astray."[25]

Once again the charge is a claim about the exercise of unusual powers and of leading Israel astray. In fact, the two points (practiced sorcery,

24. This translation (with British spellings preserved) is from Israel Epstein, ed., *The Babylonian Talmud* (London: Soncino, 1935–48). A more modern English translation appears in Stanton, "Jesus of Nazareth," 167. I do not include a discussion of a later portion of this text that engages in a wordplay allegedly involving five of Jesus' disciples: Matthai, Nakai, Nezer, Buni, and Toda. The reference is too problematic to yield much of value, though some have seen allusions at least to Matthew, Nicodemus, Boanerges (John or James), and Thaddaeus in this reference. See Bruce, *Jesus and Christian Origins*, 63.

25. Stanton, "Jesus of Nazareth," 168.

led the nation astray) appear in the same order as the earlier text from
b. Sanhedrin 43ª.

Avoid Works of Healing from the Minim (b. ᶜAbodah Zarah 27ᵇ, 16ᵇ– 17ª; t. Šeḥîṭat Ḥullin)

The evidence in this section is, at best, very indirect. Each incident
comes in a text warning Jews to have nothing to do with healing by the
minim (heretics) or healing associated with the name of Jesus, son of
Pantera. Some think this name for Jesus may be a misreading of the
Greek term for "virgin" (παρθένος, *parthenos*).[26]

In ᶜAbodah Zarah 16ᵇ–17ª, Rabbi Eliezer has just been acquitted of a
charge of associating with *minuth* (a term that means "heresy" and
often alluded to Christianity). Rabbi Akiba meets with him and wonders whether Eliezer had passed on Christian teaching at some point,
an act forbidden among the rabbis. (The mention of Akiba places us in
the early second century according to the tradition.) Eliezer then recalls that Akiba is right, for a disciple of the *minim*, Jacob of Kefar Sekaniah, told him a teaching passed on to him (by implication from
Jesus): "For of the hire of a harlot has she gathered them and unto the
hire of the harlot shall they return: they came from a place of filth, let
them go to a place of filth." The first part of the text is a paraphrase of
Mic. 1:7. The second is presented as Jesus' teaching. Eliezer admits to
liking the saying, and he is arrested for apostasy and dangerous associations.[27]

In ᶜAbodah Zarah 27ᵇ the topic is again associating with the *minim*.
Here the point is added that no one should be healed by them, even at
the risk of "an hour's life." The incident involves Ben Dama, son of
Rabbi Ishmael's sister. He was bitten by a serpent, and Jacob of Kefar
Sekaniah came to heal him, but Ishmael would not permit it, though
Ben Dama wanted to allow it. However, before Ben Dama finished
speaking, he passed away. The rabbi responded that as a result Ben

26. This entire question of the name Pantera is discussed in Bruce, *Jesus and Christian Origins*, 57–58, 175 n. 19. One talmudic text often suggested here is *b. Sanhedrin* 67ª,
which mentions a paramour known as Pandira. But any allusion to Jesus or Miriam here
is suspect, not being in the correct chronological setting, as the note in *The Babylonian
Talmud* (ed. Israel Epstein [London: Soncino, 1935–48]) on *Sanhedrin* makes clear (see
n. 12 on *b. Sanhedrin* 67ª). Thus efforts like those of Bruce Chilton to evoke this imagery
for a Jewish view of Jesus' illegitimate birth are suspect; cf. Bruce Chilton, *Rabbi Jesus:
An Intimate Biography* (New York: Doubleday, 2000), 8.

27. For this text see I. Epstein, ed., *Babylonian Talmud, Seder Nezikin: ᶜAbodah Zarah*
(London: Soncino, 1935), 85.

Dama died in purity and that "he who breaks through a fence [to protect Torah], a serpent shall bite him."[28]

These two texts indicate that the effects of Jesus' teaching, including any healing activity, were rejected by official Judaism. Such activity was seen as unclean and made one culpable for judgment. The final example combines the two traditions.

The final text is from the Tosepta, a late supplemental text to the Mishnah.[29] It also involves Ben Dama (whose full name is Rabbi Eleazer Ben Dama) and Jacob of Kefar Sama (the locale probably equals Kefar Sekaniah of the previous texts since all the figures are otherwise the same). The text also mentions Jesus, son of Pantera. Ben Dama is bitten by a snake, and Jacob comes to heal him in the name of Jesus. Rabbi Ishmael forbids it, as in the previous talmudic text. When Ben Dama says he can prove it is permitted, he drops dead. Ishmael repeats his purity and "fence" saying. This account is then immediately followed by the discussion of the trial of Rabbi Eliezer on account of the *minuth*. The account of the exchange with Akiba is repeated with one exception: with good rabbinical sensitivity, what Jesus said to him is omitted, so that the report does not repeat the crime.

These texts do not touch the life of Jesus directly, though they do underline that a healing ministry continued in the church as an extension of what Jesus had done. They also show how some traditions circulated separately but treated the same event, much like parallel texts in the Synoptic Gospels.

Similar Texts from the Fathers

Parallel evidence from the second-century church fathers provides support for the rabbinical evidence concerning Jesus' healing powers.[30] Justin Martyr in *Dialogue* 69.7 notes that Jews were arguing, "They said it was a display of magic art, for they even dared to say that he was a magician and a deceiver of the people [μάγος καὶ λαοπλάνος, *magos kai laoplanos*]." This language parallels the rabbinic material and comes in the same order as that material. The language about being a magician (ὁ μάγος, *ho magos*) does not come to Justin from the New Testament, because this term is not used of Jesus there. Justin repeats the claim that Jesus was charged with using magical arts in *First Apol-*

28. For this text see ibid., 136–37.

29. For this text see Jacob Neusner, *The Tosefta Translated from the Fifth Division Qodoshim (The Order of Holy Things)* (New York: Ktav, 1979), 74–75.

30. This section summarizes a much more detailed argument found in Stanton, "Jesus of Nazareth," 166, 171–79.

ogy 30. In *Dialogue* 108 Justin notes that Jesus was called a deceiver (πλάνος, *planos*).

Justin is not alone. Origen also discusses his debate with a pagan philosopher named Celsus in *Contra Celsum*. Origen reports Celsus's account of a Jew who directly confronted Jesus (*Contra Celsum* 1.68). The Jew challenges Jesus with a seeming concession, "Come let us believe that these miracles were really done by you." The remark is ironic, however, because Celsus explains the power by discussing the work of those who profess to perform wonderful deeds. The second-century Jew sets forth two competing options, "Since these men do these wonders, ought we to think them sons of God? Or ought we to say that they are the practices of wicked men possessed by an evil demon?" What is important here is not whether Celsus's report about a confrontation with Jesus actually happened but that the explanation reflects what second-century Jews like Celsus were saying about Jesus and his power. Here is second-century evidence about the fundamental debate over the source of Jesus' power.

The same debate shows its presence a century earlier in the New Testament. The Pharisees charged that Jesus led people astray (John 7:12, 47). The Jews said Jesus had a demon (John 10:19–21), leading to a dispute about the source of his power. In Luke 23:2 Jesus is accused of perverting the customs of the people (διαστρέφοντα τὸ ἔθνος ἡμῶν, *diastrephonta to ethnos hēmōn*), a charge very similar to "leading them astray." In Matthew 27:63–64, the chief priests and Pharisees refer to Jesus as "that deceiver" (ἐκεῖνος ὁ πλάνος, *ekeinos ho planos*). Finally, the Pharisees' charge in Mark 3:22 ties Jesus' exorcisms to the power of Beelzebul, the prince of demons. Mark 3:22 has conceptual similarities to Matthew 12:24 and Luke 11:15. In other words, the charge attested by the rabbis and the fathers parallels charges noted in the Gospels, suggesting continuity in a series of distinct witnesses. There is enough diversity in how the charges are presented that dependence on the language of the New Testament is not likely. A genuine historical echo is plausible.

Stanton's conclusion is worth citing in full:

> I have argued that the double allegation found in Justin's *Dialogue* 69:7 and in the rabbinic traditions quoted above has deep roots. In his own lifetime Jesus was said by some to be a demon-possessed magician. It is probable, but not certain, that he was also said to be a demon-possessed false prophet.
>
> Two corollaries follow. It is generally accepted that in the first and second centuries Christians and Jews were at odds about Christology and the law. It is less frequently appreciated that both the actions and teach-

ings of Jesus were a source of tension and dispute: they were assessed very differently by his later followers and opponents.

The allegations of contemporary opponents of Jesus confirm that he was seen by many as a disruptive threat to social and religious order. His claims to act and speak on the basis of a special relationship to God were rightly perceived to be radical. For some they were so radical that they had to be undermined by an alternative explanation of their source.[31]

Conclusion

This survey answers the question at the beginning of this chapter. Is the extrabiblical evidence for Jesus obscure and trivial? Hardly. The testimony of extrabiblical material raises important historical issues about Jesus. A major element of the conflict between Jesus and the Jewish leadership emerges from this material. The Roman and Syrian sources testify only to the origins of the Christian movement, how quickly and persistently it spread, and the fact of Christ's execution under Pilate. However, Josephus indicates that Jesus was a powerful and controversial figure, executed under Pontius Pilate as a so-called Christ. He was the source of bewitching teaching that caused many Jews and Gentiles to become his followers. The rabbinic material and the fathers evidence the debate that exercise of power generated. Both his power and teaching produced a major controversy for Israel. Even though Jesus began as a religious teacher on the fringe of the Roman Empire, his presence and impact had an effect the Romans noted and the Jews debated. The effect of his life is why his story in the Gospels is important to trace. To be understood and appreciated, however, Jesus' story needs to be placed in its historical context. Thus first we turn to the dates for Jesus' life as a way of seeing historical method at work. Then we turn to the history of Israel that informs the time of Jesus and the expectations of the people to whom he preached. Then we consider the culture that reacted so strongly both for and against him. Understanding Jesus' culture helps us understand the choices and illustrations contained in his message, as well as the reaction of people to him.

31. Ibid., 180.

chapter 2

A Basic Chronology of Jesus' Life

A historian who wants to retain any semblance of tension and drama in events as they unfold dare not flash forward to another, all-seeing point of view. Do so, and all tension melts away. Rather a good historian re-creates for the reader the conditions of the history being described, conveying a sense of "you were there."

That, I concluded, is the problem with most of our writing and thinking about Jesus. We read the Gospels through the flash-forward lenses of church councils like Nicea and Chalcedon, through the church's studied attempts to make sense of him.

Jesus was a human being, a Jew in Galilee with a name and a family, a person who was in a way like everyone else. Yet in another way he was different than anyone who ever lived on earth before. It took the church five centuries of active debate to agree on some sort of epistemological balance between "just like everyone else" and "something different."[1]

Our Calendar: An Indication of Jesus' Importance and an Illustration of Historical Judgment

History tells us that Jesus of Nazareth made a difference. Even the most commonly used calendar today is a testimony to his impact, dividing history into a period before and a period after Jesus (B.C.—"be-

1. Phillip Yancey, *The Jesus I Never Knew* (Grand Rapids: Zondervan, 1995), 24.

65

fore Christ"/A.D.—*anno Domini,* "in the year of the Lord"). Even those who refer to before and in the Common Era (B.C.E./C.E.) use the same break in time. But this division of time came late, some five hundred years after Jesus' life. In A.D. 525 Pope John I requested that Dionysius, a Scythian monk, prepare a calendar for the Western church. The monk modified the Alexandrian system of dating, which figured years from the reign of Diocletian, a Roman emperor who had persecuted the church. Dionysius tried to work back to Jesus' birth and mark it as A.D. 1. (The calendar became popular in the ninth and tenth centuries, but was not officially adopted until the time of Pope Gregory XIII in the late 1500s.) Later recalculating along with the discovery of fresh historical sources indicated that this diligent monk made some errors in his attempt to determine Jesus' birth date. This reconsideration of the data showed that he had miscalculated by a span of four to six years. Thus Jesus is said to have been born c. 6–4 B.C. But these differences, which this chapter will consider later, do not obscure the importance of what the change in calendar represented. The events that led to a request to redesign the calendar around the coming of Jesus are part of the history of humanity that has always had to reckon with Jesus' coming and reflect on what took place in his life.

Encountering Jesus is ultimately a reflective exercise. One meets him through the four Gospels and then assesses his story. That assessment can take place at two levels: with the Gospel narrative itself or as part of a broader historical goal to place Jesus more consciously in his larger first-century world.

Narratively, the story can be told in two ways. It can be presented as an encounter with little or no glance forward in perspective. Or it can involve a reflective mode that puts together a comprehensive point of view because the current portion of the story is told in light of knowledge of the whole story. One of the basic premises of my examination of Jesus according to Scripture is that the Gospels present him in this dual light. They show him both as he was experienced (with no flashbacks) and in a more reflective way, revealing the depth that was in part of the story in light of the rest of the story.

The Synoptics (Matthew, Mark, and Luke) generally tell Jesus' story from "the earth up," starting with a human life and then showing how his life and ministry led many to embrace him as more than human, while others rejected him. There is little or no flashback. The Synoptics tend to emphasize how he was like everyone else and yet became widely regarded as exceptional. They portray how people slowly came to realize that he might be more by the unusual nature of his life and teaching.

On the other hand, John is more reflective, telling the story "from heaven down," giving a divine point of origin in his prologue. This Jesus is the Word who was in the beginning, who was God, and who became flesh. This starting point is very different from that of the Synoptics, which begin with his miraculous birth or John's prophetic ministry. In John's Gospel, every now and then, the evangelist notes that certain things had meaning that the disciples did not realize until later (e.g., John 2:22; 12:16). In other words, there was a difference between what they experienced at the time and what they eventually came to understand about what was said or done. The very tension Yancey mentions between "like everyone else" and "something different" permeates the ways in which the Gospels present Jesus' story in Scripture. John is much more direct, from the start leaving no doubt that Jesus is very different.

In contrast, the Synoptics start with categories describing Jesus to which we can relate, even though there are unusual elements in the story. Indeed, Jesus is specially conceived, and he is presented at birth as the long-hoped-for Messiah; in other words, he is the special Promised One of God. But these three evangelists leave the more exalted understanding of Jesus to the development of the gospel story itself. They tell the story in a way people often assess Jesus, a few steps at a time. Thus, in *Jesus according to Scripture,* we shall study the developing story of the Synoptics together and then show how John connects to that account.

This is how the Gospels work as narrative. The presence of multiple Gospels allows a depth about Jesus to emerge from four different perspectives that one portrait alone could never give.

Yet to study Jesus means also to consider how we make unified, historical sense of the Gospel accounts. It is important to move from the history contained in the narrative to the big picture of how Jesus fits into the historical-cultural world in which he lived, as well as to how the various Gospel portraits relate to each other. To appreciate Jesus' story historically, we also need to set him into the history of the first century and discuss how people study him today.

The history of the development of the modern calendar illustrates nicely how historical work can help us. The scholarly, historical study of Jesus is not always right, because it is a reconstruction done by fallible people. Such study combines the evidence of various early sources, biblical and extrabiblical, in order to attempt to explain what took place. Such inquiry involves making judgments about the relationship between the pieces. It requires taking the portrait of Scripture, which presents Jesus' story faithfully, and setting that story into the backdrop

of the world from which the story emerged, a world Scripture does
not always detail for us. The sources we have that describe the world
Jesus lived in are incomplete, but they tell us enough to give us some
idea of where he fits. Some historical questions are more specific than
the information in Scripture can answer. This means that sometimes
precision in regard to the sequence, dating, or setting of events is not
as clear as we would like. We need to have patience with the tentative-
ness of historical conclusions in spots and recognize that we might
need to revise the details in light of compelling new evidence or perspectives. The presentation works with a kind of checking and cross-
checking that affects how the details of the story are seen, just as re-
checking the calendar "moved" the date of Jesus' birth from A.D. 1 to
6–4 B.C.

In other words, history in the Gospels is laid out differently from the
way we write history today. Where we would begin with Jesus' date of
birth and end with the date of his death, the Gospels just launch into
describing events. They supply dates in a way that was common for the
ancient world, connecting them to the reigns of major political or religious figures. It is here that we begin to consider where Jesus fits chro-
nologically in history.

Dating Jesus' Life

Dating Jesus' life involves understanding how the ancients reckoned
years, as well as an acquaintance with the placement of certain key
events that Scripture mentions.

Dating in the Ancient World

The ancients established dates in two primary ways. They connected
them to the length of a ruler's career, and they associated one event in
a general way to the timing of other key events. For example, in 1 Kings
15:1 the accession of the king of Judah, Abijam, is dated by the length
of Jeroboam's reign as the king of Israel in the north ("in the eighteenth
year of King Jeroboam son of Nebat, Abijam began to reign over
Judah"). This connective reckoning of kings continues throughout the
book and allows us to date many of the key figures in Israel's history.
Josephus also reckoned time this way. He writes that King Herod
began the great work of expanding the temple in the "eighteenth year
of his reign" (*Ant.* 15.380). In another text Josephus writes that the
building of Caesarea Sebaste was completed in "the twenty-eighth year
of Herod's reign, and into the hundred and ninety-second olympiad"

(*Ant.* 16.136). Such methods give us not a specific day but a range within which a specific event can be placed. Determining the date of Jesus' birth works similarly.

The Year of Jesus' Birth

In Luke 1:5 the time of John the Baptist's birth is placed in the period of "King Herod of Judea." Moreover, the Lucan account indicates that Jesus was conceived soon after John, before the Baptist was born. Matthew 2:1 agrees with this reckoning by noting that the visit of the wise men to see the baby Jesus took place "in the time of King Herod." In Luke 2:1–3 Luke relates a census "while Quirinius was governor" that he fits into the same time period as John's birth and that sent Joseph and Mary to Bethlehem. Instructed by a dream, the family goes to Egypt to escape pending danger. Finally, after the slaughter of children two years and younger by Herod, Matthew 2:19–20 notes that Joseph was instructed in a dream to bring back Jesus and Mary from Egypt. The call to return followed Herod's death. Thus in different ways Luke and Matthew show agreement about the general timing of Jesus' birth within the latter part of Herod the Great's reign.

Critics have sometimes challenged these details. They question the veracity of Luke's timing of the census and many of the historical details emerging from the infancy material. Such debates have shown up recently in television documentaries about Jesus. However, such a discussion involves more than simply noting some differences among the accounts. Let's take a closer look at this event.

The only census involving Quirinius (also spelled Cyrenius) we know about from extrabiblical material dates to "the tenth year of Archelaus's government," when Caesar removed him and placed Judah under the authority of the Roman governor of Syria, Quirinius (= A.D. 6; Josephus, *Ant.* 17.342–44; 17.354; 18.1–10). This date is too late to be tied to Jesus' birth, if Jesus was born during the reign of Herod the Great as the Gospels claim. For Herod was dead by 4 B.C. at the latest. Josephus's portrayal of this A.D. 6 census makes it look like an innovation because it involved a change of oversight and policy that was so offensive that it caused a seditious Jewish reaction against Rome. Skeptical critics cite this detail as the clearest example in Luke's Gospel of a historical error. Even some who regard Luke as normally trustworthy doubt him here.[2]

2. See, for example, Raymond E. Brown, *The Birth of the Messiah: A Commentary on the Infancy Narratives in Matthew and Luke* (Garden City, N.Y.: Doubleday, 1977), 547–56; and A. N. Sherwin-White, *Roman Society and Roman Law in the New Testament*, Sarum Lectures 1960–61 (Oxford: Clarendon, 1963), 162–71.

However, Josephus does not actually call the census itself an innovation. That is an inference critics make about his description. We also know that Josephus does not mention every census we know about from other sources. It is likely that the reason this census received Josephus's attention is that it was so disruptive. It was unprecedented because Rome administered it directly, rather than through an intermediary, like one of Herod's sons.

Other contentious issues are tied to the early census, such as how Quirinius could be associated with it, since the extant sources indicate that he was governor only later, in A.D. 6. Many proposed solutions exist. Two of the more plausible ones involve the idea that a census begun earlier under another ruler finished with Quirinius in charge, possibly in the period of 4–1 B.C., where our extrabiblical records of the Roman governors of the region have a gap. The census became associated with him as the key player at its completion. Another argues that the term translated "first" in Luke 2:2 could be rendered "before" (as in John 15:18), in which case only one census is alluded to here, the later one from A.D. 6. Neither solution is clearly preferable, but either is a possibility.[3]

These options and the fragmentary nature of our sources also reveal the care with which we should reconstruct history from the sources. The biblical materials are often prematurely judged to be erroneous, when we really cannot be sure because of the fragmentary nature of the evidence we possess. Our historical pursuit of Jesus, in terms of setting him into the larger frame of history, involves judgments about how the evidence is to be put together. Where the evidence is not complete, we should be circumspect about declaring there is an error in the biblical source, even if the exact solution to the problem surrounding the text is not entirely clear.

Even though we cannot solve the census problem, history does help with the portrait of Herod the Great as it surfaces in Matthew's account. Historical sources further illustrate Herod's murderous personality, reflected in his order to kill children two years and under. This was a horrendous act of self-preservation and paranoia that, given the size of Bethlehem, would have involved the murder of around twenty infants. One can say that his attempt to slay anyone he perceived as a threat was a constant element of his rule. He plotted the death of his uncle Joseph (*Ant.* 15.62–87), Hyrcanus of the rival Hasmonean family (*Ant.* 15.161–73), and even his own wife, Mariamne (also a Hasmonean, *Ant.* 15.218–31), not to mention his later slaying of many of the nation's elite near the time of his death (*Ant.* 17.180–81). Josephus de-

---

3. For a detailed treatment of this problem, see Darrell Bock, *Luke 1:1–9:50*, BECNT (Grand Rapids: Baker, 1994), 903–9.

scribes this final act of rage: "Now anyone may easily discover the temper of this man's mind, which not only took pleasure in doing what he had done formerly to his relations, out of the love of life, but by those commands of his which savored no humanity, since he took care, when he was departing out of this life, that the whole nation should be put into mourning, and indeed made desolate of their dearest kindred, when he gave order that one out of every family should be slain, although they had done nothing that was unjust, or against him, nor were they accused of any other crimes" (17.180–81).

But how can we date the exact time of the king's death? Once again Josephus gives us the key data. He tells us of a lunar eclipse that came during the last portion of the king's illness that led to his death (*Ant.* 17.167–81, 188–92). It is the only eclipse Josephus mentions. By astronomical calculation, we can date this to the middle of March in 4 B.C. This sets the latest date for Jesus' birth, since he was born before Herod the Great died.

What can one determine about the earliest possible date? One could place the census to a period when Herod's situation was unstable; he fell into some disfavor with Augustus in 8–7 B.C. Herod's nervousness emerges in his changing the heirs in his will a few times in his last three years. A Roman census in the final years of Herod's life is likely, especially when placed alongside uncertainty about who would succeed him. This might correlate as well with the "two-year" age span Herod specifies for slaying the infants to try to eliminate Jesus, the promised child. Working backward two years from Herod's death, the result is a birth for Jesus that falls somewhere in the 6–4 B.C. range. Given the current nature of our sources, this is as specific as we can get.

Just tracing the background of Jesus' birth shows how turbulent the period of his birth was. Jesus' homeland was subject to Rome as well as to its appointed ruler, who held onto his sovereignty with a ruthless exercise of power.

The Start and Length of Jesus' Ministry

The date of Jesus' ministry depends in part on the date of the start of John the Baptist's ministry, since John baptized Jesus before the start of Jesus' ministry.

Luke 3:1–2 names several figures who were ruling at the start of John's ministry. The dates of the following are known in terms of the timing of their rule: Herod Antipas (4 B.C.–A.D. 39), Philip (4 B.C.–A.D. 34), Caiaphas (A.D. 18–36), and Pontius Pilate (A.D. 26–36). The dates of Lysanius are not known, while Annas is probably mentioned because he is the patriarch of the high priestly family to which Caiaphas belongs. His time of rule (A.D. 6–15) had passed, but he was still an important figure as the head of this family. This places us in the later 20s to early 30s. However, Luke more precisely reckons the rule of the emperor Tiberius by noting that John began his ministry in the Roman ruler's fifteenth year.

The question remains, however, how these regal years were counted, as several systems existed side by side in the Roman world.[4] Several options need sorting out. (1) Did this reckoning count the two to three years of coregency Tiberius had with Augustus (Velleius Paterculus 2.121 and Suetonius, *Tiberius* 21, who do not agree on exactly when the coregency began [c. A.D. 11–12])? Some mention the evidence of coins that date this rise alternatively to c. A.D. 13.[5] These suboptions produce a three-year window for this reckoning. If so, the beginning of the date for John's ministry is c. A.D. 25/27, remembering that one counts years inclusively. (2) Was it counted from the death of Augustus in August of A.D. 14 or from the senate vote officially recognizing Tiberius's rule, which came a month later? (3) Was the accession year (or part of that year) included, or did the count start at the next New Year? (4) Which of three calendars did Luke use: a Roman one starting in January 1, a Jewish one counting from Nisan 1 (which would be March/April), or a Syrian one dating from October 1 (the Syrian option assumes Luke wrote to those in Antioch, which is one of the best-attested traditional options for his original audience)? These four basic questions are noted to show how complicated working with the historical data can be and how complex the judgments are that relate the biblical details to larger secular history.

Some options can be ruled out as unlikely. For example, none of our sources counts Tiberius's rule from his coregency—not Josephus, Appian, Plutarch, or Suetonius. Our evidence from coins is more disputed and thus debatable. Jewish reckoning is also unlikely, as even Jewish sources tended to date non-Jewish events in non-Jewish terms, so that no clear custom existed for reckoning in Jewish sources (e.g., 1 Macc. 1:20 reckons on the basis of Macedonian counting, while 1 Macc. 4:52 mixes calendars). Given that Luke may be Gentile and that Theophilus probably was, a Jewish reckoning is unlikely. Beyond this tentative conclusion, however, things are less clear.

Many hold that Jesus was crucified in A.D. 30. Those who favor this view suggest plausibly that Luke used a Syrian reckoning, which places

4. For more detail on the issues mentioned in this section, see Harold Hoehner, *Chronological Aspects of the Life of Christ* (Grand Rapids: Zondervan, 1977).

5. For this view see Rainer Riesner, *Paul's Early Period: Chronology, Mission Strategy, Theology*, trans. Doug Stott (Grand Rapids: Eerdmans, 1998), 40.

the fifteenth year in the fall of 27 to 28. This view notes that Luke 3:23 estimates that Jesus began his ministry when he was about thirty. It also argues for the length of his ministry running from two to three years (indicated by the number of Passover feasts John's Gospel connects to Jesus' career, John 2:13; 6:4; 11:55).

Two ways of reckoning the Roman calendar are also possible, depending on whether the three-month portion of the accession year counts as one year. If the accession year is not counted, then the time of the start of John's ministry is A.D. 29. This all but rules out an A.D. 30 crucifixion, as Jesus needs to have at least two years for his ministry (following the tightest chronology involving John's Gospel, because it requires at least two years involving three Passovers). Even if one counts from the accession directly, this only moves things back three months and leaves us with too tight a chronology for A.D. 30. Thus a decision to reckon by the Roman method likely carries with it the view that Jesus was crucified in A.D. 33, as it places the start of John's ministry in A.D. 28–29.[6]

Determining the length of Jesus' ministry depends almost entirely on data from John's Gospel, but the data do correspond to these options. The Synoptics mention only one trip to Jerusalem, the one at the end, though Luke does suggest that Jesus was in Bethany, near Jerusalem, earlier in his ministry with the visit to the house of Martha and Mary (Luke 10:38–42). As was noted, three Passovers, requiring at least two years time, are mentioned in John (John 2:13; 6:4; and 11:55 all use the term πάσχα, *pascha*). In addition, John 5:1 speaks of a feast of the Jews, which may mean a fourth Passover, hence at least three years for Jesus' ministry. Thus this reckoning requires a minimum of two years and maximum of four years for Jesus' ministry. To decide between a Syrian and a Roman reckoning requires that we also consider the data related to the year of Jesus' death. Before we consider that question, however, we need to consider one other issue that also might complicate the decision: the timing of Jesus' cleansing of the temple.

A Complicating Factor

Another issue figuring prominently in determining the date of Jesus' ministry and death is the reference in John 2:20 by Jesus' opponents that the temple (ὁ ναός, *ho naos*) was completed forty-six years previously or had been under construction for forty-six years up to this

---

6. I discuss Jesus' crucifixion date below, but the two most-discussed options are A.D. 30 and 33. This is because Nisan 14 falling on a Friday is likely only for these years, a point that rules out A.D. 31 and 32. See Hoehner, *Chronological Aspects*, 98–105.

point.[7] The allusion is to the work of Herod the Great. The opponents are responding to Jesus' claim to be able to raise up a destroyed temple in three days. The setting is the cleansing of the temple. Three factors, besides the syntax already noted, complicate determining this date.

First, there is a dispute about what is referred to here. Is the reference to the temple precincts as a whole, which can be referred to by either the Greek term ἱερόν (*hieron*) or ναός (*naos*), or is it a more specific reference to the holy inner sanctuary, which *naos* can also mean? If this more specific reference to the sanctuary is taken, then the date is at least a year and a half after the start of the work on the entire area (*Ant.* 15.421). Rounded off, two years' variation is present in this question alone.

Second, there are competing dates for when this general work began. Two come from Josephus, reflecting his own inconsistency or uncertainty. Did the work start in Herod's fifteenth year (*War* 1.401), which would be 23/22 B.C.? Was it in his eighteenth year (*Ant.* 15.380), which would be 20/19 B.C., a date that corresponds to Dio Cassius's timing of Augustus's arrival in Syria (compare Dio Cassius 54.7.4–6 with Josephus, *Ant.* 15.254 and *War* 1.399)? This raises a possibility of a three-year range in this date alone, though the bulk of the evidence suggests the c. 20 B.C. date. The additional factor of counting inclusively (any part of first year is year one) or conclusively (first year is counted only at its end), not to mention any partial year involved in or excluded from the number, adds as much as two years' difference within the options. The latest date emerging from the combination of these two issues puts Jesus' final Passover in either A.D. 29 or 30. The range of both factors together is about five years. But one other factor remains.

Third is the question of whether John refers to a separate temple cleansing early in Jesus' ministry. Is John's account distinct from the one the Synoptics mention in Jesus' last week? If this is a separate event, then this date comes near the start of Jesus' ministry. If it is the same event and has been moved forward for literary reasons to preview the opposition to Jesus' ministry, then the forty-six years should be

---

7. On the debate about how to interpret the aorist οἰκοδομήθη in John 2:20, compare Hoehner, *Chronological Aspects*, 42–43, and Leon Morris, *The Gospel according to John*, rev. ed., NICNT (Grand Rapids: Eerdmans, 1995), 176–77 n. 89. Hoehner thinks the verb means that the temple edifice was completed forty-six years earlier. Morris thinks it means that the work had been underway for the past forty-six years and was still in progress. Either interpretation is possible, and the right choice is not obvious, which further complicates the attempt to date Jesus' ministry on the basis of this verse. If Morris's position is adopted, then the options for the date are narrowed, and the only remaining question is whether or not the number forty-six should be taken as inclusive.

counted from the end of his ministry.[8] Exactly how this would affect the dating depends on how long Jesus' ministry was, a figure that varies from two to almost four years depending on how one assesses John's chronology. This would move the latest option to A.D. 36, but that date is recognized by all as too late to apply to Jesus' crucifixion, given the data we have already examined. It is also unlikely because the day of the crucifixion and burial for that year (Saturday/Sunday) does not match the possible options noted by the accounts (Friday/Saturday). What this factor also means is that another three-year variable exists within the options already noted, depending on where one places this passage. An A.D. 33 date usually places this Johannine cleansing early in Jesus' ministry, but given all of these dating variables, including the possibility of literary relocation, that conclusion is not certain either.

Again, these variables allow a range of plausible dates for the completion of Jesus' ministry from A.D. 27 to 36, with A.D. 27, 30, 33, and 36 the most common suggestions. As with other issues noted in this chapter, this imprecise and complex situation is common in attempting to relate the historical material in the Gospels to events outside the biblical material. However, the general historical placement of Jesus' ministry is not in dispute.

Turning to the four specific options, we have already suggested why A.D. 36 is not a good candidate. One can also exclude A.D. 27, since it is too early to accommodate the more likely options regarding the start of John's ministry and also requires that the earliest option for John 2:20 be correct, which is not the most likely option for that date. Thus two dates have been more frequently mentioned as marking Jesus' death, A.D. 30 and 33. To these options we now turn.

The Year of Jesus' Death

A date in A.D. 30 assumes (1) the use of a Syrian reckoning or a counting from Tiberius's coregency, (2) the date for the beginning of Herod's construction of the temple in c. 20 B.C. (assuming the precincts are meant), and (3) a short ministry (about two years) for Jesus.

None of these conclusions is certain. A Roman reckoning seems preferable over a Syrian counting, since the works of Josephus (*Ant.* 18.106, 224; *War* 2.180), Appian (*Civil War* 2.149), Plutarch (*Caesar* 62–

---

8. This is not the place to settle the question of the number of cleansings. One must note, however, the two possibilities in order to understand why the discussion of chronology is so complicated. These options can be raised without rejecting the historicity of the event. Issues of literary placement do not require a denial of historicity, especially if any specific internal chronology of the event explicitly tying it to other events in the Gospel is lacking.

67), Suetonius (*Caesar* 81.2; *Augustus* 100.2), and Dio Cassius (106.3) indicate this Roman method. Reckoning Tiberius's reign from the coregency does not seem to have been particularly common either. If Luke follows a Roman reckoning without a coregency, then an A.D. 30 date for the death is difficult, requiring too many things to happen after the fifteenth year of Tiberius as the start of the Baptist's ministry. The three uses of *naos* in John 2:19–21 are unique; elsewhere John uses *hieron* and clearly refers to the temple complex, especially the areas where Jesus taught in the temple precincts (John 2:14–15; 5:14; 7:14, 28; 8:2, 20, 59; 10:23; 11:56; 18:20).[9] If the distinction is conscious, which is plausible because Jesus is discussing a comparison of "holy" things (holy place and his physical person and presence), then this also pushes the dating two years later, moving us toward the A.D. 33 date. Finally, a two-year ministry is possible for Jesus, but one longer than three years is more likely.

If one argues for an A.D. 33 date, then this assumes (1) a Roman reckoning, (2) a reference to the "holy place" in John 2:20 with its later starting date, and probably (3) a more than two-year ministry for Jesus. The problem with this view is not so much with the chronology tied to Jesus. Rather its timing in relationship to Paul's conversion is tight. This date means that Paul was converted within two years of Jesus' death (given the data in Gal. 1). This tight time frame is possible, but it must be admitted that it is compact.

However, one more factor may favor an A.D. 33 date. The "foreign minister" for Rome during the early period of Pilate's governorship was Lucius Aelius Sejanus, who was known as anti-Semitic (Philo, *Embassy* 159–61) and served as the prefect of the Praetorian guard, commanding the elite of nine thousand strong imperial soldiers. With Tiberius on the island of Capri and having lost interest in ruling, Sejanus held a considerable amount of power.

Early in his rule, Pilate showed signs of insensitivity to the Jews that reflected the attitude of his boss, Sejanus. First, on his arrival Pilate insisted that Roman standards with images of the emperor be erected in Jerusalem, angering the Jews because the images raised the specter of idols and pagan worship in the capital (*Ant.* 18.55–59; *War* 2.169–74). Jewish persistence led Pilate to relent. Second, he took funds from the temple treasury to build an aqueduct (*Ant.* 18.60–62; *War* 2.175–77). This unpopular move prompted the Jews to protest. Pilate ordered his troops secretly to infiltrate the crowd. When the protest became loud, the troops beat the crowd with clubs, killing some. Luke 13:1 relates a third incident in which Pilate apparently ordered the beating of some

9. John Meier, *A Marginal Jew: Rethinking the Historical Jesus*, vol. 1: *The Roots of the Problem and the Person* (New York: Doubleday, 1991), 381.

Galileans as they attempted to prepare to offer sacrifices. Finally, the Roman representative issued coins for the region with a symbol indicating worship of the emperor. None of this would have enamored Pilate to Herod or to the Jews in general. Philo also records an incident involving shields with the emperor's name erected in Herod the Great's former palace (*Embassy* 299–305). It is possible this event took place after Sejanus died, so Pilate was simply showing his support for Tiberius. However, the protest brought Tiberius's rebuke for the insensitivity shown, and the shields were removed.

Sejanus was eventually suspected of garnering too much power to himself. However, he was tricked into revealing his desire and was executed in October of A.D. 31. Luke 23:12 notes the enmity Herod had for Pilate up to the point of Jesus' trial. When Pilate was considerate enough to send Jesus to Antipas, thereby finally giving his counterpart some respect, they became friends. These events make better sense in this later time frame than in A.D. 30.

Thus for these series of factors, it is slightly more likely that Jesus' death should be dated in A.D. 33 than 30.

Summary on the Dates

My detailed explanation of the dates of Jesus' life shows that we can place him within a range for both his birth (6–4 B.C.) and his death (A.D. 30–33). This general placement has much historical support. The details are important to discuss, however, to show the complexity of the historical enterprise. Even when one has confidence concerning the events Scripture portrays, placing them in the larger historical frame of the world is not always easy. It involves making judgments about how exactly the background fits. Date ranges for ancient figures are not unusual given the fragmentary nature of our data. Yet even in the absence of precise detail, important and interesting facts about the setting of Jesus' life emerge, and a solid approximation of his dates is possible.

The sociopolitical setting at the time of both Jesus' birth and death is complex. Rome and local rulers often wielded power ruthlessly. To the Romans, ruling meant exercising total power and demanding submission. Loyalty to those powers was important. Rome permitted religious freedom as long as it did not affect loyalty to the state. Protest was often dangerous and life-threatening. One thing was clear: Israel was far from free. They longed for the day when God would let his people worship him without the tensions introduced by the presence of foreign authority. The political figures associated with Jesus' birth and death show why someone like the first-century Jewish priest Zechariah yearned for the day when God's people might be able to "serve him [God] without fear, in holiness and righteousness before him all of our days" (Luke 1:74–75). Placing Jesus' ministry in historical context explains why Jews might have an interest in anyone who became associated with God's powerful presence among his people. The crucial backdrop for what motivated that hope awaits a discussion of Jewish history, culture, life, and religion.

chapter 3

Political History

How did Jesus relate to Palestinian Judaism and how was he different from other Palestinian Jews?

The issue is complicated by a wonderful problem that now confronts historians: the wealth of information that has come to the fore concerning first-century Palestine. Archaeological excavations, the discovery of the Dead Sea Scrolls, refinement of social-scientific methods for studying ancient cultures, and other factors have combined to broaden our view of Jesus' world. It was a more diverse world than we once thought. Indeed, most scholars are reluctant to speak of Judaism as a monolithic entity at all for this period. Rather, there were varieties of "Judaisms," developing trajectories, and competing ways of being Jewish.[1]

The difficulty for any historian is in achieving the right balance between Jesus' continuity and discontinuity with early Judaism. Insist on too much discontinuity, and it becomes impossible to explain why Jesus had an exclusively Jewish following during his lifetime and why so many different kinds of Jews were interested in giving him a hearing. Insist on too much continuity, and differences of the church from early Judaism, even in the church's earliest days, become very difficult to explain.[2]

1. Mark Allan Powell, *Jesus as a Figure in History: How Modern Historians View the Man from Galilee* (Louisville: Westminster John Knox, 1998), 170.
2. Ben Witherington III, *The Jesus Quest: The Third Search for the Jew of Nazareth* (Downers Grove, Ill.: InterVarsity, 1995), 122.

Why Appreciating Jewish History Is Important to Understanding Jesus

To understand Jesus and the Gospels, one must understand the complexity of Judaism in the time of Jesus. The traumas in the six centuries before Jesus marked this people, their religious practice, and their expectations. This history of engagement with foreigners explains how Jesus was understood and misunderstood. The Judaism of Jesus' time that emerged from this history is now called second temple Judaism. It is a complex entity made up of many factions and competing concerns.

To understand the impression history made on the Jewish people, we must review Israel's history as it moves from the Babylonian captivity to Persian rule to the rule of the Greeks through Alexander the Great. After Alexander, Israel was ruled by the Ptolemies of Egypt and then the Seleucids of Syria. This period from Babylon to the Seleucids runs from 586 to 167 B.C.[3] In this period, when Israel was occupied, Jews faced the central question of how they could best live in the midst of Gentiles and still be faithful to God. The various views taken on this question dominated Jewish identity for the centuries before Jesus.[4]

This brings us into the crucial time that led to a period of Israelite independence under the Maccabeans, better known as the Hasmoneans (167–63 B.C.). Many of the key Jewish groups of Jesus' time surfaced during this period, when Israel had as much political unity and independence as it had experienced since the time of David and Solomon. The final period we consider is that of Roman rule (63 B.C.–A.D. 36).[5] The complexity of Jewish identity, life, and politics during this

3. A chart of the key periods of rule over the land of Israel/Judea appears at the end of this chapter.

4. The ways in which Judaism of the Diaspora attempted to cope with the presence of Hellenism and the Gentiles is examined in John J. Collins, *Between Athens and Jerusalem: Jewish Identity in the Hellenistic Diaspora*, 2d ed., Biblical Resource Series (Grand Rapids: Eerdmans, 2000). This work also discusses the setting of many books found among the Old Testament Pseudepigrapha. On a continuum, Collins describes three basic approaches to Judaism: (1) a concern for law as expressed in the concept of "covenantal nomism" (the view that one is a member of the covenant community by birth but one maintains this position of blessing by keeping the law), (2) a pride in Jewish history that engendered ethnic pride, and (3) a moral system presented as an ethic to the Gentiles. The spectrum within Israel was even more complicated, as allegiance to the law was expressed with even more intensity by some Jews living in Israel. Collins comments that covenantal nomism, though popular, was not necessarily dominant even among Diaspora Jews.

5. Roman rule extended far beyond A.D. 36, of course, but we are following the story only through the end of Pilate's rule.

time gives us insight into how Jesus was both a hope and a threat to Jews.

The Historical Backdrop to Second Temple Judaism and the Life of Jesus

The Babylonian Exile and the Persian Period (586–331 B.C.)

No event is more devastating for a nation than to lose its freedom and autonomy, as happened when Babylon overran Israel and Nebuchadnezzar sacked Jerusalem in 586 B.C. Nothing indicates the emotional shock of the Israelites as much as the Old Testament Book of Lamentations, which begins with wailing over the fate of Jerusalem: "How lonely sits the city that once was full of people . . . she that was a princess among the provinces has become a vassal" (1:1). The cause of the nation's fate is also noted in 1:8, "Jerusalem sinned grievously, so she has become a mockery." God had judged his people because they had been unfaithful, and some in the nation understood why Israel was overrun.

The consequences for Israel were devastating, as the Babylonians were ruthless in victory. The results of invasion fragmented the nation. The Babylonian policy was to deport their enemies' elite and assimilate the leaders into Babylonian culture. They sought to degrade Israel's potential to return and reassert Israelite independence. (The policy was so prominent and permanent that a major rabbinic community for Jews resided in Babylon even a millennium later.) The new exiles were trained in Babylonian beliefs and customs, as the early chapters of Daniel indicate, even though the most faithful resisted the efforts. Those not captured and taken to Babylon fled to Egypt, a nation that was often a haven for Jews when powers overran them from the east. Jeremiah ended up with this group but warned them they would not be successful (Jeremiah 44) in their effort to preserve the nation in distinct communities while compromising their faith with the use of idols. Many of Israel's poor were left in Israel because they were not important politically.

The new reality raised new, major religious questions. How should Jews live faithfully before God when they were neither independent nor in their land? How could they be faithful to God when they had no temple? The question of how to live with foreigners and as a minority raised new challenges for Israel. Other questions also surfaced. Where is our God that such a defeat could occur? If our punishment is the product of unfaithfulness, how do we come back into blessing? How should we endure the suffering of judgment? Do we accommodate or separate or compromise as we try to live in the Gentiles' midst and yet be distinct in our worship and practice?

The questions raised by the exile remained for Israel for much of this period. Even in the time of Jesus, when the nation had been back in the land for five centuries, they were still subject to Rome and faced the question of how to interact with the presence of Gentiles and their distinct practices. The various Jewish groups Jesus encountered had different answers to these basic questions. Understanding how these groups emerged helps us appreciate the challenge in Jesus' life and message.

In 539 B.C. Cyrus the Persian overran Babylon. A wise statesman, his policy for the nations he conquered was the reverse of Babylon's. Rather than assimilation, he opted for tolerance. All nations could keep their religious and cultural practices; they would not be forced to become "Persian." Edicts of deportation were canceled, and exiles wishing to return to Jerusalem could do so. He authorized the temple to be rebuilt in Jerusalem. He even offered to help pay for its reconstruction (2 Chron. 36:22–23; Ezra 1:2–4). Ezra notes (6:3–5) that this fulfilled God's promise to Jeremiah (Jer. 29:10). The second temple was completed in 515 B.C. Haggai 2:3 suggests that the glory of the new temple did not reach that of the old, but the prophet promised that God again would show his faithfulness and presence to the people (2:4–9, 20–23). For many, this connected to the hope of a branch from the house of David that Jeremiah had predicted (Jer. 23:5; 33:15). Jeremiah 30–36 looked forward to an eschatological day when God would again work with Israel, a hope that paralleled language in Isaiah 40–66 and Ezekiel 34–36.

What should Jews do as they waited for God to act? They should turn back to being faithful and walk in the ways of the Law. The rise of figures like Ezra, Nehemiah, and Daniel showed how one should be faithful before God until the promised divine restoration comes. Here is the call to God's people. Keep the Law. Observe those practices that mark out God's people as faithful to the one true God. Discourage intermarriage with Gentiles. Such practices reflect one's identity and faithful walk. The nation understood from the exile what the consequences of unfaithfulness were.

Most of what we know about this period concerns Babylon and Persia. Archaeology also reveals that a large group of Jews gathered in Egypt at Elephantine. This group took a different approach to the faith in exile, building their own temple to keep traditional worship alive, even though this violated the prohibition in Deuteronomy 12:5 to build other temples. Thus this temple took on only the form of faithfulness; names reflecting the presence of idols and the use of the name of Anat (queen of the heaven) are also found at this site.[6] Jeremiah's earlier warning for Jews in Egypt was not being heeded. The choice of this group was to syncretize their faith.

Four other developments seem to reach back into this period. They reflect major changes in Jewish life and perspective.

1. The synagogue as a place of prayer, gathering, education, and worship probably arose initially to make up for the absence of the temple and then the problem of distance from Jerusalem after the temple was rebuilt. The synagogue was not a temple. It was an innovation rather than a violation of the Law, and it became the center of religious identity and practice. It also led to the development of teachers and rabbis who would lead the nation in instruction about the Law, which now came to be a center of religious concern. In a way, Judaism became an ethnic way of life and worship built around a nomocracy (a rule by law). That nomocracy was supported by a growing oral law, or body of tradition, designed to deal with the demands of the new and changing setting.

2. Aramaic as a dominant language emerged in this period, as Old Testament texts indicate (Neh. 8:8). This meant that Jews no longer would have direct access to the language of their Scriptures in their native tongue, even when it was read to them orally, as would have most often been the case in this period. A second key foreign tongue, Greek, would emerge later with the rise of the influence of Hellenism. It would become the language of the New Testament.

3. With no political authority, no king, and a rebuilt temple, one figure became central in Jewish religion and life: the high priest. He formerly shared authority with the king but now took on an expanded role, especially in the face of a diminution of the role of prophets. Within Israel, Judaism was becoming a temple-state, a people united in its religion and worship. Thus it was natural that the role of high priest not only involved the temple but also political authority as national representative to foreign powers.

4. The exposure to the belief systems of other nations intensified strands of ideas already present in Judaism. For example, the Persian emphasis in Zoroastrianism on dualism and the spiritual forces of good and evil led to more reflection about the nature of the cosmic conflict between good and evil beings. The intertestamental literature is full of

6. For a summary of life at this colony, see F. F. Bruce and David F. Payne, *Israel and the Nations: The History of Israel from the Exodus to the Fall of the Second Temple*, rev. ed. (Downers Grove, Ill.: InterVarsity, 1997), 107–10.

details about such figures that appear only briefly in the Old Testament. As events in history became turbulent, it seemed only natural to ask what might be going on with unseen forces that were at work. Detailed angelology and demonology emerged in some writings, especially in pseudepigraphical texts from the next few centuries. This focus on unseen forces led to the rise of both apocalyptic speculation, which is inherently dualistic (i.e., tracing the struggle of good versus evil), and to concern about the afterlife and resurrection. What happened after death became a natural topic for a people who would face persecution and martyrdom for their faith when the threats to Judaism emerged under the Seleucids and Antiochus Epiphanes in the second century B.C.

All of these features indicate how Judaism had to cope with major changes that the exile brought into its history. No longer was Israel a theocratic state in control of its political and religious environment. More than that, Jews now had to decide how they would cope with life among the nations as well as dealing with the nations in the midst of their land. How would they deal with a seemingly more powerful people who worshiped other gods and idols instead of the one true God of Israel? In the exile and after it up to the time of Jesus, Judaism was a faith dealing with constant major changes in its circumstances. Some Jews lived far away from the land; others returned to it. Many left the land to pursue a richer life that other locales could offer. All faced the question of how to be faithful to God in the midst of people who did not know Yahweh. As difficult as these transitions were, the questions only intensified when Greek civilization made its way to Israel through the presence of that great conqueror, Alexander the Great. The aftermath of the empire he established significantly added to the dilemma. When Hellenism came, Israel's unique religion and history faced even more pressure and a wider array of choices and events threatening its destruction.

From Alexander the Great to Antiochus Epiphanes (331–175 B.C.)

The world has seen few conquerors like Alexander the Great of Macedonia. His father, Philip II, had defeated Athens in 338 B.C., but Philip had great respect for Greek thinking. He had his son Alexander tutored by Aristotle, and Alexander fell in love with the ideal image of Achilles the warrior, a figure immortalized in Homer's *Iliad*. When Alexander came to power, he quickly swept across the world, conquering from the corner of northern Africa into southern Russia and as far as what is today India. Israel came under his control in 331 B.C. Everywhere he went he planted cities built on a Greek model. He hoped to bring that culture to the entire world. However, his careless lifestyle left him susceptible to disease, and he died from an intense fever at thirty-two in 323 B.C. Alexander allowed religious worship to continue as it had under the Persians, but his death set in motion forces that made Israel a buffer zone between two key parts of the empire.

When Alexander died, he had only two potential heirs, a mentally handicapped half-brother (Philip) and a son who was born after his death (Alexander). The ensuing struggle over succession left both dead, so that power fell into the hands of his generals, called the *Diadochi* ("successors"). The empire was divided into four parts, but two portions were crucial to Israel's story: Egypt, ruled by the Ptolemies, and Syria, ruled by the Seleucids.

Ptolemy and his line became rulers over Egypt and portions of the eastern Mediterranean, including Israel. They maintained that control from c. 300 to 198 B.C. They were known to Israel as the king(s) of the south, the Ptolemaic line.[7] They continued the policy of religious toleration that the Persians and Alexander had followed. They also continued to battle for territory and raised taxes to support their efforts. Here originated the basis for the hatred of tax collectors so prominent in the New Testament. They also built great cities, like Alexandria in Egypt, which became a popular home for Jews, so much so that one of the five sections of the city was entirely Jewish. They constituted a significant minority in the city. Many Jews flocked to this city to share in its economic opportunity. Here the first major translation of the Old Testament emerged, known as the Septuagint (LXX). The Jewish work *The Letter of Aristeas* gives a legendary account of how this translation came about under Ptolemy II (282–246 B.C.) as a monument to Jewish and Gentile relations.[8] The creation of the translation shows that many Jews of that time needed Scripture in a language other than the original Hebrew. The Septuagint is an important translation not only because it shows how many Diaspora Jews were assimilating into the foreign cultures in which they lived but also because many of the Old Testament citations in the New Testament reflect the renderings growing out of this version.

From Syria Seleucid and his line controlled Western Asia. The Seleucids became known as the king(s) of the north. They actively promoted

---

7. Daniel 11 discusses the period from Persian rule through the reign of Antiochus Epiphanes.

8. *Aristeas* 47–51 names seventy-two scholars who participated. The translation was completed in seventy-two days with a curse issued to anyone who changed it in any way, showing the respect some had for the translation (*Aristeas* 307–11). From this point on, dates in parentheses following a person's name give the years of regal or priestly rule.

the Hellenistic lifestyle. They also established major cities, like Antioch of Syria, which would become one of the major commercial centers of the Roman Empire. Many Jews were attracted to this new way of life; they enjoyed Greek dress, the gymnasium, theater and stadium events, as well as the societies structured around such venues. The gymnasium stressed a well-rounded person and physical fitness and promoted male exercise in the nude. This caused some Jews to seek to reverse the sign of their ethnicity, circumcision (1 Macc. 1:14–15; 2 Macc. 4:10–17). Other pious Jews reacted against this lifestyle, as 1 and 2 Maccabees clearly indicate through their detailed description of this key period. These very pious Jews became known as the Hasidim (or Hasideans). They deplored the changes, although they did not have the power at the time to stop them. The reactions to Hellenism created major splintering within Israel.

Thus Israel was caught politically between Egypt and Syria, two powerful parts of the old Macedonian Empire. Culturally, however, both parts of the empire exerted constant pressure on the religious views, identity, and practices of Jews.

Egypt and Syria constantly fought with each other; they had six periods of war during this time. For almost a century, Israel escaped the geopolitical fray, except as a source for Ptolemaic tax revenue. Finally in 202–198 B.C., the Seleucid ruler Antiochus III (223–187 B.C.) defeated Egypt when the Ptolemaic king Ptolemy V (204–180 B.C.) was an infant. The key battle was at Panion/Paneas (variously dated as 200 or 198 B.C.), near the source of the Jordan River.[9] With Israel shifting to Seleucid control, it entered a new and key chapter of its history.

The arrival of Hellenism challenged the Jewish faith with a new way of life, new prosperity, and even a new diet. Hellenism offered an alternative to Jewish life as well as the enticing possibility of participation in a growing international commerce. Some were attracted to the opportunity. They headed to places like Alexandria in Egypt and Antioch in Syria. Loyalty to Judaism and the integrity of one's Jewish identity became associated with keeping certain Jewish practices. The choice to acclimate to Hellenism or remain distinct from it is illustrated in a battle between two prominent Jewish families, the Oniads and Tobiads. The Oniads were generally pro-Jewish, skeptical about Hellenism, and held the high priesthood when the Seleucids gained control of Israel. The Tobiads were a wealthy, commercially oriented family whose roots went back to their opposition to Nehemiah. They were more open to Helle-

9. On the dispute over the date of this battle, see Emil Schürer, *The History of the Jewish People in the Age of Jesus Christ*, ed. Geza Vermes et al., rev. ed., 3 vols. in 4 (Edinburgh: Clark, 1973–87), 2:89 n. 10; he prefers the 200 B.C. date.

nism and a compromise between the two cultures. These two families, which became intertwined through marriage, and those close to them would eventually enter a bidding war for the high priesthood to gain control of the situation and retain influence with the Seleucid leaders. Differing views led to splinters within each of the families. Sometimes maintaining influence meant seeking Ptolemaic support as a counter to the other side. The mix was a lethal combination. It was this battle, along with deteriorating Seleucid relations with the growing power of Rome, that led to the traumatic events tied to Antiochus IV (175–163 B.C.), brother of Seleucid IV (187–175 B.C.), the successor to Antiochus III.

Antiochus IV is better known by two names that summarize how controversial he was. He called himself Antiochus Theos Epiphanes, which means "Antiochus God Manifest," a reference to his claim to be a divine agent. Others called him Antiochus Epimanes, which means "Antiochus the madman." The story of how he became so controversial is important to understanding Israel's history and the Jewish mind-set. The events associated with this king highlight the choices Jews had to make to preserve their faith.

Antiochus IV (Epiphanes) and the Road to the Maccabean Revolt (175–164 B.C.)

Antiochus III had just established Seleucid control over Israel; now he sought greater goals, but his efforts at expansion failed miserably when he suffered a devastating defeat against the Romans in 190 B.C. at Magnesia. This defeat, formalized in the treaty of Apamea (188 B.C.), required that the Seleucid line pay the heaviest indemnity required up to that time (15,000 talents). They had to repay the fine in just twelve years as well as to give up prosperous land and key military capabilities (elephants and ships). The result was that other territories separated from Seleucia, so the Seleucid rulers were left to raise funds from the weaker, less prosperous remaining portions of the empire. This was the political reality that Antiochus IV inherited from his brother, Seleucus IV, in 175 B.C. This desperate situation made Israel prey to the assertion of what Seleucid authority remained, as well as a source for raising the exorbitant fees the Romans demanded. Israel would have to choose between faithfulness and prosperity, purity and access to power. Eventually, it would be forced to decide between submission to Gentiles and allegiance to God.

What brought events to the initial breaking point was a three-way battle in bidding for the high priesthood.[10] One key player was Onias

10. A chart listing the succession of high priests during this period appears at the end of this chapter.

III, the hereditary high priest of the line of Zadok, a pious Oniad and ruling member of a family that had now intermarried with the Tobiads. He was the son of the highly respected Simon II (Sirach 50:1–21), who was high priest (220–198 B.C.) when Antiochus III came to power. Simon II had led work to repair Jerusalem, bringing great honor to his family and line as loyal Jews. Onias III (198–175 B.C.) inherited the priesthood from his father. The second figure was his ambitious brother, Jason, an ardent pro-Hellenist. Finally, there was an opportunistic aid to Jason, Menelaus, who had no hereditary claim to the office.

Antiochus IV came to power in 175 B.C. after the assassination of his brother, Seleucid IV. Onias III was the high priest at that time. Antiochus had spent much time in Rome and Athens and knew that he would have to pay the Romans. Onias III met with the new king in Antioch but found he had a rival in his brother Jason. His sibling argued that if the new king would select him as high priest, then he would promote the Hellenism so dear to the new ruler. Jason also offered to pay the treasury a significant sum for the honor. So Antiochus, needing money to pay Rome, appointed Jason and established a dangerous precedent for how the key office of high priest was filled. Jason did promote Hellenism in a way that shocked the pious of Israel, paying for the right to be a citizen of Antioch and for the right to send a deputation of citizens to participate in athletic games at Tyre in honor of the god Heracles. The donation was not paid to the games in honor of the god; rather it was paid directly to the king to avoid religious offense. Still the pious in Israel saw the act as the height of impiety. Some in Israel felt drawn to Egypt and the old days of the Ptolemies, when Egypt gave Israel more religious freedom. In addition, the Egyptians longed to strike back at the Syrians. Meanwhile, the Hellenist supporters in Israel continued to back Antiochus.

In 172 or 171 B.C., Jason sent his annual tribute to Antiochus through Menelaus, brother of a captain of the temple guard. Menelaus betrayed his superior and offered to pay Antiochus three hundred more talents than Jason for the right to be high priest, an offer Antiochus accepted, even though Menelaus had no hereditary right to the position (2 Macc. 4:23–29). Menelaus had trouble raising the money but managed to keep the position in part by having Onias III murdered. Antiochus was so upset by this inflammatory act that he had the actual murderer executed. Yet Menelaus escaped when he again bribed Antiochus. Some who opposed this appointed high priest were martyred. These events triggered a bloody period of Israel's history as the people struggled to be faithful.

Just after all of this, Egypt planned to invade Antiochus's territory, but he beat them to the punch and defeated them, removing them as a major political factor. He took the occasion to solidify his power with a treaty in 169 B.C. that gave him control of the region. These wars and the old treaty with Rome required funds, but Egypt now was no longer a source of income, because they had agreed to a cooperative peace. Thus Antiochus turned to the temple treasury in Jerusalem. Menelaus escorted him into the temple, an act in violation of the Law in that not only a Jewish layman entered the sacred area but also a pagan king. Collecting eighteen hundred talents, the king gathered his resources, yet escaped divine punishment. Jewish writings regarded God's toleration of Antiochus's unrighteous act as a sign of judgment on his people for their continued unfaithfulness (2 Macc. 5:15–26; 1 Macc. 1:25–28). But Antiochus was not done with Jerusalem or his policy to hellenize the country.

Meanwhile, Rome was nervous about Antiochus's rising power and sent an envoy, Gaius Popilius Laenas, an old friend of Antiochus from Rome, to confront him at Eleusis, four miles from Alexandria (Livy, *History of Rome* 45.12; Polybius, *Histories* 29.27). Popilius did his duty. When they met, he immediately handed Antiochus the Roman senatorial decree demanding that Antiochus leave Egypt. Popilius told him to read the decree before doing anything else. Antiochus responded that he must consult with his friends about what he would do. Then Popilius drew a circle in the sand around the Seleucid leader and told Antiochus not to leave the circle until he agreed to leave Egypt at once. Egypt would be Rome's. After a short pause, Antiochus submitted. Only then did Popilius shake the hand of his old friend. Rome was becoming supreme; Syria was left with a portion of its old realm.

False rumors had spread that Antiochus was dead, so Jason thought he had a chance to reclaim the high priestly office he had lost. He and a band of one thousand men tried to reclaim Jerusalem; yet after an initial success that saw Menelaus flee, they failed. News of the conflict reached Antiochus as he returned from Eleusis. The king saw the act as a rebellion against him and dispatched an army to regain control and reinstate Menelaus. The army stormed into Jerusalem, crushing the uprising. Some citizens were taken into slavery and sold. Antiochus needed stability on this Egyptian border controlled by Rome, so he acted to quell the nationalism. He issued an edict in 167 B.C. that annulled the old temple-state that had existed since the Persian period. He tried to make Jerusalem a Greek city-state. He began his actions on the Sabbath, destroyed the city walls, and built a manned citadel (the Acra) in the temple area. He commanded that the Scriptures be destroyed, that feast days and the Sabbath no longer be observed, that strict food laws be annulled, and that circumcision be discontinued (1 Macc. 1:41–64). There would no longer be specifically Jewish customs. Antiochus's whole kingdom should be one people.

The final act came in December of 167 B.C. when Antiochus erected an altar in the temple and offered pigs as sacrifices to Zeus. This act, predicted by Daniel (11:31), became the model for a later "abomination of desolation" mentioned in the New Testament (Dan. 9:27; Matt. 24:15). He commanded that Jews offer such sacrifices in various locales set up in honor of "the lord of heaven." The pious in Israel had finally seen the limit of what they regarded as an all-out pagan attack on their faith. Their reaction led to a major conflict for religious and political freedom, known as the Maccabean revolt. It began when an old priest with five sons, Mattathiah, killed an Israelite about to offer one of these commanded pagan sacrifices; he reportedly cried out, "Let everyone who is zealous for the law and supports the covenant come out with me" (1 Macc. 2:27). From the wilderness, they launched a clever guerrilla campaign. It took three years to bear fruit. During that time Mattathiah died, but his son, Judas Maccabeus, ably assumed leadership. Their eventual victory gave birth to a period of Israeli independence in the family line known as the Hasmoneans, the family name of Mattathiah's ancestor. This was the only time since the Babylonian exile that Israel had control of her political role. The Hasmonean rule started as a period filled with hope. Perhaps God was restoring his people.

The temple was formally reclaimed later in 164 B.C. The victors purified the temple by removing the old altar and building a new altar, and eight days of celebration began (1 Macc. 4:36–61; 2 Macc. 10:1–8). It is this event that is the basis for Hanukkah, the Feast of Dedication. The entire incident reflected the repeated history of God's preservation of Judaism, starting with the exodus and now seen as realized again with the Maccabees. Fresh hope emerged. Events in 164 B.C. did not end the battle for freedom; at various points the Seleucids regained temporary superiority. However, the constant battles for the Seleucid throne between various descendants of Antiochus III kept the Seleucids from totally reasserting their authority.

Direct Seleucid involvement remained until 142 B.C., when Simon, the Hasmonean leader of Israel at the time, negotiated Jewish freedom from the Seleucid Demetrius II as a reward for supporting Demetrius's effort against Trypho, who was bidding for the Seleucid throne. That Simon had obtained Roman support and protection helped to make Israel appear untouchable. Simon became known as the "great high priest and commander and leader of the Jews" (1 Macc. 13:42). He was also elected "leader and high priest forever, until a trustworthy prophet should arise" (1 Macc. 14:41). In other words, the Hasmonean line was in place to serve as both political ruler and high priest until God explicitly indicated otherwise. Yet intrigue over the throne continued for both the Seleucids and the Hasmoneans, while the Ptolemies of Egypt kept up the pressure and various key families in each nation continued to seek political power.[11] The final threat of the Seleucids was not removed until Antiochus VII met his demise at the hands of another power of the region, the Parthians, in 129 B.C. After almost forty years of struggle, Israel was finally free and on its own.

Yet for all practical purposes, the turning point in a Jewish move toward temporary freedom was with the victory in 164 B.C. It began what became known as a short golden age in Israel's history. The events also explain why the most pious in Israel were nervous about the influence of the nations in their midst. In the view of the most pious Jews, Jewish identity and faithfulness were tied with loyalty to their religious practices. The roots of the Jewish groups we meet in Jesus' life go back to this period, although they were certainly already marked by what had taken place under Antiochus IV and the Maccabean revolt.

Hasmonean Rule (164–63 B.C.)

The Hasmonean line was another name for the Maccabean descendants. The name goes back to an ancestor of Mattathiah, Hashmon. The dynasty introduced a rule that would receive mixed reviews from the nation. On the one hand, Israel was independent and its territory expanded under the military leadership of this family, but the cost both in terms of the need to raise money for the effort and in terms of the spiritual well-being of the country was immense. What the nation had feared in the leadership of foreigners, the raw exercise of political power, was now happening among its own leaders. The situation became so bad that the nation solved the problem by inviting in foreigners, the Romans, to solve it.

The precedent for the controversial combining of priesthood and political leader predated Simon. In 152 B.C. a pretender to the Seleucid

---

11. The complexity of this period is well surveyed in Bruce and Payne, *Israel and the Nations*, 159–68. The Hasmonean choice to bring the high priesthood and political rule together in one person was never popular with the most pious forces in Israel, who felt their Scripture did not permit such a concentration of religious and political power. Thus this concentration of power led to the opposition of what would become the party of the Pharisees, while the Sadducees supported a move toward political autonomy and stability. Meanwhile, the Essenes were so disturbed that they withdrew to the desert at Qumran to await God's vindication.

throne, Balas, claimed to be the younger son of Antiochus IV. He gained the support of Ptolemy VI and challenged Demetrius II. As Balas pursued his goal, he gained the support of Jonathan Maccabeus, who had succeeded Judas upon his death in 160 B.C. Balas not only proclaimed Jonathan high priest but also presented him with a crown and purple robe, signifying political power. This was a frightful precedent. The national struggle went back to Antiochus IV's willingness to put the priesthood up for sale to Jason and Menelaus. However, now a Hasmonean, from the very family that had reacted against such foreign intervention and defended the Law, was accepting in violation of the Law this dual role of ruler and high priest from a foreigner who did not even possess the right to give it. Jonathan even claimed to be Antiochus's rightful heir.

It is also possible (but not certain) that when Jonathan took hold of the priesthood, he did so at the expense of another candidate. This candidate fled into the wilderness with those loyal to him. The rejected candidate suffered persecution at the hands of the new ruler–high priest Jonathan. The candidate, unhappy with the turn against the Law, simply called Jonathan "the wicked priest." These descriptions of the other candidate appear in documents describing the "Teacher of Righteousness." This figure is known to us today as the founder of the Qumran community that produced the Dead Sea Scrolls. In other words, some, rather than accepting Hasmonean rule, chose to withdraw and live faithfully as separatists according to their understanding of the Law. Thus the origin of the Essene party may date back to here. If this is not the period of their founding, then the group most likely emerged as a reaction to one of the later Hasmoneans, among whom Alexander Jannaeus is another possible candidate.[12]

Yet when the nation ratified this move, bringing rule and priesthood together in Simon a decade later, they were expressing gratitude for all that the family had done finally to free the nation from foreign influence.[13] The nation's politics had produced, as often happens, a set of terribly conflicting choices. Hasmonean rule got off to a confused start. That confusion only deepened in the following generations. I can only trace the major lines of development and the reaction it spawned.

After Simon was assassinated in 134 B.C.,[14] John Hyrcanus ruled (134–104 B.C.) and became the beneficiary of the Parthians' defeat of

12. Numerous theories are put forward about the "wicked priest." Herbert W. Bateman IV (*Early Jewish Hermeneutics and Hebrews 1:5–13: The Impact of Early Jewish Exegesis on the Interpretation of a Significant New Testament Passage* [New York: Peter Lang, 1997], 85) has a chart of the major options with a bibliography on pp. 295–97.

13. The story is summarized in 1 Macc. 14:25–48.

14. The date of the assassination is disputed. It occurred in the Seleucid year 177 (1 Macc. 16:14), which could be either 135 or 134 B.C., although the 134 B.C. date is more likely in light of *Ant.* 13.228.

the Seleucids in 129 B.C. Now politics in Israel would have a somewhat free hand. Josephus records Hyrcanus's thirty-one-year rule as a great moment, for God gave him three privileges: government, high priesthood, and the gift of prophecy (*Ant.* 13.299).

This centralization of power was not uniformly popular, as a famous incident during Hyrcanus's rule shows. Hyrcanus knew that the pious had questions about him, but he regarded himself as pious, so he invited some of his key supporters, mostly Pharisees, to a banquet. He told them that if they saw him break one of God's laws unintentionally they should let him know. At this, one member of the pious party, Eleazar, rose to tell him that if he wished to follow God's law perfectly, he should give up the priesthood and simply be a political leader (Josephus, *Ant.* 13.288–98). In part, Eleazar raised this question because there were rumors that Antiochus IV had held Hyrcanus's mother captive and that someone had taken advantage of (i.e., raped) her. The implication was that they could not be sure of Hyrcanus's Jewish heredity, much less his priestly purity (Lev. 21:7, 13–14). Josephus describes Eleazar as a Pharisee, the member of a party of great popular influence. The event shows how this party was seen as representing the religiously and politically pious who were concerned with faithfulness to Jewish law and practice. Nevertheless, the Jewish historian describes the remarks as coming from an ill-tempered, seditious man (Eleazar). One of Hyrcanus's advisers, a Sadducee named Jonathan, made the point that the remark was a reproach against the ruler and that it reflected the attitude of the whole group. Thus he told the king to see what penalty the Pharisees would recommend for such a remark. When they recommended only "stripes and bonds" rather than death, in part because the Pharisees hesitated to give severe punishment, the king was angered, sensing disloyalty among the Pharisees. He renounced his association with the Pharisees and decreed that their practices should not be followed, with penalties for those who did. Josephus treats this event as a turning point in Hasmonean-Pharisaical relations that would play out over decades. For Josephus, the change in policy led to a rise in Sadducean influence.

The early Hasmonean period shows that the nation still faced old choices. How would Jews now live? Some, like the Essenes, withdrew and kept their faithfulness in the desert to wait for a better day. Others, like the Pharisees, continued to lobby for keeping the Law and a life faithfully reflecting Jewish identity. Still others, like the Sadducees, preferred a road of compromise, open to other ways of doing things, commercial opportunity, and support for those in power. The Sadducees held the prime positions in support of the ruling family, but the

Pharisees were a popular force, and their piety brought them much respect. As the account of Josephus suggests, the characteristics of these three major Jewish parties changed little from this time until the time of Jesus.

The rule of Hyrcanus and his immediate successor, Aristobulus I (104–103 B.C.), led to an expansion of Israel's borders. Particularly significant was Hyrcanus's brutal victory over the Samaritans, during which he destroyed their temple on Mount Gerizim (*War* 1.65). This conflict only fueled the racial distaste each group had for the other. The distaste extended back to the separation of Israel from Judah in the period of Rehoboam and Jeroboam (930 B.C.). The Judeans' disrespect for the Samaritans grew as the latter became a predominantly racially mixed people after northern Israel's fall to Assyria in the eighth century.

When Aristobulus died, his widow, Salome Alexandra, was childless. So she decided to marry one of his half brothers, Alexander Jannaeus, whom she also had released from prison. This made him in effect the ruler. Constant and expensive military activity as well as a brutal rule characterized Jannaeus's kingship (103–76 B.C.). It proved to be as oppressive as any that had come from foreign kings. His entire approach led to massive opposition by the Pharisees. Once he was pelted by citrons while trying to officiate at the Feast of Tabernacles (*Ant.* 13.372–73). In reaction he sent out mercenary troops (foreigners) to slay six hundred of his Jewish opponents. Such action left him very unpopular with many. From 94 to 88 B.C., Jannaeus faced a rebellion from Jewish leaders, who called in Hellenistic troops against Israel's king. This rebel move backfired, as many others feared where this involvement of the nations would lead. Many Jews preferred a ruthless Jewish leader to the uncertain alternative. Thus Jannaeus was able to rally forces and recover. Having asserted his power, he took the rebels captive and slew eight hundred of them before the royal palace, showing that opposition would be ruthlessly crushed. A calm settled over his rule. At the end of his life, he reportedly told his wife to make peace with the Pharisees (*Ant.* 14.401). It was advice she would follow, and the Pharisees assumed a key role again.

When Jannaeus died in 76 B.C., sixty-four-year-old Alexandra took the throne, holding it for nine years. She was so accomplished that Josephus complimented her rule, saying, "A woman she was who showed no signs of the weakness of her sex, for she was sagacious to the greatest degree in her ambition of governing" (*Ant.* 14.430). She heeded the advice of the Pharisees, and for the period of her reign all was quiet.

With her death (65 B.C.) came the seeds of what would eventually lead to Rome's entry into Israel. Alexandra left two sons, Hyrcanus II—

the eldest, who was quiet and unambitious—and Aristobulus II, who was more like his father Jannaeus and his uncle Aristobulus I. Hyrcanus was appointed successor, while the Sadducees preferred the other son, who might let them return to power. When Alexandra died, Aristobulus pounced and won a victory, although he did not slay his brother (*Ant.* 14.4–7). Their battle continued when an Idumean, Antipater, joined the fray on Hyrcanus's side (*Ant.* 14.8–13). Antipater's father had served as governor of Idumea for Jannaeus and Alexandra. Antipater was also the father of Herod the Great and would put his family and Hyrcanus in direct touch with Rome. In 65 B.C. he persuaded Hyrcanus to seek what was rightfully his. They attacked with the aid of another ally, the Nabateans, and put Aristobulus on the run (*Ant.* 14.19–21).[15]

The appearance of civil war and chaos was just the excuse the Romans needed as they sought to solidify their own expansion. Both Aristobulus and Hyrcanus offered to pay significant sums to the Roman governor of Syria, Scaurus, to be appointed. Scaurus chose Aristobulus, who also began to court the key Roman general, Pompey, as did Hyrcanus (*Ant.* 14.37–40). Finally, Pompey visited Damascus and held court for both Aristobulus and Hyrcanus. Other Jews came and asked him not to accept either of them but to abolish Hasmonean rule and allow the nation to return to its old temple structure (*Ant.* 14.41–46). The situation had gotten so bad that Israel was actively seeking help from the outside.

Aristobulus made an error in judgment. As he supported Pompey, he also built up his forces, so the Roman general became suspicious and came against him (*Ant.* 14.48–53). By the time Pompey got to Jerusalem, Aristobulus realized he would have to welcome the Roman representative, but some of his supporters did not want to concede. While Aristobulus turned himself over, his supporters refused to give up. Meanwhile, Hyrcanus's supporters welcomed the Roman general in the hope that he would now side with them. Hyrcanus's forces secured entry into parts of Jerusalem for the general, although a decisive siege to conquer the rest of the city took another three months. When the Romans finally gained full entry, many Jews were slain. Pompey himself inspected the whole temple but out of respect touched nothing in it (*Ant.* 14.72). Some Jews interpreted Pompey's victory as God's retribution against Jewish unfaithfulness (*Psalms of Solomon* 2:1–21). Pompey appointed Hyrcanus as high priest, but the turbulent period of Hasmonean independent rule was over. It was time for the Romans to run

---

15. Nabatea was a region located to the south and east of Perea, almost directly east of the Dead Sea (see the map in the front of the book, p. 2).

things. They had been invited in as Israel had proved so divided that its own rule had produced nothing but chaos (*Ant.* 14.77). Its rulers had taken to power in a way that did not differ from foreigners, and these power struggles had fractured the nation. Some opted for power, and others chose to fight for faithfulness, and still others simply withdrew to wait for a better day. To have peace would require outsiders. How to have purity remained a concern for many. For others, just to have peace was good enough.

Roman Rule from Pompey to Pilate (63 B.C.–A.D. 36)

The Romans learned major lessons from the region's previous history. They decided that divided power was a better way to govern here. Hyrcanus was high priest and had the support of Antipater (*Ant.* 14.73, 80). Antipater was shrewd; he always gave support to the local Roman ruler. Meanwhile, Aristobulus was exiled to Rome with his family. One of the sons, Alexander, managed to avoid capture, but another son, Antigonus, was exiled temporarily. They returned separately later to shake things up again, staging two brief revolts in 56–55 B.C. with Alexander leading the effort, but both failed (*Ant.* 14.82–83, 101–3). Another brief revolt followed in 51 B.C., led by Pitholaus, a Jewish lieutenant. Cassius (also known as Crassus), who was now governor of Syria, crushed the revolt. Meanwhile, in 47 B.C. Julius Caesar finally won his two-year battle with Pompey and his forces for control of Rome. Caesar gained victory over Pompey with the aid of Antipater, who along with Hyrcanus was rewarded for supporting Caesar. Such support took place even though Antigonus, Aristobulus's son, had accused Antipater of murdering his father (*Ant.* 14.140–55). Some Jews took Pompey's defeat as divine retribution for his excursion into the temple fifteen years earlier (*Psalms of Solomon* 2:22–35; cf. Dio Cassius 42.5).[16] Relations among the Jewish elite were chaotic. Rome opted for stability and the Idumean connection.

The Romans let Antipater appoint his sons to military positions. Among them was Herod, who would become known as Herod the Great, ruler of Judea during Jesus' birth. Herod proved successful and ruthless in his military efforts but upset the Jews when he executed a rebel named Hezekiah without consulting the Sanhedrin, the ruling Jewish council. Such independent action disturbed the Jews. Herod was spared only when Hyrcanus came to his defense to avoid the political chaos that punishing Antipater's son would cause (*Ant.* 14.158–84).

---

16. Pompey was murdered by the Egyptians at Alexandria, after losing a battle at Pharsalus in 48 B.C.

In 44 B.C., Julius Caesar was assassinated in Rome, leading to more political disruption in the larger empire. Cassius, Caesar's opponent with Brutus, received local support from Antipater because he was the Roman ruler with the closest ties to the region. Antipater was reappointed but then was assassinated in 43 B.C. (*Ant.* 14.281). This left power to his sons, Herod and Phasael. Things moved quickly. A major battle at Philippi took place in 42 B.C. involving Cassius against Antony and Octavian (later known as Augustus). Cassius was defeated, and the sons of Antipater were vulnerable. Yet Antony understood that they had supported Cassius because he had been Rome's agent in the area (*Ant.* 14.301–13). He realized that they could be as loyal to him as their father had been to previous rulers. Thus in 41 B.C. he appointed them joint tetrarchs (*Ant.* 14.326). This quick survey shows how chaotic the political situation was in this period.

It got worse in 40 B.C. While Octavian and Antony were fighting politically, but not yet militarily, for control of Rome, the Parthians invaded Judea and captured the son of Aristobulus II, Antigonus. The Parthians' success allowed Antigonus to depose Hyrcanus (*Ant.* 14.365–66). To ensure that Hyrcanus would not return to the high priesthood, Antigonus had Hyrcanus's ears mutilated, disqualifying him from the priesthood (Lev. 21:17; *Ant.* 14.366). Phasael was captured, and he committed suicide (*Ant.* 14.369). Herod fled to Rome to wait for a better opportunity. Antigonus was king and high priest for three years, until the Romans returned and drove out the Parthians in 39 B.C.

Herod took advantage of his exile by ingratiating himself to both Antony and Octavian. The Roman Senate appointed him king of the Jews in 40 B.C. (*Ant.* 14.377–85). He returned to battle for his kingdom with their crucial support in hand. Victory came in 37 B.C., and Antigonus was sent to Antony as a captive (*Ant.* 14.477–91). He was eventually beheaded (*Ant.* 15.8). Josephus calls this "the end of the Hasmonean family," and for all practical purposes it was, in terms of major male heirs (*Ant.* 14.491). Herod now had an uncontested hand in Judean affairs, although the intrigue left him forever suspicious of any potential or rumored enemies. Near the end of his reign, his many sons conspired for the succession, and he executed some of them, including two descended from the Hasmoneans. Octavian, now called Augustus Caesar, is rumored to have said in a late text that it was better to be Herod's pig than his son (Macrobius, *Saturnalia* 2.4.11, c. A.D. 400, which makes it too late for us to be certain of its veracity).

Herod solidified things after the situation in Rome became clear. He married a Hasmonean daughter, Mariamne, to try to appease the Jews for his all but exterminating the line (*War* 1.240–41). Although he claimed to worship according to Jewish practice, he was ethnically not a Jew. After appointing Aristobulus to the high priesthood because of pressure from Alexandra, Mariamne's mother and daughter of Hyrcanus II, Herod was rumored to have had him drowned to prevent further hereditary trouble (*Ant*. 15.55). Alexandra would never forget this and eventually persuaded Cleopatra in Egypt to take up the cause against Herod. Antony, who by now was under Cleopatra's spell, called Herod to face a trial for murder (*Ant*. 15.62–63). Herod escaped only by paying a huge bribe and because Antony was not confident that another competent ruler could be found (*Ant*. 15.75–76). Herod never felt entirely secure in his power. The potential Egyptian threat was removed when Antony and Cleopatra were finally defeated by Octavian in 31 B.C. at the sea battle of Actium (*Ant*. 15.161). Herod told the new Caesar that he would be as faithful to him as he had been to Antony (*Ant*. 15.189–93), and so Octavian reappointed Herod, who finally had some sense of security in his rule. Herod would now be Rome's client-king, serving and collecting taxes for them. His family would serve strictly at their pleasure.

The result was a quarter century of relative peace—except for family division and strife. There were also numerous building programs (*Ant*. 15.331–41). Herod built fortresses and palaces and even undertook a major renovation of the temple precinct. Cities (some on a Greek model), roads, and aqueducts increased commerce. A temple was dedicated to Caesar at Caesarea Maritima, which later became the capital for Roman rule (*War* 1.414). Games and festivals were established in the emperor's honor (*Ant*. 16.136–41). These foreign practices "departed from the native customs" (*Ant*. 15.267–68). Such honoring by the "client-king" to his patron served to underscore the client's loyalty. All of this cost money. Taxes were raised by the now infamous tax collectors to make sure Rome and Herod had their due honor.

When Herod died in 4 B.C., he had three sons in his will, two by his Samaritan wife, Malthace (Archelaus and Antipas), and one by Cleopatra of Jerusalem (Philip).[17] Although the Jews did not want Archelaus (*Ant*. 17.314), he was appointed by Rome to rule Judea (Matt. 2:22). Antipas received Galilee and Perea. Philip received the area northeast of the Sea of Galilee (Luke 3:1). None was given their father's title of king (*Ant*. 17.317–18). Philip and Antipas were called tetrarchs, while Archelaus was given the title of ethnarch, a lesser title. Archelaus was deposed by the Romans in A.D. 6, having done nothing to gain Jewish support (*Ant*. 17.342–44). Antipas remained in power through the time of Jesus, whom he examined in those fateful days that led to the crucifix-

---

17. A chart of Herod the Great's descendants appears at the end of this chapter.

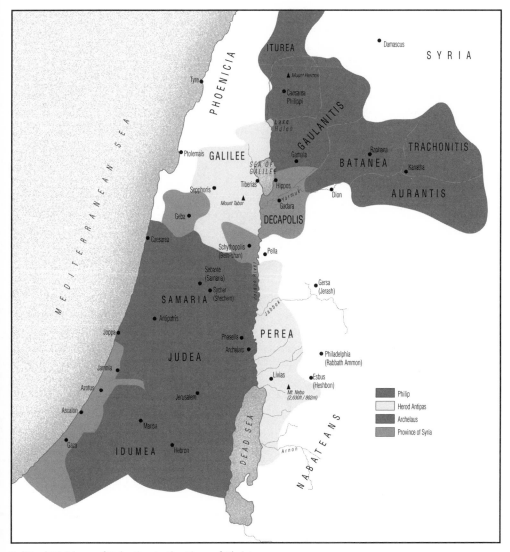

Political Divisions of Palestine in the Time of Christ

ion (Luke 23:6–12). Little is known about Philip, except that he also built cities to honor the Romans (*Ant.* 18.28).

With Archelaus's fall in A.D. 6, the Romans took direct control of affairs in Judea (*Ant.* 17.354; 18.1–10). They appointed prefects to keep the peace and directly collect the taxes, an act that was controversial, for it only underscored that Israel was under foreign control. They also sought to uphold Roman culture. It was in this role that Pilate found himself in A.D. 26. We possess today a brief dedicatory inscription of a theater at Caesarea referring to Pontius Pilate as a prefect of Judea. It also shows that the building was dedicated to Tiberius as a *Tiberium*, a "religious" building, indicating how politics and national religion mixed together in Roman culture. Some Jews found such cities and dedications in their land disturbing, although the extent of Roman power meant they could do nothing to stop it. Pilate would serve ten years. He was also responsible to appoint the high priest, but by Pilate's time Annas and his family had shown themselves to be trustworthy to the Romans. Therefore, Caiaphas, Annas's son-in-law, was solidly in place as high priest, a role he held from A.D. 18 to 36 (*Ant.* 18.26, 35). He would preside at Jesus' examination by Jewish leaders.

Pilate's rule came with controversy. He did not care for the Jews and loved to show the nation that Rome was in control. Twice he deeply offended Jewish sensibilities. The first time was when he placed the emperor's image and military standard in Jerusalem (*Ant.* 18.55). Caesar had previously refused to allow such an act, knowing that it would upset the Jews because they saw it as a violation of the second commandment. Pilate took away the offending items when protesting Jews voluntarily lay down before his soldiers, who had drawn their swords to execute them during their protest. The nonviolent, self-sacrificial act so impressed Pilate that he changed his mind (*Ant.* 18.57–59). The second incident involved his placement of the emperor's golden votive shields in Herod's palace in Jerusalem, an act seen as sacrilegious. Here a Jewish letter to Tiberius Caesar was enough to reverse Pilate's act (Philo, *Embassy* 38 §§299–305). Philo gives a long description of just how cruel, corrupt, and insensitive Pilate was and hence how unpopular he was with the Jews. Josephus also shows Pilate's cruelty, relating a massacre of Samaritans when they caused him trouble (*Ant.* 18.85–89). One of the prefect's duties was to keep the peace. Many Jews still desired to be loyal to their God and resented Rome's presence. The prefect's actions only underscored to many Jews how different and disrespectful to God the nations were.

Pilate's rule had the support of the Jewish elite, consisting of the high priest and the Sadducees, who controlled the Sanhedrin. They kept power by their support of Rome, as the prefect appointed the high priest. They also maintained power by their regulation of temple commerce, an activity that involved the entire nation. Compromise, commerce, and reality seemed to favor this course. Though the Pharisees might have wished for something different, the previous experience of national independence under the Hasmoneans did not make them anxious to do anything radical.

The nation's chaotic history since the Maccabean revolt served to keep alive the hope that God might act again for his people. The question of how God's people might be faithful to God and implore him to respond led to many different approaches to Judaism and contentions within Israel. Judaism in the time of Jesus may have shared faith in one God, but it was far from one faith in practice or priorities.

Conclusion

Jewish history since the exile had brought Israel in closer touch with the nations. Little about that history made them comfortable with this association, except for the few at the top of the social strata who benefited from such relationships. Various factions emerged. The very pious split into two camps, the separatist Essenes and the Pharisees, who tried to be faithful and yet stay in the sociopolitical fray to influence the nation. The more aristocratic Sadducees preferred compromise and a level of cooperation to keep their place. Every now and then during the Roman period, some would rise up and call for independence, but such political zealotry surfaced mostly after the time of Jesus.[18] The sources indicate the struggle to maintain Jewish identity and peace throughout the entire period. How could a Jew be faithful in the midst of Gentile rule? All that could mark one out as Jewish were the practices associated with life and worship. Some chose to abandon such a life, preferring Hellenism. Others tried to combine the two. Others fought to be distinct.

Many devout Jews believed that God had judged the nation for unfaithfulness to the covenant, and the price for such unfaithfulness was the resulting centuries of chaos. They viewed any relationship to outsiders, like the Samaritans or Gentiles, with suspicion. Jesus was born into such a chaotic sociopolitical climate. Understanding that history helps us see how what he said offered hope on the one hand and challenged cherished views on the other. To get the full picture of the background, however, one also needs to look at the sociological and cultural elements of first-century Jewish life. It is here, especially among the various hopes for how God would rescue the nation from the chaos of recent history, that Jesus' message fits. He drew on the one thing many

18. For a list of "social bandits" from 47 B.C. to A.D. 195, see K. C. Hanson and Douglas E. Oakman, *Palestine in the Time of Jesus* (Minneapolis: Fortress, 1998), 91. Josephus has no mention of a bandit in the Judean-Galilean region from 4 B.C. to A.D. 48.

Jews were most concerned about—how one could and should be faithful to God and how God would claim his people for his own again. It is here that Jesus' answer was both distinctive and unifying of the hope that the Hebrew Scriptures had articulated for God's people.

Periods of Rule over the Land of Israel/Judea
(all dates are B.C.)

Persian Period	Ptolemaic Egypt	Seleucid Syria	Hasmonean/ Maccabean Judea
Cyrus, 559–530			
Cambyses, 530–522			
Darius, 522–486			
Xerxes (Ahasuerus), 486–465			
Artaxerxes I Longimanus, 464–424			
Darius II Nothus, 424–404			
Artaxerxes II Mnemon, 404–358			
Artaxerxes III Ochus, 358–338			
Darius III Codomannus, 336–330			
(Persia conquered by Alexander the Great, 330)			
	Ptolemy I Lagi (or Soter), 323–285	Seleucus I Nicator, 312–280	
	Ptolemy II Philadelphus, 285–246	Antiochus I Soter, 280–261	
		Antiochus II Theos, 261–247	
	Ptolemy III Euergetes, 246–221	Seleucus II Callinicus, 247–226	
		Seleucus III Soter Ceraunos, 226–223	
	Ptolemy IV Philopator, 221–203	Antiochus III the Great, 223–187	
	Ptolemy V Epiphanes, 203–181	Seleucus IV Philopator, 187–175	
	Ptolemy VI Philometor, 181–145	Antiochus IV Epiphanes, 175–163	Judas Maccabeus, 164–160
		Antiochus V Eupator, 163–162	
		Demetrius I Soter, 162–150	Jonathan, 160–143
		Alexander Balas, 150–145	

Persian Period	Ptolemaic Egypt	Seleucid Syria	Hasmonean/ Maccabean Judea
	Ptolemy VII Physcon, 145–117	Demetrius II Nicator, 145–138 (Antiochus VI Epiphanes Dionysus, 145–142)	Simon, 143–134
		Antiochus VII Sidetes, 138–129	John Hyrcanus, 134–104
		Demetrius II Nicator (2d term), 129–125	
			Aristobulus I, 104–103
			Alexander Jannaeus, 103–76
			Salome Alexandra, 76–67
			Aristobulus II, 67–63
			Hyrcanus II, 63–40
			Antigonus Mattathias, 40–37

Note: Adapted from J. Julius Scott Jr., *Customs and Controversies: Intertestamental Jewish Backgrounds of the New Testament* (Grand Rapids: Baker, 1995), 75, 80–81, 83.

High Priests from the Pre-Maccabean Period to the Time of Christ

House of Zadok	Onias II c. 245–220 B.C.
	Simon II c. 220–198 B.C.
	Onias III c. 198–175 B.C.
Appointed by Antiochus IV (Seleucid king)	Jason (brother of Onias III) 175–172 B.C.
	Menelaus 172–163 B.C.
Appointed with approval of Lysias, regent for Antiochus V (Seleucid king)	Alcimus 162–160 B.C. (d. 159 B.C.)
Apparently no high priest 159–152 B.C.	
Appointed by Alexander Balas (Seleucid king)	Jonathan (the Hasmonean) Maccabeus 152–143 B.C.
Israel's independence negotiated between Simon Maccabeus and Demetrius II (Seleucid king) 142 B.C.	
Hasmonean/Maccabean High Priests (all but Hyrcanus II held kingship and priesthood simultaneously)	Simon 140–134 B.C.
	John Hyrcanus 134–104 B.C.
	Aristobulus I 104–103 B.C.
	Alexander Jannaeus 103–76 B.C.
	Hyrcanus II 76–67 B.C. (during rule of Queen Salome Alexandra)
	Aristobulus II 67–63 B.C.

Appointed by Rome, supported by Antipater (Idumean; Roman supporter)	Hyrcanus II 63–40 B.C.
	Antigonus 40–37 B.C. (d. 37 B.C., beheaded by Roman Antony; end of Hasmonean line)

After this time, high priests were appointed either by Herodian rulers (37 B.C.–A.D. 6 and A.D. 41–65) or by Roman legates or prefects (A.D. 6–39). The family of Annas I, high priest from A.D. 6 to 15, dominated these appointments for six decades until Annas II in A.D. 62. Caiaphas, son-in-law of Annas I, was high priest during the time of Christ and held the post from A.D. 18 to 36, the longest tenure of a high priest during the Roman period.

Note: For a summary of information relevant to this chart, see F. F. Bruce, *Israel and the Nations: The History of Israel from the Exodus to the Fall of the Second Temple,* rev. David F. Payne (Downers Grove, Ill.: InterVarsity, 1997), 116–204, 235–36.

Herod the Great and His Descendants

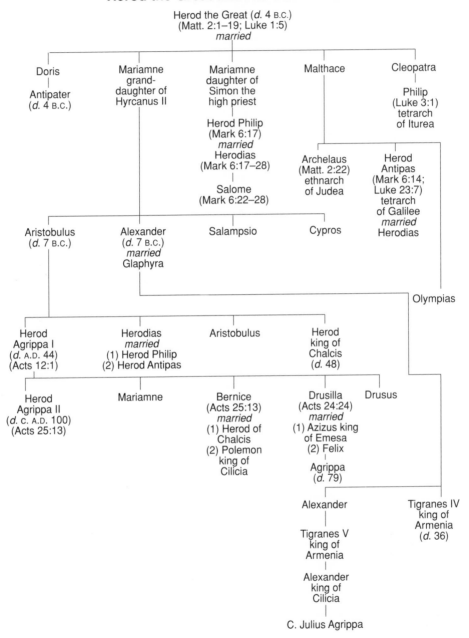

Herod the Great (*d.* 4 B.C.)
(Matt. 2:1–19; Luke 1:5)
married

Doris
Antipater
(*d.* 4 B.C.)

Mariamne
granddaughter of
Hyrcanus II

Mariamne
daughter of
Simon the
high priest
Herod Philip
(Mark 6:17)
married
Herodias
(Mark 6:17–28)
Salome
(Mark 6:22–28)

Malthace
Archelaus
(Matt. 2:22)
ethnarch
of Judea

Herod
Antipas
(Mark 6:14;
Luke 23:7)
tetrarch
of Galilee
married
Herodias

Cleopatra
Philip
(Luke 3:1)
tetrarch
of Iturea

Aristobulus
(*d.* 7 B.C.)

Alexander
(*d.* 7 B.C.)
married
Glaphyra

Salampsio

Cypros

Olympias

Herod
Agrippa I
(*d.* A.D. 44)
(Acts 12:1)

Herodias
married
(1) Herod Philip
(2) Herod Antipas

Aristobulus

Herod
king of
Chalcis
(*d.* 48)

Herod
Agrippa II
(*d.* c. A.D. 100)
(Acts 25:13)

Mariamne

Bernice
(Acts 25:13)
married
(1) Herod of
Chalcis
(2) Polemon
king of
Cilicia

Drusilla
(Acts 24:24)
married
(1) Azizus king
of Emesa
(2) Felix
Agrippa
(*d.* 79)

Drusus

Alexander
Tigranes V
king of
Armenia
Alexander
king of
Cilicia
C. Julius Agrippa

Tigranes IV
king of
Armenia
(*d.* 36)

Note: From J. Julius Scott Jr., *Customs and Controversies: Intertestamental Jewish Backgrounds of the New Testament* (Grand Rapids: Baker, 1995), 98. Used by permission of Baker Book House Company.

Rulers of Palestine

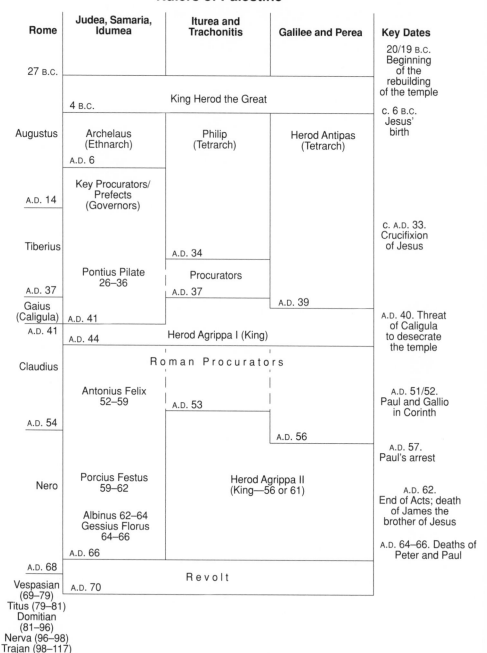

Rome	Judea, Samaria, Idumea	Iturea and Trachonitis	Galilee and Perea	Key Dates
27 B.C.				20/19 B.C. Beginning of the rebuilding of the temple
	4 B.C. King Herod the Great			c. 6 B.C. Jesus' birth
Augustus	Archelaus (Ethnarch) A.D. 6	Philip (Tetrarch)	Herod Antipas (Tetrarch)	
A.D. 14	Key Procurators/ Prefects (Governors)			
Tiberius		A.D. 34		C. A.D. 33. Crucifixion of Jesus
A.D. 37	Pontius Pilate 26–36	Procurators A.D. 37		
Gaius (Caligula) A.D. 41	A.D. 41		A.D. 39	A.D. 40. Threat of Caligula to desecrate the temple
	A.D. 44	Herod Agrippa I (King)		
Claudius	Roman Procurators			
	Antonius Felix 52–59	A.D. 53		A.D. 51/52. Paul and Gallio in Corinth
A.D. 54			A.D. 56	
				A.D. 57. Paul's arrest
Nero	Porcius Festus 59–62	Herod Agrippa II (King—56 or 61)		A.D. 62. End of Acts; death of James the brother of Jesus
	Albinus 62–64 Gessius Florus 64–66			A.D. 64–66. Deaths of Peter and Paul
A.D. 68	A.D. 66			
Vespasian (69–79)	A.D. 70 Revolt			
Titus (79–81) Domitian (81–96) Nerva (96–98) Trajan (98–117) Hadrian (117–138)				

chapter 4

Sociocultural History

It is fundamental to recognize that the biblical texts convey meanings derived through a specific culture and particular social arrangements. For the most part, ancient documents refer to their contemporary social systems only indirectly. They assume that their readers share their world and know what they mean by patron, what sort of taxation is in effect, or how a certain faction fits into the social matrix. Our difficulty as modern, Western readers is to relate meaningfully to documents that are the products of a radically different world in terms of institutions and values. We do not share important social understandings with the writers of these texts. Because our social and cultural experiences do not match those of the biblical authors, we can be seriously misled about what they mean.[1]

Anyone who has lived in another culture knows the shock of recognizing that things are done differently from what one is used to. Culture is a strange mix of social values, practices, and institutions that carry with them unexpressed but established ways of negotiating through life. Cultural life involves perception, feeling, acting, believing, admiring, and striving, as well as how someone does all these things.[2] To those who are at home in a given culture, all these ways of life are taken for granted. But to those on the outside, they may seem strange, inexplicable, or incomprehensible. These cultural expectations or practices are often not defended or justified; they simply are the way things are

1. K. C. Hanson and Douglas E. Oakman, *Palestine in the Time of Jesus: Social Structures and Social Conflicts* (Minneapolis: Fortress, 1998), 4.
2. Bruce J. Malina, *The New Testament World: Insights from Cultural Anthropology*, 2d ed. (Louisville: Westminster/John Knox, 1993), 15–17.

done or have been done for centuries. The experience for the outsider is expressed by the phrase "being a stranger in a strange land" (Exod. 2:22). Culture is complex because while not everyone embraces it or establishes it, all are affected by it. Even where culture is challenged or rejected, the dominant elements of a culture provide the backdrop and impetus for the reaction. Finally, cultural expectations are not the same for everyone. A person's social standing, the amenities of life in a given setting, and other social, economic, religious, and political realities of life often affect how one relates to the culture.

Add the passage of time, and the complexity increases. The cultural world underlying the time of Jesus is far different from life in the twenty-first century. The goal of this chapter is to point out some of the more fundamental features of first-century life in Israel and Galilee that help us to better understand the Gospels. My subsequent study, *Jesus according to Scripture*, will discuss other instances in contexts where specific texts raise them. For now I survey issues related to population; geography, travel, and agriculture; values; life expectancy and literacy; family and home; politics and power; economics; religion; and key sects of Judaism. What I consider here is a mixture of features, some Greco-Roman in their roots, others grounded in Judaism. The world of Jesus and the Gospels was a mixed cultural world, where Hellenism and Judaism existed side by side in a variety of combinations, as the earlier historical survey showed. The days of arguing that many particular cultural features were only Jewish or Hellenistic have long passed. Many aspects of the culture, such as issues of honor and shame or political structure, were too mixed to be seen as simply one or the other.[3]

Population

Population in the ancient world is difficult to calculate. We do not have multiple sources for the same time period and locales across the Roman Empire. The remarks of ancient historians are often seen as exaggerated. Their numbers are usually rejected on the basis of estimates made on analogies about population density or on what population an area could agriculturally sustain. Another problem is that the historians who make estimates are often centuries removed from the period in

---

3. On the elements and influence of the Greco-Roman world, see James S. Jeffers, *The Greco-Roman World of the New Testament Era: Exploring the Background of Early Christianity* (Downers Grove, Ill.: InterVarsity, 1999). For the argument that Hellenistic and Jewish culture had become intermixed, see Martin Hengel, *Judaism and Hellenism: Studies in Their Encounter in Palestine during the Early Hellenistic Period*, trans. John Bowden, 2 vols. (Philadelphia: Fortress, 1974). This point is the burden of his entire study.

question. For example, a Christian historian, Bar Hebraeus, the son of a converted Jew, tells us in the thirteenth century that there were 7 million Jews in the Roman Empire at the time of Claudius (A.D. 41–54). However, he appears to have confused the number of Jews with the number of Roman citizens mentioned in the census he consults.[4] Thus in this section we deal with ranges and estimates put together on the basis of circumstantial evidence and probabilities based on density estimates.

Estimates for the Roman Empire indicate that in the time of Augustus (27 B.C.–A.D. 14) the population may have been anywhere from 70 million to 100 million.[5] Rome itself had a population of around a million, making it the largest city of the period.[6] The estimated number of Jews in the empire also varies widely, ranging from 1 million to 8 million.[7] A larger figure may be more likely than a lower one, given how widespread the Jewish population was. What is largely agreed upon is that about one-quarter to one-third of the Jewish population lived in Israel, while the rest were dispersed. For example, a huge contingent of Jews lived in Alexandria, a city whose population at the time was several hundred thousand.[8] One of the five sectors of the city was entirely Jewish, and another sector was largely Jewish.

4. For details see Victor Tcherikover, *Hellenistic Civilization and the Jews* (Philadelphia: Jewish Publication Society of America, 1961), 292. He refuses to make any estimates.

5. M. Cary, *A History of Rome: Down to the Reign of Constantine*, 2d ed. (London: Macmillan, 1954), 507. Other estimates fall slightly lower, to around 60 million.

6. Jo-Ann Shelton, *As the Romans Did: A Sourcebook in Roman Social History*, 2d ed. (New York: Oxford University Press, 1998), 1. She notes that London did not exceed 1 million until A.D. 1800.

7. Tcherikover, *Hellenistic Civilization*, 292–93, 504–5 nn. 81, 86. He cites "prophetic" remarks in the *Sibylline Oracles* (c. 160 B.C.) that "the whole land and sea will be full of you" (3.271), as well as a statement of Josephus that "there is no people in the world among whom part of our brethren is not to be found" (in remarks of Agrippa, *War* 2.398). In another place, Josephus says, "The Jewish race is scattered over the entire world among its local inhabitants" (*War* 7.43). He also cites the Greek geographer Strabo as declaring in 85 B.C. that the Jew "had reached every town, and it is hard to find a place in the world where this race has not penetrated and where it has not obtained a hold" (*Ant.* 14.115). Finally, Philo speaks of the nation's wide expansion throughout the world (*Flaccus* 7.46—"no one country can hold them"). Perhaps Acts plays off similar imagery, making Rome "the ends of the earth" (Acts 1:8; 28:14–30).

8. Though his number is considered a little high, Philo says there are one million Jews in Egypt alone (*Flaccus* 6.43). Josephus puts the population of Egypt at 7.5 million, excluding Alexandria (*War* 2.385). This city was one of the largest in the empire, along with Antioch of Syria, a locale prominent in Acts. The estimate for Alexandria runs from 500,000 to 750,000, while Antioch of Syria is estimated to have had up to 500,000. Many Jews also lived in Antioch. Athens and Tarsus were important locales of culture and education. Other cities of possibly 100,000 include Ephesus, Philippi, Thessalonica, and Corinth. Jews were plentiful in many of these locales; see Craig Blomberg, *Jesus and the Gospels* (Nashville: Broadman & Holman, 1997), 55.

Estimates for Palestine also vary. Figures run from 700,000 to 2.5 million.[9] The size of the largest city in the region, Jerusalem, has been the subject of much controversy. Part of the problem here is that when the feasts were held, people streamed in from the entire region and beyond. Most estimates for Jerusalem range from 25,000 to 200,000.[10] A figure of up to 100,000 might be correct.[11] During the feasts, its size would have at least doubled. The major cities of Galilee have less variation in the range of estimates. An estimate of 200,000 seems to fit with the region as a whole, while estimates for the major cities of Tiberius and Sepphoris run from 15,000 to 25,000.[12] Capernaum, Jesus' ministry headquarters, is estimated to have had from 6,000 to 12,000.[13]

The bulk of Jesus' ministry took place in largely rural Galilee in towns and villages. The moderately sized city of Capernaum served as the center. It is interesting that Sepphoris, a major pro-Roman, Galilean fortress city and council seat built on a Greek model, is never mentioned in the Gospels as a locale for Jesus' work despite the fact that it was just a few miles north of Nazareth. Jerusalem represents the most urban site for Jesus' work. It also is a logical place for confrontation because the Jewish leadership tightly controlled worship at the temple and its accompanying commercial elements. It was, after all, the central religious locale for the nation and the Jewish faith.

Geography, Travel, and Agriculture

Geography

The regions of Judea, Samaria, and Galilee touch on the edge of the Mesopotamian Fertile Crescent in the north and stretch to desert land

9. Nikos Kokkinos, *The Herodian Dynasty: Origins, Role in Society, and Eclipse* (Sheffield: Sheffield Academic Press, 1998), 73.

10. The low-end figure comes from the additional note in Joachim Jeremias, *Jerusalem in the Time of Jesus: An Investigation into Economic and Social Conditions during the New Testament Period*, trans. F. H. Cave and C. H. Cave, 3d ed. (Philadelphia: Fortress, 1969), 84. For a range of estimates, see Wolfgang Reinhardt, "The Population Size of Jerusalem and the Numerical Growth of the Jerusalem Church," in *The Book of Acts in Its First Century Setting*, vol. 4, ed. R. Bauckham (Grand Rapids: Eerdmans, 1995), 240–43. As Josephus notes, the third-century Greek historian Hecataeus of Abdera estimated the population of Jerusalem in about 300 B.C. as 120,000 (*Ag. Apion* 1.197).

11. See Reinhardt, "Population Size of Jerusalem," 245–57.

12. Harold Hoehner, *Herod Antipas: A Contemporary of Jesus Christ* (1972; reprint, Grand Rapids: Zondervan, 1980), 52. He also notes that villages would have averaged around five hundred or so. This would have been the size of many of the towns in which Jesus' disciples ministered within Galilee. The lower estimates are from Richard A. Horsley, *Galilee: History, Politics, People* (Valley Forge, Pa.: Trinity Press International, 1995), 166, 320 n. 28.

13. Horsley (*Galilee*, 166) is again on the low end here.

in the south.[14] Thus the more fertile portion of the land is dominated by valleys running on either side of the Sea of Galilee down to the Dead Sea or down the coastal plain, except for the hill country, which runs through the middle of the region and divides the land. The land is set between the Mediterranean Sea on the west and a series of wildernesses to the northeast, east, and south. Winds from the west supply moisture for crops, while wind from the east brings dryness, and southerly wind brings heat. As one moves north, closer to the sea or higher up in elevation, the climate becomes more moist. Rainfall varies from a little over an inch a year in the southern or eastern desert to forty-plus inches in the mountains of Upper Galilee.[15] Winter is the rainy season, while summer is drier.

The country has a coastal plain by the Mediterranean Sea. The portion of this plain south of Mount Carmel is known as the Plain of Sharon. Fishing in the "Great Sea," farming of grain and vegetables, and forestry dominate this region. Farther south, as one moves inland from the Mediterranean in Judea toward Jerusalem, some cattle but more sheep would be found in the valleys southwest of the city.[16] Grain was also grown much farther north in the Esdraelon Valley, a valley in southwest Galilee that separated Galilee from Samaria to the south. This valley is also known as Jezreel. Most of Jesus' ministry took place north and east of this valley in an area extending from Nazareth to Caesarea Philippi in the north and to Gergesa and Gadara to the east and south of the Sea of Galilee. Much of this area was quite hilly, except for the sloping area east of the Sea of Galilee. This sea was also known as Gennesaret or Tiberius.[17] On its north-northwestern shore was Capernaum, which was his ministry center. Jesus also ventured up the northern coastal plain beyond Galilee into the area between Sidon and Tyre. His Judean ministry focused on the Bethany-Jerusalem area. John the Evangelist notes that John the Baptist spent time in Perea to the east of the Jordan (= "on the other side of the Jordan," John 1:28 NIV), and he describes Jesus traveling through Samaria (John 4:4).

14. This section is best read with a good map of the land at hand (see pp. 2 and 110). Almost any good Bible atlas would also suffice. I note one because it has a good selection of maps: Yohanan Aharoni et al., eds., *The Macmillan Bible Atlas*, 3d ed. (New York: Macmillan, 1993).

15. Sean Freyne, *Galilee from Alexander the Great to Hadrian, 323 BCE to 135 CE* (Wilmington, Del.: Glazier, 1980), 5.

16. Aharoni et al., eds., *Macmillan Bible Atlas*, 166 (map 224).

17. Tiberius, on the western shore, was a major Galilean city that Herod had built up on a Greco-Roman model. Sepphoris was also a major Galilean city, though we have no record of Jesus' ministry in either locale.

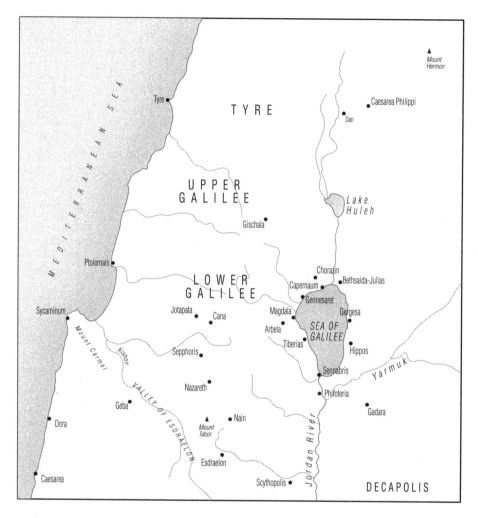

Galilee in the Time of Christ

The Galilean region is more rugged than the southern area of Judea, while the hill country in the southern region has peaks that reach only to about 2,000 feet, with Jerusalem at 2,600 feet. This range can be described as foothills and is known as the Shephelah, which also contains a narrow valley bounded on the other end by the Judean mountains. It runs from Beersheba in the south up to Jericho and extends into Samaria. Farther north in Galilee, peaks often reach 2,000 to 4,000 feet as they stretch northward toward Mount Hermon, which at 9,200 feet is the highest. This peak lies between Dan and Damascus, just northeast of Dan. In contrast stands the terrain farther south on the eastern border of the land. Running south from the Sea of Galilee to the Dead Sea by way of the Jordan River, one goes from 685 feet below sea level to 1,275 feet below sea level. Thus one can see how quickly the central hills of Galilee drop off toward the south and east.[18] This dramatic drop-off explains the weather in some of the events in Jesus' ministry as he was on the Sea of Galilee. Winds can rush down with a tunnel effect descending as they go, resulting in huge, dangerous storms.

Ancient Israel did not cover a large area. From Dan in the north to Beersheba in the south is about 150 miles. From the Sea of Galilee to the Dead Sea is about 65 miles. The east-west width from the Sea of Galilee to the Mediterranean is 28 miles, while the Dead Sea is 54 miles from the Mediterranean. The Sea of Galilee is also relatively small, 13 miles in length and about 7 miles at its widest point.

Travel

Most major trade routes ran along the coastal plain from north to south. Roman highways were made of cobblestone and allowed one lane of chariots to pass on each side. Most people traveled by cart, animal, or foot. Numerous smaller routes existed outside the main trade routes. Most roads were simply dirt. Travel speeds ranged from 7 miles a day for wagons to 20 miles a day on foot, but from 25 miles to 50 miles a day for a soldier in a hurry. Thus a journey from Lower Galilee to Jerusalem took about three days on foot. Inns provided lodging but could be dangerous, so people often relied on hospitality, which was held in high regard. People often stayed in homes with friends or relatives. The hill country in the center of the land made movement from east to west more difficult, especially in the northern regions, although one route, known as the Ridge Route, allowed movement north and south through the hills and offered smaller valleys running east and west along the way. However, to avoid Samaria, many Jews did not take this more central route, opting often to journey down the eastern side of the Jordan to go south through Perea in the east.

Agriculture

The valleys were fertile and the source of grain, vines, olives, and vegetables. Sheep and cattle were somewhat plentiful in Judea. Fishing dominated the Mediterranean coast and the Sea of Galilee.[19] A fishing

18. J. Julius Scott Jr., *Customs and Controversies: Intertestamental Jewish Backgrounds of the New Testament* (Grand Rapids: Baker, 1995), 43–44.

19. E. F. F. Bishop, "Jesus and the Lake," *Catholic Biblical Quarterly* 13 (1951): 398–414.

boat on the Galilean Sea might be twenty to thirty feet long and could hold several men. One discovered example measures 26.5 feet long, 7.5 feet wide, and 4.5 feet deep.[20] Figs and dates were grown in Judea. Some forests were also preserved on the edge of the coastal plains. The economy was rather limited in scope, with agriculture (grains and vines) and shepherding being among the more important pursuits. Thus landownership was a key to wealth; most people simply worked the land on behalf of others. The geography and agriculture also explain the kind of imagery Jesus used; his examples often came from everyday life in the land.

Values

To speak of values in ancient culture means that one considers what issues drive decisions and life choices. It is common to regard ancient society as based on an honor-shame approach to life.[21] Honor was the key cultural value—how a person was seen by other social groups, especially those that matter to the person. Honor was a claim to worth and was bound up in the basis for such a claim. It should be noted that this kind of psychological-anthropological focus may reflect more of a self-reflective modernist perspective than the ancient practice. Nonetheless, the concern about honor before others and, for many, about a reputation before God (or the gods) does seem to have been a major factor in ancient life. One was responsible to maintain honor for the self, the family, and the groups with which one identified.

Reputation, social status, actions, and gender play a role in this pursuit of honor. Honor is a "social rating which entitles a person to interact in specific ways with equals, superiors, subordinates, according to prescribed cues of the society."[22] It becomes particularly important in the confrontations that come with opponents in religious or ideological clashes. In such disputes an observer has to judge who has the high ground, and oftentimes, who has the social leverage. Part of the goal of the Gospels is to present Jesus' stature and authority as a means of commending him, showing that he, best of all, knows the way to God.

20. Shelley Wachsmann, "The Galilean Boat," *Biblical Archeology Review* 14.5 (1988): 18–33.

21. For a description of this standard as it applies to a Gospel, see Bruce J. Malina and Jerome H. Neyrey, "Honor and Shame in Luke-Acts: Pivotal Values of the Mediterranean World," in *The Social World of Luke-Acts: Models for Interpretation*, ed. Jerome H. Neyrey (Peabody, Mass.: Hendrickson, 1991), 25–65. See also Malina, *New Testament World*, 28–62.

22. Malina and Neyrey, "Honor and Shame in Luke-Acts," 26.

In presenting Jesus as credible and authoritative, the Gospels seek to elevate him to a place of honor, one worthy of respect, even though the people he confronts have seemingly honorable status. The appeal takes place not only at the theological level of elevating his person as Son of God but also in the character of his ministry as a person who cared for humanity and served as an example of how to live. In other words, the Gospels and their description of Jesus appeal to the highest standards and concerns of ancient existence as they present Jesus' life, ministry, and significance.

Some honor was "ascribed," that is, passed on as a result of social status, family background, and/or religious affiliation. "Acquired" honor is different. It involves a reputation obtained through action, achievement, or prowess. Honor can be individual or collective. Collective honor, honor of the group, was more important generally in the ancient world than in more individually focused societies like the modern West.[23] This is what made religious identity or even religious subgroup identity so important. Worth came from the group to which one was connected. Allegiance to the group was paramount. This is why certain actions, such as the threat of separation from the synagogue for aligning with Jesus, had so much social force. It is why the debates about theology and practice were significant. The issue was about not only who was right or what was true but also which way of life appropriately honored God and reflected the way people who seek to honor God should live. Each side in this debate claimed to be honoring God, providing a way by which God would honor faithful people. The very religious nature of the discussion shows how different this debate is from many elements of our own culture, where separate compartments often box out religion from life practices or everyday actions.

At a more mundane level, actions between people were also assessed in terms of honor and social standing. This meant that certain values like hospitality and reciprocity were highly honored among those of equal status. If an equal was kind to you, then you should return equal kindness. Just being human meant being hospitable, especially to family, friends, or group members. Those who belonged to a different group or who disdained such values could be ignored. Commendation might be necessary to make a case for receiving them, such as happened with the centurion commended to Jesus by the Jewish elders in Luke 7. A lesser social status could be a reason for treating someone with less deference. Those on the fringe of society could be ignored. This often meant that those higher up the social scale could be less con-

23. Malina, *New Testament World*, 63–89.

cerned with justice and fairness for those of lesser status. Though Judaism tended to affirm justice for all, especially through its prophetic tradition, the influence of status and power, especially as they were exercised in the Hellenistic world, tended to blunt such an ideal. The rule of the Hasmoneans shows how even Jewish leaders applied power ruthlessly. Still, honor was often ascribed automatically to a person's elders, men, parents, patrons-masters, those of high social standing, and religious leaders.

Another important ancient reality was that most people's positions in life were relatively fixed. Not much possibility existed for changing greatly a person's social standing and status except in the very limited cases of those in the upper classes.[24] These upper classes represented two to four percent of the population. "Rags to riches" did not exist. Access to goods was very limited, especially in villages. Those who controlled the larger urban areas also dominated the use of and access to resources. Patron-client relationships, where the patron held all the rights, ruled the day. Benefits a patron could provide were protection and limited care. The client must faithfully work for and support his patron.

The society was patriarchal (Wisdom 7:1–2; Philo, *Special Laws* 3.169–71, 178). Thus men controlled the key public roles in society. Those women who did possess honor usually received it because of their position in a significant family or because they came to have influence over a man of significance. Women of character and modesty could receive respect (Proverbs 31), yet women were often viewed as a grave threat, especially beautiful women (Sirach 42:12–14). The pious saw them as sources of temptation.

Life Expectancy and Literacy

Life expectancy in the ancient world averaged about 20 years, but if one reached the age of 5, then that expectancy went up to 40 years.[25]

24. Malina (*New Testament World*, 90–116) speaks of the "perception of limited good" in the ancient world, which drives one merely to maintain one's social status. It might be better to speak of "perception of limited goods." One's advance might have to come at the expense of another, since resources were limited. Reciprocity, returning a favor or act with an equal act, was often expected and served as a way of protection as well as to communicate that advantage was not being gained. On the other hand, it was often regarded as quite honorable to be a good and beneficent patron, though it was not required.

25. Hanson and Oakman, *Palestine in the Time of Jesus*, 14. Members of elite families tended to live on average twenty years more than others.

The marriageable age was much younger than in the modern West. Women were wed as early as 12 or 13, while men married from about 18 for Jews (*m. ʾAbot* 5.21) to their 20s or early 30s for those of Greco-Roman background. Such marriages were mostly arranged by the family and included significant exchanges of property for families who had means. Upper-class marriages were often between relatives or key families, forming social, political, and economic alliances.[26] Thus honor, wealth, and status in the family were passed on from one generation to the next.

Another key difference from modern Western culture is that literacy was limited. Education was largely restricted to males and to the upper classes. The value of instructing women was debated (*m. Soṭah* 3.4), and it generally occurred only in upper-class homes.[27] Most information came orally, not by written word. Basic instruction for Jews took place in the synagogue and through the family. It came to an end during the middle teens, when a person entered into a trade.

This brief survey of values shows how different life in the first century was from life in the modern West. Appreciating these differences helps us understand why certain issues were pursued so tenaciously and passionately. Honoring God and having honor from him is what drove many of these debates. This type of piety was also seen as commending a person before humanity.

Family and Home

Kinship was the most significant of human relationships in the ancient world. I have already noted how marriage was used to solidify social status. Herod the Great, an Idumean leader, married Mariamne, a Hasmonean princess, to add to his claim of legitimacy. The custom of betrothal and dowry shows how marriage was not just social but also economic. Betrothal was arranged about a year ahead of the marriage and was a legal process (*m. Ketubbot* 4.4–5). The dowry was supplied by the bride's family to help provide for her transfer to the husband. In effect, it was the daughter's inheritance provided early to her new family. An indirect dowry also went from

26. Ibid., 34–35. They trace thirty-nine marriages of Herodian family members and note that twenty-two marriages fell within the family, while twenty-seven fell outside (accounting for multiple marriages). Of the twenty-seven marriages outside the family, involving fourteen Herodians, only six were to people of unknown background.

27. On the role of women see Joachim Jeremias, "Appendix: The Social Position of Women," in *Jerusalem in the Time of Jesus*, 3d ed. (Philadelphia: Fortress, 1969), 359–76.

the groom's family to the family of the bride.[28] Thus marriage was a socioeconomic arrangement.

Honoring family in Jewish life was next to honoring God, because honoring mother and father is part of the Ten Commandments. An honorable family tree was also important, which is one of the reasons two of the Gospels present genealogies of Jesus early on. Family lineage could be considered either biological or adoptive. Biological lineage refers to physical parentage. Adoptive lineage means that the child was legally part of the family but not biologically descended. Both forms carried full familial rights, so the issue of a person's household was important.

Children were considered a blessing and an economic benefit, able to help the family labor pool. Generations often lived together within a household, possibly including extended families. Nevertheless, until they became useful, children were better seen but not heard.

Families tended to worship as groups. Often the father's faith determined that of the whole household, both family and servants.[29] However, the presence of Jesus led to a potential conflict between loyalty to God, in allegiance to Jesus, and loyalty to family, which often rejected him. The pressure this conflict introduced was immense.

The average home in Palestine was quite simple.[30] It had two stories in effect, because the area on the roof served as a second story. Steps gave access to the roof. Wooden beams set on mud (adobe) or stone walls supported the roof, which itself generally consisted of reeds, thorns, or clay. Most homes had a central room where family activities took place and where a fire might be lit when heat was needed. Floors were packed dirt or pebbles and dirt. Any internal division for rooms in the house was provided by thin walls made of curtains or mats. Many homes had a few rooms. Multiple small homes would often share an

28. Hanson and Oakman (*Palestine in the Life of Jesus*, 38–43) cover dowry and indirect dowry, which could include money, houses, land, and slaves. For mishnaic texts covering the contract amount and the marriage ceremony, see *Pesaḥim* 3.7 (betrothal meal at father-in-law's home); *Ketubbot* 4.7; 5.2 (the *ketubah*, the fee she gets if he dies or divorces her); *Šebiʿit* 7.4 (what can be eaten at the ceremony, e.g., a blemished animal); *Ḥallah* 2.7 (the dough offering for the wedding; cf. Num. 15:20); *Yebamot* 7.1 (slaves in the dowry). The celebration usually lasted seven days. Tobit 6:10–8:21 describes a marriage, the giving of the dowry, and a fourteen-day celebration. Despite some unusual details, the marital practices described in Tobit accurately reflect the culture.

29. S. C. Barton, "Family," *DJG*, 226.

30. Scott, *Customs and Controversies*, 246–47. For a description of an ancient site in Capernaum that contained homes, see Jack Finegan, *The Archeology of the New Testament: The Life of Jesus and the Beginning of the Church*, rev. ed. (Princeton: Princeton University Press, 1992), 107–9. One home at this site measured seven by six-and-one-half meters.

inner court where various items were stored, animals sheltered, cisterns kept, garbage collected, and toilets might be located. Furniture was minimal: mats for sleeping, maybe an oven, a table, and possibly a few chairs. Wealthy and middle-class homes had raised beds for sleeping. Local wells or cisterns storing rain provided water. Small homes might have only one window, which could be a security problem, although it did allow for air circulation. Only larger homes, usually containing a large or wealthy family, had a more complicated layout, with multiple rooms and a private central courtyard.[31] At night, lamps, lanterns, or torches could provide light. Utensils were of clay, stone, or glass, unless one was wealthy, in which case they might be made of bronze, copper, silver, or gold.

Initially, Jesus' ministry was often in small homes (e.g., the scene with the paralytic, Mark 2:1–2). However, he quickly became so popular that it was impossible to continue to meet in houses. The many significant meals of his ministry, most of which Luke describes, must have taken place in larger homes to accommodate the crowds.

Politics and Power

Most of what is central about ancient political power has been suggested in the client-patron relationship noted above.[32] For example, the Herodian family would have viewed the emperor and Rome as patrons to be honored. In a real sense, Herod was a client-king. Much of the building Herod did in honor of his patron served to show his loyalty and solidify this relationship. Thus he named a city, Caesarea, after Augustus. Herod also built up Sebaste, better known as Samaria, in his honor as well as constructing a harbor tower to honor Augustus's dead stepson, Drusus. He built a temple to Augustus and to Roma, the patron goddess of the city of Rome. Herod celebrated musical and sporting festivals in Augustus's honor every fifth year to commemorate his victory at Actium, which brought him to power. There also was his work on the temple and his building of his own palaces. These were expensive undertakings, and the populace bore the expense. It was for political reasons like these that taxes were unpopular.

31. S. Safrai ("Home and Family," in *The Jewish People in the First Century*, ed. S. Safrai and S. Stern, Compendia rerum iudaicarum ad Novum Testamentum 1.2 [Philadelphia: Fortress, 1976], 728–92) has a detailed treatment of all aspects of family and home. Houses are described on pp. 730–32.

32. Hanson and Oakman (*Palestine in the Time of Jesus*, 72) give a chart summarizing the elements of this relationship.

In addition, the high priest, appointed as he was by the Roman prefect, also had a client relationship to Rome, serving at the prefect's pleasure. The high priest, along with the prefect, also had a responsibility to make sure life went smoothly, because the prefect was required to keep the peace and make sure that taxes were collected and paid to Rome. Rome did permit the high priest to control the administration of the temple area and sacrifices, but if things got unruly, Rome would take control. One means of control was the right to execute criminals. The most severe rite of execution, crucifixion, was a power Rome kept to itself. Crucifixion was not only an aspect of the rule of law against criminals but also an expression of political power and a reminder of that power by example. To be crucified was to face the ultimate public shame.[33] It was regarded as so torturous and shameful that Romans were excluded from being crucified.

Society was highly stratified and hierarchical. A few families held all the power, with the aristocracy composing no more than 4 percent of the population.[34] The absence of social mobility meant that certain families maintained power for generations. What mobility there was came from association with the major families within the upper classes. The group that supported the upper class and had access to them may have composed up to 7 percent. Some estimates of these first two groups are smaller, comprising no more than 6 percent together. The religious class (priests and scribes) and others able to make more than a subsistent existence as artisans or craftsmen may have been as much as 15 percent. They were the closest thing to a middle class in the ancient world. Jesus' family with their carpentry background may have come from this class. Most people, as high as 70 percent, eked out a living, usually working someone else's land, while the bottom 10 percent lived on the fringe of society and were ignored, near starvation, and expendable. Mixed in among the dominant class but often enjoying better living conditions were the slaves of the wealthy. They were usually prisoners of war and often helped in the home of the master. In general, slaves were found in non-Jewish homes or in Jewish homes that had adopted Hellenistic ways.

33. Martin Hengel, *Crucifixion in the Ancient World and the Folly of the Message of the Cross* (Philadelphia: Fortress, 1977), 22–38. Hengel notes that other forms of execution included decapitation, being fed to wild animals, and cremation, but crucifixion was regarded as the supreme death penalty and the most horrific. See Cicero, *In Verrem* 2.5.168.

34. Hanson and Oakman (*Palestine in the Time of Jesus*, 69) speak of an "aristocratic empire." The estimates of the breakdown of various strata vary, so the numbers together may not equal 100 percent.

For Jews, most of the power emanated from Jerusalem and from the high priesthood. The dominant religious-political power resided in the Sadducees, who had worked out their relationship to Rome and had a major role in commercial endeavors, though the Pharisees held enough public respect to be a factor in major deliberations. Of course, both Jewish groups had to honor the presence of Rome as represented by the prefect, as well as the role the Herodians played as Rome's "ethnic" client-rulers. The major role of the elite was to control life and commerce as well as to help support the collection of taxes and contribute to keeping the peace. For Jews, this commercial activity would have included issues tied to the worship at the temple and its prescribed role as a locale for sacrifices. As already noted, most people did not belong to these groups and simply tried to survive.

Economics

Economics in the ancient world can be summarized by one phrase: "trickle-up economics." Money and goods flowed to the elite with next to nothing left for anyone else. It is estimated that in agrarian societies the top 5 percent of the population may generally control 50 to 65 percent of the goods.[35] In Israel this would include the patrons of the land, the emperor and his agents, the prefect, other key families, and the elite priests. They exercised control through their imperial and private estates, where land was owned and worked. The temple also generated significant funds. The elite did not labor; they managed affairs. Included in this elite were rulers, soldiers, scribes, and administrators. The ideal for them was the contemplative life.

Others earned their wages with their hands. Crops on average yielded about ten to fifteen times what was sown. Sixty-five to seventy percent of the land was used for agriculture. Rulers also controlled fishing. They sold fishing rights to brokers (tax collectors), who in turn hired the fishermen. Some fishermen worked together in a kind of cooperative. They certainly lived better than many, but they were not well off or "middle class." They fished with a rod and hooks on flaxen line, flaxen nets, traps, or tridents. Nets were most common in Galilee. Fish caught in Galilee went out to the entire region of Palestine through a network of processors and marketers. Fish were processed for preservation and transported as cured, pickled, salted, or dried (*m. Nedarim* 6.4).[36] Other artisan specialties included pottery,

35. Ibid., 113–14.
36. For this entire section, see ibid., 101–12.

metalworking, cloth weaving, leather working (sandal making), woodworking, and oil and wine making.

The masses worked for the elite. Only artisans or other craftspeople had the ancient equivalent of small, independent businesses. They constituted a minority of the labor force. Stewards helped manage the affairs of the elite and often received a portion of the benefits for their work. Sources of labor were limited to what humans or humans with animals could produce. Many people were day laborers, hired in the marketplace for a day at a time. They would help on large estates as needed. Commerce involved some currency, but bartering was much more common than in the modern West.

Taxes operated at multiple levels, because both Rome and the temple needed support. Roman taxes included a "soil" tax on what was grown, a head (poll) tax, a market tax on what was sold, a transit tax, a shipping tax, taxes for roads and aqueducts, and a tax on rental revenue. In addition, taxes for Jerusalem included the tithe, a head tax, and expenses for sacrifices or vows. Taxes varied depending on the commodity. The state collected grain and fruit to support its services. Grain sent to the state ran from 25 to 35 percent, but this was gathered periodically, not every year, while fruit was provided at a 50 percent rate on the same basis. Such taxes were draining (*Ant.* 16.153–55). The basic Roman crop tax appears to have been about 12.5 percent when figured on an annual basis (*Ant.* 14.203—a quarter of the harvest every other year).[37] It is hard to estimate what the total percentage of all taxes was, because it would depend on how much commerce one participated in. Nonetheless, figures of up to 33 percent are not unrealistic, with Jerusalem getting about 15 percent of the total. This situation led to discontent among some, and occasionally to public uprisings, although this seems to have been more common in the decades following the time of Jesus. Money and commerce were often a means of controlling people in this culture, and its structure explains the trickle-up effect.

The temple also generated economic interests. The ruling priests administered the sacrifices, which required thousands of animals a year. The conversion of money from one currency to another also generated income. It is suggested that the priests' decision to move some of this activity to within the temple court is what contributed to Jesus' action to cleanse the temple.[38] Some have described the feel of the temple as

37. E. P. Sanders, *Judaism: Practice and Belief 63 BCE–66 CE* (Philadelphia: Trinity Press International, 1992), 166–67. I follow his more conservative estimates versus the 40 percent plus of others.

38. Victor Eppstein, "The Historicity of the Gospel Account of the Cleansing of the Temple," *ZNW* 55 (1964): 42–58; Craig A. Evans, "Jesus' Action in the Temple and Evidence of Corruption in the First-Century Temple," in *Society of Biblical Literature 1989 Seminar Papers* (Atlanta: Scholars Press, 1989), 522–39.

almost like a slaughterhouse but with a sense of sacred awe for what was taking place. All this was designed to picture the reality of what sin cost, in terms of both life and money.[39] It explains why some Gospel imagery pictures sin as debt. In this culture, sin brought economic consequences if one offered sacrifices to deal with it.

Issues of life and commerce were difficult, except for the privileged few. Understanding how the culture worked helps the Gospel reader appreciate the illustrations Jesus used when it came to issues involving money. It also explains why those who collected the money were disliked. That Jesus reached out to the fringe of society and the poor showed his concern for all people, not just the most powerful.

Religion

Six themes are important in thinking about Jewish faith: Sabbath, purity, temple, feasts, calendar, and messianic hope. With the exception of the issue of messianic hope, each of these areas is related to practice as it is presented in the Law. Before I treat these themes, however, it is important to highlight three other fundamental aspects of Jewish belief and identity: monotheism-election, covenant-land, and circumcision. These three religious issues explain why some were so loyal and meticulous about such practices.

Three Fundamental Beliefs

Monotheism-Election. Israel believed there was only one true God, in contrast to the belief of their neighbors in multiple gods (Deut. 6:4–6). Nothing was more fundamental to Israel's faith than that this God was the creator of heaven and earth, the God who had chosen and had redeemed and would redeem Israel. The Abrahamic promise, as outlined in Genesis 12:1–3 and developed in that book, presented the fundamental Jewish belief that Israel was a uniquely elected people of the one true God. That election was underscored in the covenant relationship God had formed with the people through Moses, a covenant relationship that called for the nation to be a unique people set apart for God (Exod. 19). This sense of corporate election was something each sect in Judaism held to, although to varying degrees. For the most pious groups like the separatist Essenes and the Pharisees, this election and the covenant relationship that emerged from it required the pursuit of

39. Sanders (*Judaism*, 49, 104–18) describes the process of sacrifice and gives the details of how the animal was slain (see esp. 105 and 107).

holiness from all the people, both lay and priesthood. The Sadducees, who held only the Torah in high regard, were much more flexible in how the standards of holiness should be applied. They rejected the oral Torah, traditions fundamental to the approaches of the Pharisees and Essenes. Nationalist movements were motivated by their sense of Israel's uniqueness to seek independence for the chosen nation. This sense of election and the responsibility to be a distinct people undergirded virtually all aspects of Jewish life.

Covenant-Land. One of the commitments God made in covenant was the promise of access to a land of blessing that God would give to his people (Gen. 12–13; Joshua). One of the traumas of Jewish history was that foreign countries had overrun the land and the sacred temple. Indeed, such humiliating defeat had occurred on numerous occasions as Babylon, Syria, and Rome had defeated the nation and desecrated the holy temple. On each occasion the explanation for defeat was the unfaithfulness of the people (Lamentations; 1 Maccabees; *Psalms of Solomon*). It was always seen as awkward that the nations were so thoroughly present in the land God had given to Israel. Israel still hoped for the day when they would dwell in the land again in independence and peace. In the view of the pious, the only way back would be for the people to return to a faithful walk with God.

Circumcision: The Mark of a Unique, Covenant People. A unique people often engage in unique practices. One of these distinctive marks for Israel was circumcision, established as an affirmation of accepting the promise made to Abraham (Gen. 17).[40] When some Jews moved to accept the rise of Hellenism and tried to reverse the sign of their identity, other Jews were shocked by this renunciation of an act so central to Jewish identity (1 Macc. 1:12–15). "They had joined with the Gentiles and sold themselves to do evil" (1 Macc. 1:15). This Maccabean text indicates how circumcision was a matter of fundamental identity for pious Jews. The other unique Jewish practices were merely an extension in their minds of this commitment to walk with God. In a sense the cry of Matthias during the Maccabean revolt reflects the key attitude, "I and my sons and my brothers will continue to live by the covenants of the ancestors. Far be it from us to desert the law and the ordinances" (1 Macc. 1:20–21). For Jews seeking to be faithful and hoping for God's blessing, this attitude was a basic part of their religious iden-

---

40. Although others may have sometimes practiced this rite (Arabs, Egyptians, and some pagan priests), Judaism was especially identified with this practice. D. R. de Lacey ("Circumcision," *Dictionary of the Later New Testament and Its Developments*, ed. R. P. Martin and P. H. Davids [Downers Grove, Ill.: InterVarsity, 1997], 226) suggests that evidence for the practice outside of Judaism may not be accurate.

tity. Their election and unique position meant that they must be faithful. Such faithfulness was expressed in various practices that showed the uniqueness of their people.

Six Other Important Concerns

Sabbath. One of the more fundamental marks of Judaism is its keeping of the Sabbath as an expression of God's day of rest in the creation (Exod. 20:8–11; Deut. 5:12–15). It is seen as a sign that God has set apart his people, a reminder of their relationship to him (Exod. 31:13). The writer of *Jubilees* 2:17–22 notes that the day is an indication of God's unique relationship to Israel. Preparing food or drink, drawing water, bringing in or taking out work were prohibited, as were sexual relations or doing any business on the Sabbath (*Jubilees* 50:6–13). Similar lists could be found at Qumran in the Damascus Rule document (CD 10–12; 4Q267, frags. 17–18; 268, frag. 3; 270, frag. 10). After the time of Christ, the Mishnah has a famous text, "the forty less one," where thirty-nine things are explicitly prohibited on the Sabbath (*m. Šabbat* 7.2). Such detail shows how seriously many took this day of rest. Only that which preserved life might be done on the Sabbath. In fact, it was debated for a time whether a person could fight a war, even in retaliation, on the Sabbath. Fighting in self-defense was eventually permitted. Here was a day that marked Israel as a unique people. The Sabbath was dedicated to reminding them of their special relationship to God. It was truly a day set apart from others.

Purity. This backdrop of being a unique people also explains one of the more difficult features of second temple Jewish faith for modern people, the issues tied to purity.[41] It represents a mentality about sacred space that is hard for modern Westerners to comprehend.[42] For those to whom the entirety of the Law was important, these practices were not to be taken lightly, because the Law had grounded them in the recognition of the uniqueness of God's people (Lev. 20:24–26). The practices were part of an important walk of faithfulness, an expression of

41. For this section see Scott, *Customs and Controversies*, 254–55; and Malina, *New Testament World*, 149–83.

42. The closest analogy I can find to this in a modern context is the Japanese custom of taking off one's shoes on entering a house and wearing either socks or slippers indoors. On a recent visit to Japan, I was often caught off guard by the immediate and strong reaction of some Japanese when I forgot the custom and came indoors in my shoes or put my slippers on in the wrong order. The reaction to my error was fueled by a worldview that saw something "unclean" in what I was doing. Needless to say, after a few such encounters I became much more sensitive about how I entered a Japanese home.

identity. That such distinctions appeared in the Torah (Lev. 11–22) made these practices important to follow. In Jesus' time, with the land now filled with people for whom purity was not an issue, how to cope with the more complex situation intensified the need for additional guidance. Thus by the time of the completion of the Mishnah in c. A.D. 170, a whole unit (order), *Teharot* (cleannesses), was given over to treating such questions.

Once again, various groups took various approaches. The Sadducees limited these restrictions to the priests, while Pharisees took the view that all who wished to keep the obligations should do so. Essenes required them of their entire group, lay or priest.

The distinction between clean and unclean was not related to sin. Rather, the view was that certain food, practices, emissions, or contacts made one "common" or profane. Being profane disqualified one from entering into worship of God and coming into contact with those dedicated to him, worship that required sacred space. Thus uncleanness, even when part of a natural process such as childbirth or the menstrual cycle, rendered a person unable for a period of time to enter into the sacred space of the sanctuary to worship God. Such concerns led to the desire to wash hands and utensils and to avoid contact with lepers or with the dead (human and animal). Ritual baths were common among many, while debate arose about whether uncleanness could be transmitted by insects that were unclean, like flies. Certain foods were kosher and others not, often because of associations of some animals with pagan practices and sacrifice. The mentality tried to communicate a respect for God and a sense of creating some space that was more pure and sacred than most of the more common space that was a part of the everyday world. The attitude underlying this view was that God calls his people to live in an ordered world of his creation and to recognize the boundaries he has set for his people.

Temple. I have mentioned the political and economic role of the priesthood. Here I reflect on the importance of the temple itself. Three elements of the temple are important: its demarcation of space, the sacrifices, and the feasts. I shall consider the calendar, which regulated temple worship, after I discuss the feasts.

The layout of the temple reinforced all these views about sacred space.[43] By all estimates, the full temple area was huge; the expansion started by Herod in 19 B.C. (*Ant.* 15.380, 420–21) was not completed until A.D. 63 under Agrippa (*Ant.* 20.219). Most of this was finished earlier; the sanctuary took a year and a half and the porticoes and outer

43. For this section see Sanders, *Judaism*, 55–76. Sanders's discussions on pp. 47–145 are an excellent summary of temple activity in this period.

courts eight years. Dimensions of the four walls ran: 900 feet (south) by 1,550 feet (west) by 1,000 feet (north) by 1,500 feet (east), a perimeter of nine-tenths of a mile. The area enclosed was thirty-five acres. It was far larger than Greek temple complexes.

While some portions of the complex were available to all, access became more restricted as one approached the center of the temple at the Holy of Holies, where God was said to dwell. On the outer rim of the large complex was the Court of the Gentiles, available to anyone except "women during their impurity [menstrual cycle]," as Josephus notes (*Ag. Apion* 2.102–5). More restricted was the temple area, which was limited to Jews; the entrance from the south was marked with signs like one found that read, "No foreigner is to enter within the forecourt and the balustrade around the sanctuary. Whoever is caught will have himself to blame for his subsequent death."[44] The priests were allowed to police this area and possibly even had authority to carry out a summary execution (*War* 6.126).[45] It was probably the only circumstance in which they were granted the right of execution from the Romans. Next came the Court of the Women, open to all Jewish women (*War* 5.199). It was built so women could look into the Court of the Priests from a gallery (*m. Middot* 2.5). Up a set of fifteen steps, the men proceeded and passed through a gate in the wall into the Court of the Israelites. This is where males who were not priests or Levites would gather. From this place they could hear the singing of the Levites or watch the priests work. In the porticoes around it were various rooms, like the treasury rooms, while over these walls on a second story were the dormitories for officiating priests, a privy room, a bath for cleansing, and storage rooms. Next came the Court of the Priests (Exod. 30:17–21; *m. Tamid* 1.4). The altar, shambles (where animals were slain), and laver were restricted to the priests. Here is where sacrifices were offered.

Then came the two key sanctuaries, which sat under a single 150-foot-high roof. Twelve steps preceded the entrance to the first sanctuary, the Holy Place. In here were the lampstand, table of shewbread, and altar of incense. The second sanctuary was the Holy of Holies, which was separated by a curtain and was about 30 feet square. Josephus describes it as containing "nothing whatever" by this time and as

44. Peretz Segal, "The Penalty of the Warning Inscription of the Temple of Jerusalem," *Israel Exploration Journal* 39 (1989): 79–84.

45. Violation of the temple precinct by Gentiles may be the only case when Jews were permitted to execute someone on their own. Otherwise, the right was left to Rome. See Darrell Bock, *Blasphemy and Exaltation in Judaism and the Jewish Examination of Jesus*, WUNT 2/106 (Tübingen: Mohr, 1998), 7, 11–12; and Josef Blinzler, *Der Prozess Jesu: Das judische und das romische Gerichtsverfahren gegen Jesus Christus auf Grund der altesten Zeugnisse dargestellt und beurteilt*, 4th ed. (Regensburg: Pustet, 1969), 229–42.

"unapproachable, inviolable, invisible to all" (*War* 5.219). Here the high priest could enter only once a year. Thus the closer one got to the center of the temple, the more restricted the access, the more sacred the space. Most of the religious activity of the temple took place in the open air outside these sacred sanctuaries. The very orderliness and regulation of space was seen as speaking to the orderly design and sacredness of God.

The temple was run by a group of around twenty thousand priests and Levites (*Ag. Apion* 2.108), who were divided into twenty-four groups (*Ant.* 7.365; *m. Sukkah* 5.6). Priests offered the sacrifices, while Levites assisted them.[46]

Beyond the instruction of Exodus–Deuteronomy, what we know about first-century sacrifices comes from Josephus, Philo, and the Mishnah. The Mishnah is still a good source of older practice, although a few of the debates may reflect the controversies of the second century. Sacrifices came in various types: with meal, wine, birds (doves or pigeons), or animals (sheep, goats, or cattle). They could be offered for the community or for an individual. They could be for worship, communion, thanksgiving, purification, atonement, or feasting. Some were burned up and others eaten. It was usually the priest who ate the sacrifice, although Passover lambs and one class of sacrifice were shared with the person and family who provided the sacrifice.

Twice a day the community, as represented by the priest, provided a whole burnt offering for the nation, at nine in the morning and at three in the afternoon (Exod. 29:40; *m. Tamid* 4). These sacrifices were doubled on the Sabbath. The entire offering was consumed by fire as something given totally to God.

Individual offerings took various forms. Individual burnt offerings (Lev. 1:4) were voluntary offerings made for atonement as gifts to God. Such an offering required a sheep, goat, or cattle. Sin and guilt offerings are treated in Leviticus 5. These were offered not just for sin but also for cleansing. Sin offerings could cover sins done in ignorance (Lev. 4:27–35), while guilt offerings appear to cover sin done consciously (Lev. 6:2–7; Josephus, *Ant.* 3.230–32; Philo, *Special Laws* 1.226, 235). Sin offerings could be a lamb, a kid, or two birds for the less affluent. The male worshiper placed his hand on the offering and confessed what sin it was for (Num. 5:7; Lev. 26:40). Women also could present offerings to a priest or a Levite, who would carry it to the altar (Lev. 12:6; *Letter of Aristeas* 95; Aristeas discusses the help of Levites for all sacrifices).

46. For this section see Sanders, *Judaism,* 103–18.

Peace offerings (Lev. 3:1–16) were divided between the altar, priest, and offerer, who could share it with family. These offerings accompanied a feast and were sometimes called thanksgiving offerings or welfare offerings. If they marked the completion of a vow, they were called votive offerings. Thank offerings were eaten on the day of the offering, while votive and freewill offerings could be eaten over two days. In all cases, the animal offered was unblemished.

Sacrifices served to underscore a person's relationship to God. They made the point that sin was costly and showed the offerer's gratitude for God's graciousness. Although other nations also sacrificed, the combination of individual and community worship reveals how identity in Israel had both national and personal dimensions of responsibility.

Feasts. The bulk of the national sacrificial activity took place at feast time, especially at the three great pilgrimage feasts: Passover (closely connected to Unleavened Bread, which followed it), Weeks (firstfruits offered fifty days after Passover), and Booths (or Tabernacles, tied to the Day of Atonement and falling five days after it).[47] Though all three were originally required as times of pilgrimage for males, most Palestinian Jews made one trip a year to Jerusalem, with Passover being the most common feast for the journey (*Ant.* 17.214). To this should be added the important Day of Atonement (Yom Kippur), when the nation annually offered a comprehensive sacrifice for its sin. Other feasts, such as Purim and Hanukkah, also dot the Jewish calendar.

Passover and the Feast of Unleavened Bread are so closely connected that one name can refer to the other feast or cover both celebrations (*Ant.* 3.248–49). This is because Passover falls on the fourteenth of Nisan (in March/April), while Unleavened Bread follows it from the fifteenth to the twenty-first (Lev. 23:4–8; Deut. 16:1–8). This combined feast commemorates the exodus (Exod. 12:29) and the provision of God during that time. While this feast was originally to be celebrated only in Jerusalem, it appears that its celebration spread out by the first century. *Jubilees* attempts to insist on the feast's celebration in Jerusalem (49:16, 18, 20–21), and Philo discusses the practice as well (*Special Laws* 2.145–149; *Questions on Exodus* 1.10; implied also in Josephus, *Ant.* 14.260).

Pentecost, the Feast of Weeks, celebrates the firstfruits of the harvest and comes fifty days after Passover (Lev. 23:9–21; Deut. 16:9–12). It is an agricultural holiday and celebrates God's provision. It falls in late spring or early summer. Two loaves of bread from the first harvest are presented to God to underscore that God owns the land (Deut. 26:1–

47. For this section see Scott, *Customs and Controversies*, 156–57; Sanders, *Judaism*, 131–45.

15). It was generally the least attended feast, coming so close to Passover.

The Feast of Booths, also known as Tabernacles, commemorates the wilderness wanderings and the end of the harvest (Lev. 23:33–43; Deut. 16:13–15). It falls between the fifteenth and the twenty-first of Tishri, placing it in September/October. It comes five days after the Day of Atonement (Lev. 16; 23:26–32). For seven days, Israelite males live in booths to remember the journey. A festival day added onto the end makes the celebration eight days total. It was a popular festival (*Ant.* 15.50); families built the booths each year, and children enjoyed the occasion. There was much music and celebration associated with it (*m. Sukkah* 5.4). Community sacrifices were prominent; thirteen bulls and fourteen lambs were offered on the first day, with the number reduced by one each day until the end of the celebration (Num. 29:12–34; *Ant.* 3.264).

The Day of Atonement is a day of fasting and penitence. It runs from sunset to sunset as a day of solemn rest (*m. Yoma* 8.1). Here the nation fasts together, and sacrifice is offered for their sin. This is the one day on which the high priest entered the Holy of Holies (Lev. 16:1–14; *m. Yoma* 3.8 gives the confession of the high priest for his sins before he goes in). The end of the convocation leads into a great celebration, which Sirach 50:14–21 describes.

Also to be noted is the Feast of Trumpets on the first of Tishri (Lev. 23–25). The sounding of the trumpets marks the beginning of the civil year. Other feasts include Purim, which celebrates the preservation of the nation under the Persians. Also known as the Feast of Esther (Esth. 9:18–32), it is celebrated on the thirteenth to the fifteenth of Adar (February/March). Hanukkah, or the Feast of Lights, commemorates the victory of Judas Maccabeus during the Maccabean War and his restoration of the temple on twenty-five Chislev (November/December) in 164 B.C. It is celebrated on that day (1 Macc. 4:36–59; John 10:22).

These feasts served to bind the nation together, allowed them to worship God, and recalled what he had done for them. They were another affirmation of the unique relationship Israel had with God by covenant.

Calendar. Most of Israel operated on a lunar calendar.[48] Because a lunar month is 29.5 days, this required adjustments to get a balance in the calendar that would fit a 365-day year. Most Jews inserted a thirteenth month every three years to get the balance. The extra month was known as second Adar and came after every 36 lunar months. Qumran, however, used a solar calendar that ran for 364 days (or 365). It had parallels to reckoning in *Jubilees* and *1 Enoch*. This means that some of their festivals fell at dif-

---

48. M. D. Herr, "The Calendar," in *Jewish People*, ed. Safrai and Stern, 2:834–62.

ferent times from the rest of the nation. However, Qumran's separation from the Jewish temple kept this from being a major problem.

Jewish days were reckoned from sunset to sunset, and the daylight hours were counted from sunrise to sunrise, so the third hour was approximately 9 A.M., while the ninth hour would be 3 P.M. Nighttime was calculated by night watches, which could be figured on either three-hour (four watches) or four-hour (three watches) increments.

Messianic Hope. Many of the issues suggested by this section await treatment in the consideration of Jesus' life and ministry.[49] Yet one point needs to be made here: Judaism did not have a single view of messianic hope in this period, although the predominant view, for those who had a hope, was of a Davidic regal figure.[50] This Davidic view is clearly articulated in *Psalms of Solomon* 17–18, where the hope is for a wise, powerful king who will exercise God's judgment and vindication. Both religious and political vindication were anticipated. Through him, victory, peace, and wisdom would come to God's people as Gentiles were vanquished. On the other hand, the Qumran community, which had reacted negatively to the Hasmonean blending of kingship and priesthood, apparently anticipated a pair of messianic figures, one priestly (a Levitical messiah) and the other regal. This expectation appears to have drawn its belief from Numbers 25:10–13. Numerous texts note such a hope: *Testament of Reuben* 6.7–8; *Testament of Judah* 21.1–5; *Testament of Dan* 5.10–11; *Testament of Joseph* 19.5–11. Qumran expectation held that this priestly figure would be predominant over the political messiah (*Messianic Rule* = 1QSa; see esp. 2.20; 4QpIsaᵃ 8–10.23; CD 6.11; 12.22–23; 13.20–22; 14.18–19; 19.9–11; 19.34–20.1).

Works written at or just after the time of Jesus also speak of a figure who is an eschatological judge of humanity, the Son of Man (*1 Enoch* 39–71, esp. 46:1–5; 48:2–7; 62:3–14; 63:11; 69:27–70:1; 71:17; *4 Ezra* [= 2 Esdras] 13). He also appears to have messianic qualities but is seen in more transcendent terms than a mere king. So the Son of Man represents yet another expression of eschatological hope.

49. For a concise introduction to key elements of intertestamental Jewish theology, see Scott, *Customs and Controversies*, 265–352.

50. Three key recent surveys make this point: Jacob Neusner, William S. Green, and Ernest Frerichs, eds., *Judaisms and Their Messiahs at the Turn of the Christian Era* (Cambridge: Cambridge University Press, 1987); John J. Collins, *The Scepter and the Star: The Messiahs of the Dead Sea Scrolls and Other Ancient Literature*, Anchor Bible Research Library 10 (New York: Doubleday, 1995), who argues that the Davidic expectation was the more prevalent view; and Gerbern S. Oegema, *The Anointed and His People: Messianic Expectations from the Maccabees to Bar Kochba*, Journal for the Study of the Pseudepigrapha Supplement Series 27 (Sheffield: Sheffield Academic Press, 1998), who shows just how complex and diverse interpretation of the messianic idea was.

Associated with the eschatological time was the expectation of a prophetic figure. Sometimes it is hard to tell whether this was another way to refer to the Messiah or whether he was seen as a distinct figure like Moses or Elijah (1 Macc. 14:41; *Testament of Levi* 8.14–15; Philo, *Special Laws* 1.11 §§64–65; 4QTest; 1QS 9.11; Sirach 48:1–11).

Important to note is that the term *messiah* (or simply "anointed one") as an eschatological technical term is not prominent in the Old Testament. The term itself appears thirty-eight times in the Hebrew Bible but is rarely a technical term for a future figure. It often simply designates someone as anointed. It refers twice to the patriarchs, six times to the high priest, once to Cyrus (Isa. 45:1), twenty-nine times to the king (including Saul, David, and an unnamed Davidic king in Ps. 2:1–2), and once to an eschatological figure (Dan. 9:25–26). The term is absent from the Apocrypha, yet so much of the Old Testament looked forward to the eschatological day of vindication or to a period of peace through a great, victorious rule that there always remained the hope for many that one day God would complete his promise through such a figure. This hope surely fueled some of the speculation that surrounded both Jesus and John the Baptist. It is the lack of explicit reference to this figure and the variety of images associated with the end-time hope that led to the competing views in Jewish end-time expectations. Although many hoped for such days, some Jews did not appear to be interested in such speculation. The Sadducees seem to have had little concern for such beliefs. Those who liked the Herodian house and the status quo also had little concern for messianism. Other Jews were simply too busy coping with everyday life to be concerned about such questions. Thus as in many other areas of Jewish religious culture, there was quite a variety in Jewish faith during this time. How those differences lined up in general terms leads us to consider the various sects within Judaism at this time.

Despite such differences in Jewish expectations, it is hard to overestimate the role of messianic hope in understanding Jesus and his ministry. In all the differences that swirled around Jewish expectations, the basic hope that God would deliver his people and bring them peace was present in every expression that vied for acceptance. Jesus' teaching about the kingdom and the approach of the promised blessing of God aroused in his followers this messianic hope—and also left them wondering during his lifetime about how exactly he was bringing it. The coming of John the Baptist and the general longing of Jews for release from Rome also fanned this hope. What was contemplated was deeply rooted in the Hebrew Scriptures, which promised and prophesied the day of God's decisive deliverance through God's comprehensive rule and a hoped-for shepherd (Isa. 9–11; 52:13–53:12; Amos 9:11–15; Ezek-

iel 34–36; Dan. 2 and 7). Exactly how Jesus related to this previously expressed hope was a burden of his ministry. The later preaching of the
early church explained what God had accomplished through Jesus in a
way that brought the various elements of what Jesus did into clear
view. In a real sense, the key to understanding Jesus fits into this particular aspect of Jewish hope, even though the way Jesus realized such
expectation differed from the way Jews had come to hope the decisive
deliverance would come. The detailed treatment of the Gospel texts will
show just how fundamental this background is to understanding Jesus.
Indeed, one can argue that without a careful appreciation of not only
the Jewish but the Old Testament backdrop to Jesus, one cannot understand the depth of his claims.[51] The early church's claim that Jesus fulfilled prophetic expectation, as well as the explanation of the significance of many of Jesus' actions, is rooted in this future hope.

Key Sects

Before examining the various groups within Judaism, I need to make
one point: most people in the first century did not belong to any of the
groups I shall mention. Rather, these Jewish parties represented the
more significant groups who influenced religious and political policy.
The variety of groups and the allegiances they represent show how
complex second temple Judaism was.

The Aristocratic Class and the Sadducees

The most powerful group in first-century Judaism was the Sadducees and the aristocratic class to which they belonged. Although not all
aristocrats were Sadducees, it is possible that all Sadducees came from

51. A number of New Testament scholars suggest that many of these Old Testament
ties were fabricated later by the early church to make Jesus' ministry appear to fit the
Old Testament. Although there is no doubt that the depth of these connections came to
be more fully appreciated by the early church after Jesus' death and resurrection, these
accounts and the events they portray give sufficient evidence that the backdrop of this
expectation was inherent in these events themselves. They are not the product of a later
projection back into the life of Christ. Many of Jesus' actions intended to evoke this background. One of the goals of my treatment of specific texts is to focus on this fundamental
backdrop. In some critics' quest to explain the Gospels on the assumption and basis of a
Hellenistic background, this Jewish and especially scriptural backdrop is often severely
understated. In fact, such doubt usually reflects a worldview or belief that questions the
possibility of prophecy. My view is that the record shows that what the early church developed and preached about Jesus was inherent in what he did and what he sought to
accomplish. It was the expression of the realization of things God promised long ago.

the aristocratic class.[52] The priests, including the high priest, would have come from this party. The problem is that we possess no documents that come directly from Sadducees. All we have is filtered largely through Pharisaical or Qumranian eyes. However, the history that we possess does give insight into their views.

Josephus tells us that they believed that the soul dies when the body dies, they followed only the Torah, they were known for disputing, and their position was checked to some degree by the popularity of the Pharisees (*Ant.* 18.16–17). Elsewhere he tells us that they had no belief in fate and thought that God was distant from the personal details of human actions in terms of being a determinative being (that is, they advocated freedom of the will). They denied a resurrection and the immortality of the soul as well as punishments and rewards in Hades (*War* 2.164–65).

The Pharisees

The Pharisees are the most-discussed group in ancient materials. They are mentioned in Josephus, the Apocrypha, the Pseudepigrapha, and the Dead Sea Scrolls. They are mentioned as far back as Jonathan Maccabeus (*Ant.* 13.171). The incident between Eleazar the Pharisee and Hyrcanus (ruled 134–104 B.C.), discussed in chapter 3, is the earliest event at which the Pharisees are present, and Sadducees also are mentioned as present there (*Ant.* 13.288–98). The struggle between these two groups has a long history.

Josephus says that the Pharisees had a more austere lifestyle, followed their reason, and respected their elders. They affirmed fate and freedom of the will, immortal souls, and reward and punishment in a future judgment. They held to a resurrection and eternal punishment as the result of that judgment. They believed that their virtuous behavior commended them to the people (*Ant.* 18.12–15; *War* 2.162–63). Josephus was a Pharisee, so his portrait of them is favorable (*Life* 2.12), but it still contains the thrust of what they believed. They also were concerned that the Law be faithfully lived out; they sought to interpret it "with exact skill" (*Ant.* 17.141–42) and were "experts in the laws of their own country" (*War* 1.648). They had a reputation for being precise. The Pharisees and their scribes became the caretakers of the oral law.

The Essenes

We know less about the origins of the Essenes. It seems likely that this group represents the inhabitants at Qumran. If so, then many with-

---

52. Sanders, *Judaism*, 318. Josephus states that the Sadducean doctrine was known "only to a few males," but they were "foremost in worthiness" (*Ant.* 18.16–17).

drew and became separatist in reaction to the Hasmonean rule sometime between 150 and 140 B.C. There is also some evidence that a few
remained in Jerusalem. Josephus first mentions the group in association with a prediction by Judas the Essene of the assassination of Aristobulus I in 104 B.C. (*War* 1.78–81; *Ant.* 13.311–13).

The Essenes lived a simple life and worked the land (Philo, *Good Person* 76–77; *Hypothetica* 11.8–9). They held all things in common (*Good
Person* 86–87; *Hypothetica* 11.10–11). Josephus confirms this, saying
that they practiced holding goods in common and were hospitable to
those of the group who visited a village (*War* 2.122–25; *Ant.* 18.20). Josephus argues that they had an extraordinary piety before God (*War*
2.128). They also held that all things are ultimately God's. They believed in the immortality of the soul and a judgment including rewards.
They made use of washings, offered sacrifices in their own way, did not
marry, and did not have servants (*Ant.* 18.18–22).

The Herodians

This group is mentioned only in the New Testament (Mark 3:6;
12:13; Matt. 22:16), although Josephus mentions "partisans of Herod"
(*Ant.* 14.450; *War* 1.326). These Herodians supported the client-king
and his family and were pro-Roman.

The Nationalists (Zealots)

Although part of this group became powerful and were known as
Zealots in the 60s of the first century, various movements pressed for
Israel's freedom from Rome. Josephus calls this group the "fourth phi-
losophy" (*Ant.* 18.23–25). Josephus argues that they agreed religiously
with the Pharisees. They believed that only God was their Ruler and
Lord, and they were willing to die for their belief. He holds this group
primarily responsible for the problems that eventually led to Jerusalem
being overrun in A.D. 70 (*Ant.* 18.7–8).

Summary

These groups are the major parties in first-century Judaism. They reflect the variety and complexity of Jewish belief. Most Jews did not
have such affiliations but were affected by the practices espoused especially by the Sadducees, who controlled the temple, and the Pharisees,
who had a sympathetic following among many as representative of the
best of Jewish faith. Society could be divided into four levels: the elite
upper class, those who supported the elite (known in sociological terms

as the retainers), the nonelite lower stratum, and finally those who were struggling to survive.[53]

Those who allied themselves to Jesus appear to be primarily of the nonelite social stratum (carpenters, fishermen). However, the presence of tax collectors (Matthew, Zacchaeus), a few people tied to the Herodian house (Joanna, wife of Herod's steward—Luke 8:1–3), and the priestly leadership (Joseph of Arimathea) show that Jesus' reach spanned the classes.

Conclusion

The culture of first-century Judaism was quite complex. It was a far different culture in many ways from the life most people live today in many parts of the industrialized world. This overview of life, commerce, politics, and religion helps us to see some of the key issues of Jewish life, issues that will also surface in the reports of Jesus' own ministry. They involve questions of Jewish belief and identity, things that were also a matter of contention in Jesus' own life and ministry. To understand Jesus' ministry more comprehensively, a reader of the Gospels must be acquainted with the Jewish culture, the Jewish leadership, and the people Jesus addressed. However, a full appreciation of this background should not get too distracted by the various strands of expression that were clearly part of first-century Judaism. Rather, Jesus' ministry drew on a basic hope of divine deliverance that expressed itself with some variety in the period. Almost all Israel still longed for God's decisive act on behalf of his people. It is this hope that John the Baptist and Jesus preached. It is through this hope that they are best understood. How these two messengers of God tell their story needs careful attention, for in its telling surprises emerge. These two messengers pull together into one cohesive salvation-historical plan that which many Jews had seen only as unrelated or competing pieces of the puzzle. The Hebrew Scriptures had prepared for this expected day of deliverance. Jesus argued that with him it had arrived. In a profound way, this is why Jesus must be read "according to Scripture."

53. For an informative sociological look at first-century Judaism and the Jesus movement, see Ekkehard W. Stegemann and Wolfgang Stegemann, *The Jesus Movement: A Social History of Its First Century*, trans. O. C. Dean Jr. (Minneapolis: Fortress, 1999), 99–213. This work is far too skeptical of the biblical materials and sees Jesus in social terms as a leader of a charismatic movement that deviated to some degree from Judaism, separated itself into a "counter worldview," and was shaped and motivated by concerns growing out of its roots among the poor; but the work is still full of important discussions of the structure of ancient Jewish society.

Part 2

Methods for Studying the Gospels

There is an on-going discussion about critical methods. But this hardly accounts for the extent to which scholarly conclusions differ; there is now considerable agreement among Protestant and Roman Catholic scholars about appropriate tools and methods to be used in exegesis. The presuppositions adopted either consciously or unconsciously by the interpreter are far more influential in New Testament scholarship than disagreements over method.[1]

The sum of this discussion is that critical study of Scripture can clarify the message that authors were trying to communicate either by showing how the author came to produce his or her work (through examining sources) or by clarifying the context in which the message was communicated. But it cannot increase the authority of Scripture or find new material of the same level of authority. And while critical methodologies have undoubtedly led to a doubting of biblical authority by some, that is not their necessary conclusion, but one resulting from assumptions connected to them or perhaps even a misuse of them.[2]

1. Graham N. Stanton, "Presuppositions in New Testament Criticism," in *New Testament Interpretation: Essays on Principles and Methods*, ed. I. Howard Marshall (Grand Rapids: Eerdmans, 1977), 60.
2. Peter H. Davids, "Authority, Hermeneutics, and Criticism," in *New Testament Criticism and Interpretation*, ed. David Alan Black and David S. Dockery (Grand Rapids: Zondervan, 1991), 31–32.

The way out of the quandary [concerning critical method] is neither to continue to use the historical-critical method as classically conceived nor to abandon it outright because of its destructive past, but rather to modify it so as to make it more appropriate to the material being studied. . . .

The historical-critical method is indispensable to any adequate and accurate understanding of the Bible, but only where it is tempered by an openness to the possibility of supernatural causation in the historical process. Without this tempering of method it is clearly inappropriate and ineffective, given the fact that the Bible is after all the story of God acting in history. In short, without this tempering the method can only be destructive. One of the great challenges facing evangelical scholarship is precisely that of modifying the historical-critical method so that it becomes productive and constructive.[3]

Because the Bible is a divine-human book, it must be treated as both equal to and yet more than an ordinary book. To deny that the Bible should be studied through the use of literary and critical methodologies is to treat the Bible as less than human, less than historical, and less than literature.[4]

How shall we study the Gospels? Should we merely read them for their individual content and not consider their relationship to one another? How does one engage a topic in which various versions of the same events are presented often in varying contexts and with both similarities and differences in wording? How did we get to and how do we make sense of this complex state of affairs? One of the most potentially intimidating and confusing aspects of Gospel study is the mixture of differences and similarities that we find among the evangelists.

I. Howard Marshall defines historical criticism as "the study of any narrative which purports to convey historical information in order to determine what actually happened and is described or alluded to in the passage in question."[5] Critical studies in New Testament, which involve more than historical criticism, examine the historical processes of both the events described and the reading and production of the texts we possess. Rightly or wrongly, scholars over the years have used historical criticism to try to sort out the nature of the Gospels as we have them and make specific historical judgments about the content of the Gospels. The disciplines associated with this approach have a checkered and hotly debated history. The citations opening this chapter bring to

3. Donald A. Hagner, "The New Testament, History, and the Historical-Critical Method," in ibid., 86, 88.
4. Black and Dockery, editors' preface, in ibid., 14.
5. "Historical Criticism," in *New Testament Interpretation*, 126.

the surface elements of the controversy. At work are not only methods but presuppositions about how they should be applied, especially in assessing documents where claims appear about divine activity. Almost all of the work in Jesus studies today, whether conservative, moderate, or liberal, makes use of this kind of study to varying degrees. Thus the student must sort out what presuppositions about the Gospels a writer or scholar is working with as well as possess an awareness of what methods are being used. This requires an appreciation of an approach's strengths and weaknesses, so that the student can assess how well or poorly they are being applied. We cannot hope to do this completely in a survey chapter. Whole books treat these themes. Among evangelicals there is much discussion about how much or little one should use these approaches.[6]

Nonetheless, I need to introduce these methods because of their importance to the contemporary discussion about Jesus, as well as the potential merit their judicious use brings to understanding the Gospels. Any approach that helps us to understand better the nature of the Gospels and how they might work is worth considering. The debate also will help us sort out what we know, what may be only likely, what is useful information, and what is speculative or wrong.

Thus I survey the history of the three quests for the historical Jesus. Then I examine historical criticism in general and the presuppositions that have affected its use. Next I treat the methods associated with criticism that relate to Gospel study as it has emerged in the last two hundred years, namely, source, form, redaction, and its closely related cousin, tradition criticism. As I treat each area, I introduce the outlines of the history of Gospel criticism for each method, picking up the story from the nineteenth century. With each topic I consider the range of approaches within each discipline and a little of the rationale for each approach. To achieve some sense of the historical flow, I move from source to form to redaction criticism, because this was the historical sequence in which the methods emerged.[7] One should note, however,

---

6. One of the better sources discussing methods applied to the entire New Testament is David Alan Black and David S. Dockery, eds., *Interpreting the New Testament: Essays on Methods and Issues* (Nashville: Broadman & Holman, 2001). I shall note solid resources for each method in each chapter of this part of the book. The majority of these methods are applied to the Synoptic Gospels especially, since the overlap in their material allows for more options in studying them.

7. Tradition criticism will not be treated in terms of its history, for it is merely tracing the history of a particular unit of Gospel material through its various Synoptic expressions. In contrast, redaction study considers the activity of a single evangelist. Under tradition criticism I consider, rather, the so-called criteria of authenticity, which are the general rules critics use when trying to assess if a saying goes back to Jesus.

that the original order of sequence in constructing the Gospels differs from the order in which the criticisms developed. The former began with individual units of the oral period based on the events in Jesus' ministry. Next came their recording in sources. Then came any editing the Gospel writer did to the materials he drew from to construct his Gospel (so form, source, then redaction; the result of the whole sequence makes up the tradition history of any piece of material). One must also note, however, that some Gospel material may be the report of the author himself, containing elements that reflect his eyewitness involvement in these events. At least those Gospel portions tied to Matthew and John need not involve an oral stage. One final method is literary criticism. The study of Gospels as narrative has entered into prominence more recently, especially in North America. For some it is a complement to historical study, while for others it is a replacement of it.

The consideration of these means of understanding the Gospels will reveal why people say such a variety of things about the same texts. In addition, approaching the text with an appropriate sense of the methods' limits can lead us to ask key questions about that passage. The answers to such questions help us appreciate the message of the Gospels more clearly, whether one chooses to see the Gospels written in a particular sequence or simply to consider their accounts side by side.

chapter 5

The Three Quests
for the Historical Jesus

While the so-called "New Quest" was still cautiously arguing about presuppositions and methods, producing lengthy histories of tradition out of
which could be squeezed one or two more drops of authentic Jesus-ma-
terial, a quite different movement was beginning in a variety of places
and with no unified background or programme. Fortified by the Jewish
materials now more readily available, these scholars worked as historians, under no doubt that it is possible to know quite a lot about Jesus of
Nazareth and that it is worth while to do so—the two things which the
orthodox Bultmann school had denied. This movement of scholarship
has become so pronounced that it is not fanciful to talk in terms of a
"Third Quest."[1]

This chapter traces the history of the historical study of Jesus. Roots of
this method are tied to the historical-critical reading of Scripture, a
movement whose checkered history is the topic of the next chapter.
Such study engages all the methods covered in part 2. However, there
is a basic orientation that has allowed many scholars of Jesus to agree
that this study had three key phases: an "antidogmatic" first quest; a
second, "new" quest grounded in historical and tradition criticism as
well as in Greco-Roman background; and a third quest rooted in the
study of Jesus in his Jewish context. This third quest searches for a

1. Stephen Neill and Tom Wright, *The Interpretation of the New Testament 1861–
1986*, 2d ed. (Oxford: Oxford University Press, 1988), 379.

more unified, coherent explanation of him and the data we have about him.

Jesus has always been the object of intense study. People have discussed and debated what his ministry was all about and what context best describes him. This has been the case especially since the Enlightenment and the rise of skeptical criticism. Such study tried to separate the confessed Christ of the Bible, who was seen as the early church's theologically biased presentation, from the "historical" Jesus. The claim was that by looking for the historical Jesus one could find the emphases of Jesus' own message in his original historical context.

The distinction between the Jesus of history and the Christ of faith suggests a view that what we have in the Gospels is too heavily overlaid with later perspectives. What the debate conceals, however, is the complexity inherent in doing history. Significant events are rarely one-dimensional. Part of what makes certain events significant is their very complexity, in which the ramifications of a saying may clearly emerge for listeners only much later, a point John 2:22 and 12:16 acknowledge. In addition, the realization of an event's impact later does not necessarily mean that that impact or the seeds for it were absent in the original setting. Thus while it might be the case that what the evangelists sometimes present explicitly was implicit in the original setting, that distinction does not mean that the evangelist distorts the event's description or historical character.

For example, the discussion of purity in Mark 7:1–23 is often seen as reflecting a period after the time of Jesus (and even after that portrayed in Acts 10, where Peter is careful about not eating unclean foods until he gets a vision). Mark 7 is said to reflect such a later period in the early church when the cleanliness of food was no longer a major issue in contrast to the distinction that had been made and practiced for centuries previous in Judaism. But this is not the only way to explain the text. The note in Mark 7:19, "cleansing all food," gives an implication of Jesus' remarks that explains how the church eventually came to make less of such distinctions, once the church understood and appreciated the saying's import. History should not be read so flatly that roots in the time of Jesus are argued as not addressing issues that took on additional weight or specificity later in the church.[2]

2. Another example is found in the Matthean and Lucan Great Commissions. If we take the remarks and place them next to issues raised in Acts, we can conclude that it took the disciples a while to appreciate that taking the message to the nations meant more than just preaching to proselytes or God-fearers among the nations or just to Diaspora Jews living among the nations. The disciples did not get the full import initially.

We can now trace the history of the quest for the historical Jesus. It is often presented in three phases, or "quests."

The First Quest

The first quest was an attempt to be "historical" by noting how the scriptural accounts were not coherent and then seeing what remained. The argument, grounded in an excessive rationalism, was that one should separate the dogma in the account from its historical core, if any remained. The first quest is generally associated with G. E. Lessing's posthumous publication in 1774–78 of the work of Hermann Reimarus in his *Fragments* (1694–1768), although he was not identified as the author until 1813.[3] Reimarus, a Deist, argued that the perspective of Jesus in the Gospels differed from that of the apostles in the Epistles. Jesus taught and preached very much as a Jew. However, his death led the apostles to develop the idea of a suffering redeemer around him. Reimarus argued that the disciples stole Jesus' body and that a perspective arguing for an alleged resurrection had also infiltrated the Gospels, so that finding the real Jesus would take careful historical work.

Next came the work of David Friedrich Strauss (1808–74) in 1835–36, when he published *Das Leben Jesu* (*The Life of Jesus Critically Examined*). The book was so controversial it cost Strauss his private tutor's post at Tübingen. Strauss challenged two approaches to Jesus of the time: one was conservative, which he called "supernaturalism," and the other rationalistic, which he called "naturalism." He claimed that rationalism tried to retain the history of the Gospels, explained naturally, while rejecting the supernaturalism claimed by the early church. He rejected this "half-measure." He opted for the "mythic" and gave the impression that very little attributed to Jesus actually took place, although he did believe that Jesus regarded himself as the Messiah. He especially challenged the historical character of John's Gospel. Here was a radical statement that the value of Jesus was not in the history the Gospels portrayed but in the value the church attributed to him.

3. H. S. Reimarus, *Fragments*, ed. C. H. Talbert, trans. Ralph S. Fraser, Lives of Jesus Series (Philadelphia: Fortress, 1970). The most significant study of the first quest is Albert Schweitzer, *The Quest of the Historical Jesus: A Critical Study of Its Progress from Reimarus to Wrede*, trans. W. Montgomery (New York: Macmillan, 1959 translation of 1906 book). He studied several works and concluded that the quest had been a failure as each author had reconstructed Jesus in an image favorable to that author's predilections. Schweitzer chose to see Jesus as closely connected to his Jewish environment. For him Jesus erroneously expected God's vindication to come in his lifetime; when Jesus saw it would not come, he shifted his attention to meeting his death and explaining it.

The last work of the first quest was William Wrede's *Das Messias-geheimnis in den Evangelien,* published in 1901.[4] Wrede argued that Mark had imposed the "secret" as a device to camouflage the fact that Jesus' ministry was not messianic, even though the church preached him as such. Thus Jesus' instruction in Mark that the disciples and others not speak of his messiahship (Mark 1:23–25, 34, 43–44; 3:11–12; 5:43; 7:36; 8:30) was a theological construction of the evangelist. What made this work significant is that it represented a skeptical salvo against the Gospel that most scholars had accepted as both the earliest and most historically credible. If Mark could not help us find the historical Jesus, then maybe the historical figure was lost in the theological overlay of the Gospels. For many scholars, this was the situation at the start of the twentieth century. Nothing showed this more than the work of Rudolf Bultmann (1884–1976), who believed that we could know little about Jesus other than that he lived. The first quest had traveled the road of rationalistic historical study and had come to a dead end.[5] To use another image, it had dug a massive ditch between the historical Jesus and the Christ of faith.[6] It led to fifty years with no concentrated effort to write about the life of Jesus, a period that has been dubbed by some as the period of "no quest."

The So-Called No Quest Period

To call this period one of "no quest" is probably an overstatement. There were signs in other corners of scholarly Jesus study that those working with less skeptical presuppositions thought we could know

4. *The Messianic Secret,* trans. J. C. G. Greig (London: J. Clarke, 1971). Not all work in the first quest was negative. Johannes Weiss (*Jesus' Proclamation of the Kingdom of God,* trans. and ed. R. H. Hiers and D. L. Holland, Lives of Jesus Series [Philadelphia: Fortress, 1971 translation of 1892 work]) defended the general picture of the Gospels by considering the Jewish backdrop to Jesus' message and argued that Jesus preached the approach of the kingdom. Meanwhile, Martin Kähler (*The So-Called Historical Jesus and the Historic, Biblical Christ,* trans. and ed. Carl E. Braaten [Philadelphia: Fortress, 1964 translation of 1892 work]) argued that the preached Christ and historical Jesus were so intertwined in the Gospel material that no method could separate the strands. This added to the sense that the quest was failing. See Blomberg, *Jesus and the Gospels,* 179–80.

5. The key study on the first quest is Schweitzer, *Quest of the Historical Jesus.* He concluded that the first quest was a failure and had reached a dead end in part because it failed to take Jesus' Jewishness and Jewish context seriously enough.

6. Scot McKnight, "Who Is Jesus? An Introduction to Jesus Studies," in *Jesus under Fire,* ed. Michael J. Wilkins and J. P. Moreland (Grand Rapids: Zondervan, 1995), 52–72, esp. 54.

much more about Jesus. In fact, this has been true throughout the history of the quest.[7] In Britain T. W. Manson in 1939 argued that there was a structure to Jesus' teaching that had a solid claim to reaching back to him.[8] He represented a far more moderate use of criticism that was typical of British scholarship. Its roots extended back to the nineteenth-century days of B. F. Westcott, F. J. A. Hort, and J. B. Lightfoot, who had successfully challenged the more radical German theories of the nineteenth century.[9] The form-critical work of Vincent Taylor also fit into this more moderate critical approach. Others, like Adolph Schlatter in Germany (1852–1938), challenged the critics by appealing in principle to careful study of the Jewish background of Jesus' life and showing how the Gospels fit historically and culturally into the background they claimed to portray. Jesus studies today in some circles have come back to these points made by earlier pioneers. Thus the pursuit of the historical Jesus did not stop with the failure of the first quest. Rumblings continued that indicated that such study was not going to be abandoned, despite its complexity and difficulties.

The Second Quest

The "New," or "Second," quest was far less radical than the first quest had been. It was started in the 1950s by students of Bultmann. They argued that the results of the first quest and Bultmann's agnosticism about Jesus were far too overdrawn. Ernst Käsemann made the plea for a new, more fruitful quest in his essay, "The Problem of the Historical Jesus."[10] The classic study to

7. This point is nicely made by Stanley Porter, *The Criteria for Authenticity in Historical-Jesus Research: Previous Discussions and New Proposals*, JSNTSup 191 (Sheffield: Sheffield Academic Press, 2000), 28–62.

8. *The Teaching of Jesus*, 2d ed. (Cambridge: Cambridge University Press, 1935). He wrote that though the critical method had the danger of finding only the Jesus one was looking for, such study still needed pursuing. He proceeded on the belief that "the only way of safety is to go forward in the face of dangers, in the faith that the truth as it is in Jesus will disclose itself like all other truth to patient inquiry and religious insight" (5). He considered such themes as God as Father, God as King, the issue of the kingdom, the final consummation, and the ethics of Jesus in general, in relation to law, and in relation to sin and forgiveness.

9. The story of this debate as it applies to the whole of New Testament study is found in Neill and Wright, *Interpretation*. It is this more moderate British tradition that influenced scholars like C. H. Dodd, F. F. Bruce, C. F. D. Moule, J. D. G. Dunn, I. H. Marshall, and Graham Stanton in the last half of the twentieth century.

10. This study is in his *Essays on New Testament Themes*, trans. W. J. Montague (London: SCM, 1964 translation of 1954 work), 15–47.

emerge from this work was by Günther Bornkamm.[11] It was less radical than most work by first questers. He still rejected the idea that Jesus thought of himself as Messiah but regarded much of Jesus' teaching, especially the ethical portions and those treating the kindness of the heavenly Father, as authentic. For Bornkamm, Jesus was a transcendent personality who called people to repent. Second questers make much use of many of the critical methods, such as form, redaction, and especially tradition criticism. They do so usually requiring the burden of proof to fall on the need to show authenticity. This approach is the one into which the Jesus Seminar falls.[12]

One other feature has come into play in the discussion associated with the second quest. It is the tendency to argue that canonical and noncanonical texts should not be distinguished as historical sources.[13] In one limited sense, this point is valid. Each text must be taken on its own terms and assessed for its historical value. Noncanonical sources may have important historical points to make about the Jesus tradition and its use in the various communities of early Christianity. But in practice what has often happened is that noncanonical and even heterodox sources, like the *Gospel of Thomas*, are given an inflated historical role in the development of the Jesus tradition and placed in a position of greater prominence than the canonical Gospels. The result is that points made in the canonical Gospels are often challenged or rejected in part because of evidence from *Thomas*. So the Jesus Seminar has appealed to *Thomas* as an important mid-first-century source, even calling one of their major publications *The Five Gospels* to make the point.[14] They did so despite the fact that most New Testament scholars and historians of the early church regard *Thomas* as a heterodox early-second-century source. The emphasis has distorted the results of the seminar in a way that has been heavily criticized by conservatives and non-

11. *Jesus of Nazareth,* trans. Irene and Fraser McLuckey with James M. Robinson (New York: Harper, 1960).

12. For concise critical assessments of the seminar, see Richard Hays, "The Corrected Jesus," *First Things* 43 (May 1994): 43–48; Luke T. Johnson, *The Real Jesus: The Misguided Quest for the Historical Jesus and the Truth of the Traditional Gospels* (New York: Harper & Row, 1996), 1–27; Darrell L. Bock, "When the *Jesus Seminar* Meets *Jesus under Fire:* On Whose Side Does History Fall?" *Princeton Theological Review* 4 (1997): 3–8.

13. This approach is prominent in the work of Helmut Koester, *Introduction to the New Testament,* 2 vols., Hermeneia: Foundations and Facets (Philadelphia: Fortress, 1982).

14. Robert W. Funk, Roy W. Hoover, and the Jesus Seminar, *The Five Gospels: The Search for the Authentic Words of Jesus: New Translation and Commentary* (New York: Macmillan, 1993).

conservatives.[15] Any effort to make *Thomas* a source equal in value to the Synoptics or Q (see chap. 7) or to date it with them is decidedly unhistorical. Here is one reason many scholars, whom the seminar claims to represent, reject their work.

The Third Quest

Yet the second quest is not the only major approach left in considering issues tied to the historical Jesus. More recently, an effort has emerged to focus on the Jewish background of Jesus' life and ministry. One proponent of such concerns was Joachim Jeremias (1900–1979), who argued for evidence of authenticity in Jesus' teaching by considering the Aramaic backdrop of Jesus' teaching.[16] Even earlier precursors are the massive Jewish parallels collection of Hermann Strack and Paul Billerbeck (Strack: 1848–1922; Billerbeck: 1853–1932), and the work of Adolph Schlatter (1852–1938) and Gustav Dalman (1855–1941).[17] Significant in Britain was a seminal study by George B. Caird entitled *Jesus and the Jewish Nation.*[18] This emphasis on Jesus' Jewish roots grew into what is becoming known as the third quest, an approach that runs alongside the second quest but works more seriously with Jewish backgrounds than either of the earlier quests.[19]

In general, those who participate in the third quest have tended to see far more historicity in the Gospels than either of the previous quests, showing a renewed respect for the general historical character of the Gospels. This is not to suggest, however, that the third quest has

15. For example, Richard Hays called this element of the seminar's work "an extraordinarily early dating," "a highly controversial claim," and a "shaky element in their methodological foundation" (Hays, "Corrected Jesus," 44–45). In 1960 Robert Grant and David Noel Freedman said of *Thomas*, "What we find in Thomas, however, is a warping of the lines laid down in our gospels." After summarizing its teaching, they say, "Such a doctrine is essentially Gnostic, not Christian." See *The Secret Sayings of Jesus* (1960; reprint, New York: Barnes & Noble, 1993), 113.

16. *New Testament Theology: The Proclamation of Jesus,* trans. John Bowden (New York: Scribner, 1971 translation of 1971 German work). Jeremias also engaged in several other studies of issues in Jesus' life such as Jesus' view of the Gentiles, his use of parables, life in Jerusalem at the time of Jesus, and the Last Supper.

17. H. L. Strack and Paul Billerbeck, *Kommentar zum Neuen Testament aus Talmud und Midrasch,* 6 vols. (Munich: Beck, 1922–28); A. Schlatter, *Der Evangelist Matthäus,* 3d ed. (Stuttgart: Calwer, 1948). Gustav Dalman, *The Words of Jesus,* trans. D. M. Kay (Edinburgh: Clark, 1902).

18. London: Athlone, 1965. Caird's work reintroduced a concern to take seriously the corporate and national dimensions of Jesus' claims.

19. This is important to note. The second and third quests now run alongside one another rather than coming one after the other with a clean break between them.

reached a consensus or that it is fundamentally conservative. Some efforts at studying the Jewish background have argued for only a moderate amount of historicity. For example, E. P. Sanders sees Jesus as a reformer of Judaism, who offended the leadership by his associations and religious practices.[20] For him, however, it is doubtful that Jesus saw himself as Messiah. Other writers, like Marcus Borg and Geza Vermes, fit into this part of the spectrum, placing Jesus in a Jewish but nonmessianic context.[21] Bruce Chilton also challenges numerous elements of a traditional reading of Jesus, and the works of John Meier and Paula Fredricksen also belong on this side of the third quest spectrum, although they straddle the line between portraying Jesus as prophet and as Messiah.[22]

However, numerous other studies have produced more conservative results and have defended a messianic consciousness for Jesus. N. T. Wright sees Jesus also retelling Israel's story and recasting it as he declares the opportunity for Israel to come out from spiritual exile while also opening up the promise of God to the nations.[23] His work attributes a significant amount of historicity to the Gospels, a far cry from the ditch that ended the first quest. Others who argue for a messianic Jesus include Peter Stuhlmacher, James D. G. Dunn, Marinus de Jonge, and Markus Bockmuehl.[24] Many conservative and moderate evangelical schol-

---

20. *Jesus and Judaism* (Philadelphia: Fortress, 1985).

21. For a sense of the variety in such nonmessianic proposals, see Blomberg, *Jesus and the Gospels*, 182–85.

22. Bruce Chilton, *Rabbi Jesus: An Intimate Biography* (New York: Doubleday, 2000). Other important studies are harder to peg but tend to emphasize Jesus' role as a prophetic figure that produced a belief in him as Messiah. In the first two volumes of his projected multivolume work (*A Marginal Jew: Rethinking the Historical Jesus*, Anchor Bible Reference Library [New York: Doubleday, 1990, 1994]), John Meier expresses uncertainty about Jesus' messianic understanding; but in a later article ("Dividing Lines in Jesus Research Today: Through Dialectical Negation to a Positive Sketch," *Interpretation* 50 [1996]: 355–72), he argues that it is probable that some were given good reason to think that he was the Messiah, although he avoids any clear discussion of what Jesus himself thought. Similar in tone is Paula Fredricksen (*Jesus of Nazareth, King of the Jews* [New York: Knopf, 1999]), who argues that a messianic fervor among Jesus' followers at Passover time led to a predominantly Roman reaction against him and produced his crucifixion without leading in turn to the execution of his followers. These disciples responded to his prophetic message of the near, even contemporary approach of the kingdom. These three studies possess keen observations of Jewish background but also are somewhat skeptical about the biblical materials themselves and Jesus' own messianic intentions. My critique of their general method follows shortly.

23. *Christian Origins and the Question of God*, vol. 2: *Jesus and the Victory of God* (Minneapolis: Fortress, 1996).

24. These writers are treated in Ben Witherington III, *The Jesus Quest: The Third Search for the Jew of Nazareth* (Downers Grove, Ill.: InterVarsity, 1995), 214–18.

ars are contributing to this work with specialized monographs and articles on aspects of Jesus' life. Among them are Craig A. Evans (treating issues tied to the last week of Jesus' life and the Jewish roots of his message), Martin Hengel (concentrating on early Christology, discipleship teaching, and the use of Psalm 110), Robert Webb (on John the Baptist), E. Earle Ellis (on the stability and form of early traditions), Scot McKnight (on Jesus' appeal to issues associated with Israel as a nation), Craig Blomberg (on the reliability of the Gospels), Ben Witherington III (on early Christology and the teaching of Jesus), Robert Stein (on the key titles of Jesus), Brent Kinman (on the entry of Jesus into Jerusalem), Darrell Bock (on the Jewish examination of Jesus), and Grant Osborne (on the resurrection traditions).[25] Some of this work is ongoing or recently published. Historical Jesus studies, covering the spectrum I have noted within the third quest, are now coming out almost every year.[26]

It remains to be seen what the second and third quests will yield in terms of detail. Emerging from segments of this study are some clearly constructed bridges that connect the historical Jesus and the preached Christ to roots in Jesus' life. The ditch created by rationalist criticism may be filling in. Some of these carefully nuanced studies show the Gospels as credible, dependable sources of Jesus' life and ministry.

Critiques like that of G. B. Caird, former professor of New Testament at Oxford University, raise questions about the more skeptical approaches to Jesus.[27] He notes the following errors in many critical ap-

25. This list does not even note the number of technical commentaries on each of the Gospels that conservatives have produced that show awareness of and interact with these developments in Jesus studies. Here the work of D. A. Carson (Matthew), Robert Gundry (Mark), Craig Blomberg (Matthew), Donald Hagner (Matthew), William L. Lane (Mark), C. B. Cranfield (Mark), Robert Guelich (Mark 1–8), Craig A. Evans (Mark 8–16), I. Howard Marshall (Luke), John Nolland (Luke), Robert Stein (Luke), and Darrell Bock (Luke) could be noted as evangelical treatments of these Gospels that also interact with historical-critical study. For bibliographic information on these commentaries, see the bibliography at the end of the book. Key works on John's Gospel are also listed there as well as a few key studies like those noted here. An important collection of studies is found in Bruce D. Chilton and Craig A. Evans, eds., *Authenticating the Activities of Jesus* (Leiden: Brill, 1999). The work of Ellis, Evans, Hengel, Stein, and Witherington comprises a large body of articles and monographs. Blomberg's work is a defense of the historical reliability of the Gospels. McKnight's work focuses on the key themes of Jesus' teaching as they relate to Israel. Others in the list have produced important monographs addressing crucial aspects of Jesus' career.

26. Another recent treatment of the latest period is Mark Allan Powell, *Jesus as a Figure in History: How Modern Historians View the Man from Galilee* (Louisville: Westminster John Knox, 1998), who covers a whole range of second and third questers of the past few decades.

27. G. B. Caird, *New Testament Theology*, completed and ed. L. D. Hurst (Oxford: Clarendon, 1994), 245–59.

proaches to Jesus studies: (1) They assume that "the Jesus of history was a different person from the Christ of the Church's faith." (2) They erroneously treat the issue of "Christology as though it is exclusively a question of Jesus' relationship to God, in traditional terms a question about his deity." He goes on to note that Jesus' relationship to the human race is also an important aspect to understanding his work. His fourth point below will elaborate on this problem. (3) He challenges the belief that the gospel tradition is made of layers that can clearly be peeled apart. Caird also rejects Bultmann's skeptical position that those layers "in which whatever betrays the specific interests of the church . . . must be rejected."[28] He argues correctly that the links between Jesus and the church are tighter than this distinction suggests. (4) Such studies argue that one must start where the evidence is least in doubt. He notes that such "sure" starting points actually cover a competing range of options; he looks at several of them and finds reason to question their role as a foundation for such a quest. Caird argues that the starting point must be the background of Jesus' own age and era. It is especially important to understand how Jesus addressed Israel and how, as a result, he came to be crucified. This is why I have stressed Jewish sources and culture in this introduction to the background for studying Jesus in Scripture. It is also the reason I will focus in special detail on the events of the Passion week in my subsequent study of the text.

My work in Jesus studies shows that skeptical treatments of Jesus tend to work with other emphases that go beyond an excessive severing of the Jesus of history from the Christ of faith. These additional tendencies also lead to a misreading of the text.

1. They tend to treat Mark and Q as the historical base for Jesus, with additional material being almost automatically regarded as coming from the "early church" (i.e., later than Jesus). This results from an excessive attachment to multiple attestation. It is as if the material that Matthew, Luke, or John add on their own is inherently suspect. However, it is this very material that in part surely caused them to write their Gospels. If they were merely repeating what was already there, then why write? Anyone looking at any of the four Gospels knows these authors made choices about what to include, exclude, or emphasize, but this use of editorial choice should not lead to a judgment that what is added is necessarily suspect or automatically late. Indeed, we have no good criteria to assess the roots of this unique material. It is often the case, then, that suppositions about the credibility of the Gospels or

28. In this quoted portion, Caird (ibid., 348) critically cites the remarks of Rudolf Bultmann, *Jesus and the Word*, trans. Louise Pettibone Smith and Erminie Huntress Lantero (1934; reprint, New York: Scribner, 1958), 12–13.

a particular evangelist color whether such material is accepted or rejected as likely going back to Jesus.

2. Another tendency is to regard narratives that are dependent on Old Testament citations and allusions as late products of early church reflection. However, the idea that Jesus understood, presented, and explained himself without reference to Israel's Scripture is suspect for one appealing to be in a line with God's promised activity. Contrary to the view of many critics, sophistication in working with Scripture is not necessarily a sign of later reflection. Indeed, one would expect Jesus to explain and legitimate his claims through a grounding in Scripture.

3. The result of such assumptions is that the Gospels are played against one another in a kind of either/or mode, where one picks one account or the other (or doubts both). The implied, more skeptical formula is often "difference = contradiction." There is little attempt by critics to see if the accounts can work in a complementary relationship. This complementary approach is not merely harmonizing the passages; the correlation of passages still requires careful examination and judgments about relationships. Harmonization does not always result when texts are read in a complementary way, since the conclusion may be that the texts do not overlap as harmonization tends to argue. The complementary approach is an alternative way to weigh the evidence of these texts and will be an emphasis of my study. My hope is that this was of working with the texts will produce a coherent understanding of each passage's similarities and differences. Such a reading can also produce a coherent understanding of Jesus' key emphases, even where scholars debate how details fit together.

4. On the other hand, many critics, when faced with differences, also tend to shy away from any form of harmonizing, regarding each Gospel as functioning independently in terms of its story line. This leads to a type of "divide and conquer" approach in reading the texts, where one Gospel is almost always seen to give a challenge or represent a contradiction to the Gospel with which it is compared. This pitting of the Gospels against one another often involves, in an ironic way, an excessively literal kind of reading. The method used to pursue a point in the text is often to seek a precise correlation to something outside the Gospels in the background. Where such correlation exists, the result is helpful. Where we lack it, critics often reject the point of the Gospel text. There also tends to be a rejection of the Gospel portrait if the point of background does not match exactly, excluding the likelihood that Jesus worked creatively with such background. But our ancient evidence is piecemeal, so we must exercise care not to strain what evidence we do have through too narrow a sieve. This type of critical,

literal reading suggests that what the evangelists wrote was all they knew, when it seems clear the evangelists did make choices in presenting their material, in some cases consciously assuming knowledge of another version of the account without necessarily rejecting that account. As I demonstrate in *Jesus according to Scripture*, the various ways in which the details of the Passion and resurrection accounts can be unified shows that assuming a contradiction is not the primary way to handle such differences. The Evangelists' choices need not represent opposition to what others said but can also serve to supplement or nuance the earlier presentation. I often use the illustration of a husband and wife discussing their courtship. They will certainly be sensitive to different details in the same event and may even discuss different events, but that need not mean that one of them has erred in giving his or her version of the story. We may even have greater insight into the events and characters by having both versions of such events. The skeptical pitting of the Gospels against one another ignores that it is likely the Gospel writers did know the basic outlines of Jesus' story and the emphases of his teaching. Such knowledge came from their exposure to the church's oral tradition, especially if the roots of the Gospels are tied to apostolic tradition. Too much is made of such differences under the auspices of a careful "critical" reading.

5. The result of these tendencies in the use of critical tools is that the Jesus that emerges is often seen in a prophetic light, but not in a messianic one. This Jesus ceases to possess a uniqueness of claim that can make good sense of his crucifixion, the ultimate historical reality that any student of Jesus must be able to explain in terms of cause(s). Thus any study of Jesus that does not regard Jesus as having made some level of unique claims surely understates the thrust of his life and ministry. Such a study will fail to deal with the one fact that virtually no one contests, namely, that he was crucified with a note that he was charged with claiming to be "King of the Jews."

My subsequent study, *Jesus according to Scripture*, focuses on the texts to see if a basic pattern for understanding Jesus emerges. It does so to see if a complementary reading of the texts can help us appreciate Jesus. At the end of that study, I gather together the major themes that emerge from this type of approach. I highlight those themes that are most prominent across the Gospels. In doing so, I hope that a coherent portrait of Jesus' claims emerges, even if scholars debate aspects of the details. I also hope to show how Jesus, as the Gospels present him, connected to the already revealed scriptural promise that was part of Israel's Scripture. In that respect, my subsequent work belongs to the third quest, although in focusing so heavily on Scripture, it is not a historical work in the technical, critical sense.

chapter 6

Historical Criticism

The heart of scientific method is verification. Historians cannot achieve verification, since the events have disappeared into the past. History cannot be reenacted. There is something amusing about the spectacle of historians seeking absolute verification. Proximate verification must depend on the testimony of witnesses and the evidence of past documents fairly and honestly analyzed. The documents of ancient history are available largely on a chance (not a rational or equal or deliberative or extensive) basis, whereas evidence of physics are everywhere available for current experimentation. These factors limit historical inquiry so as to make it nonanalogous with physics.[1]

The historical study of ancient events is fraught with difficulty. The events studied are not repeatable. There is no instant replay. The evidence we have from the ancient world is piecemeal. The culture it emerged from differs from our own. Ancients think differently from moderns or postmoderns. In assessing history, one's presuppositions about whether there is a God and what God can or cannot do are important when reading documents claiming that God speaks and is actively at work. In other words, historical work has its limitations and boundaries. It deals with probabilities and possibilities based on the attempt to explain coherently the various kinds of data it treats. Given these hurdles and limitations, it is no wonder that the historical method itself has been a hotly contested area of scholarly debate, espe-

1. Thomas C. Oden, *After Modernity . . . What? Agenda for Theology* (Grand Rapids: Zondervan, 1990), 123.

cially for those who are open to God's presence and activity within his creation.

Its Roots

My consideration of the history of criticism in this section treats only the emergence of the broad discipline, a story that runs from the Renaissance to the nineteenth century. This story explains why so much of what is called criticism has served to undercut the message of Scripture, and it traces the major philosophical-ideological moves that brought it there. A focused survey of historical criticism in the Gospels comes in subsequent chapters with the survey of methods associated with Gospel study.

The initial survey in this section shows how the historical study of the Bible has produced both approaches that have advanced our understanding of the nature and meaning of Scripture as well as approaches that have sought to undermine Scripture. It is the second dimension of this history that I concentrate on here, in order to better evaluate the strengths and weaknesses of the methods associated with criticism.

The earliest roots of historical criticism reach back into the Renaissance and Reformation. The expectation emerged that the Bible should be read like any other piece of ancient literature. This meant understanding a work in its historical context, because a major emphasis of the period was to work with ancient sources to understand ancient history appropriately.[2] Erasmus and John Colet were among the key figures here. With such a concern, discussion began about the origin of documents, because some ancient documents were shown not to be so ancient after all. In 1440 Lorenzo Valla proved that the Decree of Gratian attesting to the donation of Constantine was a forgery on the basis of various internal and historical criteria. Thus the study of ancient documents at large led to the application of criteria to assess the nature of the biblical material as well. In 1567 Matthias Flacius Illyricus wrote the *Clavis Scripturae Sacrae* as the first hermeneutical text seriously discussing theory in interpretation. He argued that the reader should pursue the "literal" sense, which he defined as the "sense that it conveyed to its original readers." He also argued that apparent contradictions can be explained

2. Edgar Krentz, *The Historical-Critical Method*, Guides to Biblical Scholarship (Philadelphia: Fortress, 1975), 8. The second chapter of this work is especially helpful. See also F. F. Bruce, "The History of New Testament Study," in *New Testament Interpretation*, ed. I. H. Marshall (Grand Rapids: Eerdmans, 1977), 29–34.

if the reader observes carefully the purpose of the biblical text (*scopus*) and uses the analogy of faith as a guide.[3] The real goal was an interpretation that was historically sensitive. Illyricus pursued the history of the text and yet worked with the view that the Bible was ultimately a unity. Faith and the historical study of Scripture were not automatically opposed. Luther and Calvin also worked with such a view of the text.

Starting in 1543 with the Copernican revolution and then with Kepler's work in the seventeenth century, "methodological doubt" began to emerge within discussions of method in the humanities. Science began to challenge the way many had read the Bible. At issue was the church's belief that Scripture taught that the earth was at the center of the creation. The perception of how the Bible should be read changed as new perspectives raised questions about how it had been read. The problem here was that some of the challenges were raising appropriate questions about how the text should be understood; yet in doing so, scholars were elevating human reason to a point where for some it began seriously to challenge whether people could trust the content of Scripture, at least in terms of the immediate cultural, "commonsense" impression it made about the earth being at the center of the universe.

A major philosophical shift in the culture was part of a series of events that eventually led to the Enlightenment of the eighteenth century. An intense rationalism became the order of the day as Descartes (1605–1650) began to reason for existence, starting from methodological doubt and what one could know as a certain foundation. His conclusion became famous—"I think, therefore I am." Others, like Spinoza (1632–77), began to question those elements of the Bible that were rooted in the miraculous. All of this happened in the context of the brutal Thirty Years War (1618–48), a Europe-wide war that revealed the worst of what passion over religion can produce. Some, surveying the carnage, argued that another way needed to be found for people to think about one another. Spinoza was explicit that Scripture had to be subjected to reason and that such reason needed to be absolutely unfettered from religious sanction. When it came to miracles, Spinoza argued that they were just a common Jewish way of referring everything to God in disregard of secondary causes.[4] Revelation ceased to be a cat-

---

3. Krentz, *Historical-Critical Method*, 10.

4. Krentz (*Historical-Critical Method*, 14 n. 25) cites the following quotation from Spinoza: "I must . . . premise that the Jews never make any mention or account of secondary or particular causes, but in a spirit of religion, piety, and what is commonly called godliness, refer all things directly to the Deity. . . . Hence we must not suppose that everything is prophecy or revelation which is described in Scripture as told by God to anyone."

egory for him, and interpretation was a rational, not a theological, discipline. Here began a great divorce, where the nature of the biblical material and its claims became suspect through appeal to preset definitions in the name of what human reason claimed to be able to assert on the basis of its own judgment. Others, like Richard Simon (1638–1712), argued that the Bible was full of internal contradictions. Thus some claimed that writing historically and interpreting rationally undermined Scripture's integrity.

Others, like Hugo Grotius (1583–1645), developed interpretive methods, working carefully with the meaning of terms and considering the historical setting of individual New Testament writings. John Lightfoot (1602–75) pursued the benefit of Jewish studies as a way to enlighten the historical setting of the New Testament. His study of rabbinic materials opened avenues for better understanding the context of some New Testament teaching. Johann Jakob Wettstein (1693–1754) began to consider the variations in manuscripts that led to the development of textual criticism, the study of the exact wording of the Greek New Testament. When Johann Albrecht Bengel (1687–1752) confronted the thirty thousand variants of John Mill's (1645–1707) evaluation of the Stephanus (1550) third edition of the Greek text, he gave his life to thoroughly studying the history of these variants.

In sum, in the history of the historical study of Scripture, some have used it as a tool to challenge Scripture, while others have used it to enhance their understanding of Scripture in its historical context. In the process, each side has claimed to be historical about its pursuit.

Its Origin

Historical criticism began to emerge as a formal discipline with the attempt by Johann Salomo Semler (1725–75) to study the New Testament in its historical, sequential development. Johann David Michaelis (1717–91) emphasized the historical character of the work as distinct from a theological approach to the documents. Thus he pursued the question of the date, authorship, and setting of the New Testament books, a discipline we know today as New Testament Introduction. It is at this point that historical study began to take up seriously the question of the sequential relationship of the biblical books. It is also at this point that the historical-critical method began to focus on specific interpretive issues within the New Testament, including specific issues related to the Gospels that I shall pick up later in this chapter.

It is also during this time that the Enlightenment began to dominate the philosophical world, although by the time of its arrival, most of the significant moves in elevating the use of reason and a human spirit independent of dogmatic concerns had already been made.[5] In 1774–78 Gotthold Ephraim Lessing (1729–81) published Hermann Samuel Reimarus's (1694–1768) fragments on the life of Jesus, which recorded the Deist's challenge of the historical connection of the Gospels to the apostolic teaching about him. There developed from the "ditch" an alleged divorce between apostolic teaching as reflected in the Gospels and Jesus' teaching. Lessing was responsible for the hypothesis of this "ugly ditch," which stated that the "accidental facts of history" could not cross the ditch to become the "necessary truths of reason." Thus history in which God was active in the events was disqualified as a source in the interaction between religion and reason. Religion and the mind became separated by a secular wall. This view was counter to what Jews had claimed as they looked back to their family roots in Abraham, Isaac, and Jacob as well as when they considered a great redeeming event like the exodus. It was also counter to what Christians had claimed as they proclaimed the reality of Jesus' resurrection as a basis for their teaching about him and his offer of unending life with God. Here was a second great divorce: religion and history need not be in contact with one another, as exalted reason had blocked the way. This opened the door to the view popular among many critics today that the gospel story was valuable as a lesson even if the events did not happen. This divorce between history and gospel was unprecedented for the church.

5. For a critical analysis of the origin of historical criticism, see Eta Linnemann, *The Historical Criticism of the Bible* (Grand Rapids: Baker, 1990). Another analysis adding many "isms" to the philosophical backdrop is F. David Farnell, "Philosophical and Theological Bent of Historical Criticism," in *The Jesus Crisis: The Inroads of Historical Criticism into Evangelical Scholarship*, ed. Robert L. Thomas and F. David Farnell (Grand Rapids: Kregel, 1998), 85–131. This chapter reviews ten philosophical strands that affect the backdrop to the emergence of criticism. Especially helpful is the discussion of Hobbes through Hume (pp. 87–100). However, the chapter's implication that there is an absence of concern over the philosophical roots of such criticism among evangelicals today is off the mark (see, e.g., the citations by evangelicals and others I cited at the start of part 2). As a whole the book overreaches when it suggests that the independence of each of the Gospels solves all these interpretive problems or that anyone attempting to work with these methods will inherently misuse Scripture because of the historical biases of criticism. Different suppositions that include the role of God will produce different results through these methods.

Its Dominant Suppositions

As much of criticism became wed to a view that God does not act within the world he created, it was forced to explain the events that Scripture portrayed in terms other than those that the Bible presented. Much of what has been called historical criticism has operated with all or some of the following suppositions. (1) Miracles do not happen, so such texts need other explanations of their origin. (2) The books of Scripture are human works, not an inspired, ultimately united collection of texts. This rules out attempts to harmonize discrepancies or look for a unified message and theology. It does away with the attempt to work by the analogy of faith as Illyricus had done. (3) Problems and discrepancies in the text indicate the human character of these works. In addition, the nature of the sources, which one can determine by examining the texts, often precludes considering that certain events were repeated in distinct settings. Attempts to affirm miracles, to harmonize passages, or to consider the possibility that certain events could have happened more than once and be recorded distinctly within the tradition were rejected as injecting "dogmatic" claims into the historical process. But it is just as dogmatic to be able to claim by definition what God can or cannot do in his creation or in works that he had a hand in creating.[6] Thus each of these suppositions involves basic worldview claims that are not scientifically proven but merely asserted. They reflect preferences in a culture that had disengaged itself from divine involvement and causality. These suppositions contain fundamental questions about how God involves himself in his creation. Any approach based on them is in fundamental opposition to the text to be examined historically. This inevitably produces distorted results, because the analyzed events are altered to fit the worldview and biases of the interpreter.

Perhaps nothing illustrates the suppositions more vividly than Ernst Troeltsch's 1898 essay, "On Historical and Dogmatic Method in Theology," which summarizes how many undertook historical criticism at

---

6. I state the point about divine authorship in this way simply to make the point that if inspiration does exist, then how can one by definition claim that it is wrong to see if these works can be brought into harmony? This does not make every harmonization correct, but it does show that the attempt to rule it out is also incorrect. On this question, see I. Howard Marshall, "Historical Criticism," in *New Testament Interpretation*, ed. Marshall, 132–35. As he says at one point, "The historian who believes in the possibility of the supernatural cannot divorce his faith from his historical judgment" (135).

the turn of that century.[7] He sets forth three basic principles as virtual foundations.

1. *Methodological doubt* argues that history achieves only probability. As a result, religious tradition must be subjected to criticism. In this principle the echo of Lessing is reaffirmed that the details of history cannot conform to the necessary principles of reason. To the extent that this principle engenders an intense skepticism about sources or the possibility of divine activity, it is problematic. This kind of divorce between what history can teach us and the claims of divine activity undercuts the Christian belief that the world and history do matter for humanity, especially in those revealed events central to the movement of divine promise and the realization of salvation.

On the other hand, I would note that we must differentiate between what we know from history or the text and the way we reconstruct history. It is possible that our findings and views are not the final or complete word. More data about the world, terms, or concepts reflected in the text can help us appreciate Scripture better. Neither our knowledge of history nor our knowledge of Scripture is exhaustive. Because none of us is omniscient, there is always room to learn more about Scripture from understanding the backdrop to Scripture. To examine critically the basis of our views and understanding of history, aware that we have not said everything that could be said, is a healthy check against possible blind spots in our reading of history. Thus, rather than applying our doubt to the text, there is nothing wrong with examining carefully our own understanding in studying the text. This is *not* methodological doubt as Troeltsch explained it, but it is a self-critical dimension of our own work that may make us more careful in the end. Part of what makes history difficult to deal with and be certain about are our own limitations of knowledge and sources, not necessarily limitations in the data itself. Relating what the text says to the larger historical world into which it fits is not always easy, even when one understands the text itself reasonably well.

2. *Analogy* is what makes criticism possible and sets the standards we apply to assessing events. How things happen in the present determines what we can say about how things happened in the past. Yester-

7. I note the summary in Krentz, *Historical-Critical Method*, 55 n. 1, which cites the German original, *Zur religiosen Lage, Religionsphilosophie und Ethik von Ernst Troeltsch*, 2 vols., Gesammelte Schriften (Tübingen: Mohr, 1913), 2:729–53. A shorter version of Troeltsch's views in English are in "Historiography," *Encyclopaedia of Religion and Ethics*, ed. James Hastings, 13 vols. (New York: Scribner, 1922), 6:716–23.

day is like today.[8] Thus the claimed absence of the supernatural today is the basis for excluding it in the past. By definition, this excludes any form of special divine involvement in events.

3. Analogy is closely tied to the third principle, *correlation* or *mutual interdependence*. It argues that all historical phenomena are so tightly related that a change in one point affects other points that led into it or lead out from it. In other words, all history is a chain of causes and effects.[9] These operate from within the world in such a way that miracles and salvation history as expressions of divine design and activity are excluded, because principles one and two have ruled it out. So these principles reveal the skeptical impact that the Enlightenment and the philosophical developments preceding it had on criticism.

Assessment and Conclusion

The two results stated by Edgar Krentz are that Troeltsch's approach makes every individual event uncertain, a kind of historical relativism, and that Christianity loses its uniqueness. Krentz is saying that the possibility of a claim of an exclusive revelation is denied by a definition that treats all history as limited in what it can teach us. But Troeltsch's skeptical use of the historical-critical method is not the only option.[10] The student should not merely walk away from considering the text historically because of the bias inherent in many critics' practice of histor-

8. Troeltsch ("Historiography," 718) says, "On the analogy of the events known to us we seek by conjecture and sympathetic understanding to explain and reconstruct the past."

9. Troeltsch (ibid.) says, "The sole task of history in its specifically theoretical aspect is to explain every movement, process, state, and nexus of things by reference to the web of its causal relations."

10. Krentz, *Historical-Critical Method*, 55–56. See his assessment of Troeltsch on pp. 56–61. He notes, for example, an excessive approach to analogy, where "an overgeneralization of a warrant leads to a constriction of the historian's viewpoint so that it is no longer possible to encompass all of reality" (57). As he discusses the debate between Van Harvey and J. H. Hexter, Krentz states that even philosophers of history debate these points, so that "historical method is anything but a carefully defined and agreed on set of axioms and presuppositions" (61). In particular Hexter argues that one must free historical inquiry from the "stultifying effect of the positivist rules of historical method" (139; like those expressed in Troeltsch). See Hexter, *Doing History* (Bloomington: Indiana University Press, 1971), 139–42; see earlier as well (69–76). Distinctions must be made between facts and explanations of facts with warrants supporting the explanations and room left open for the theological claims made in narratives. See Krentz's discussion of ten benefits of historical study (*Historical-Critical Method*, 67–72). In the end, historical discipline cannot replace faith or force one to believe. What it can do is give a better understanding of the claims of the text and help us to appreciate the possible relationship of events to one another.

ical criticism. A case can be made that a form of "critical realism" offers much to the study of history and historical method that can avoid many of the pitfalls of more skeptical approaches.[11]

Still tracing the history of criticism, one can easily see why those in the church who have a high regard for Scripture have viewed criticism skeptically. But this awareness that many have practiced historical criticism in a way that by definition distorts the content of Scripture does not demand that one cease to engage the text historically or consider how it emerged. Although historical criticism has often given erroneous answers to historical questions, it has often asked the right kinds of questions but pursued answers in misdirected ways. Many of the questions raised by critics had already been raised centuries earlier. The judicious use of these methods can in some cases give us better answers than were previously given. Some of the methods used to ask the questions have merit when they are shed of those elements that deny divine activity, because they lead to more careful observations about the text.

The doctrine of inspiration affirms the use of sources (e.g., Luke 1:1–4). It also recognizes the reality that the Gospels were produced in a sequence that can be assessed historically. This opens up the possibility of considering the sources of the Gospels and the Gospels' relationship

11. A careful treatment of these philosophical issues as they relate to criticism is C. Stephen Evans, *The Historical Jesus and the Jesus of Faith: The Incarnational Narrative as History* (Oxford: Clarendon, 1996). Chapter 8 ("Critical History and the Supernatural," 170–202) deals explicitly with the positions of Troeltsch and one of his modern followers, Van Harvey. The study defines well the benefits and limits of history and historical study. Another beneficial summary of these issues is Ben F. Meyer, *Critical Realism and the New Testament*, Princeton Theological Monograph Series 17 (Allison Park, Pa.: Pickwick, 1989), esp. 59–143. Critical realism is also discussed in N. T. Wright, *Christian Origins and the Question of God*, vol. 1: *The New Testament and the People of God* (Minneapolis: Fortress, 1992), 32–46. On p. 35, Wright defines it: "This is a way of describing the process of 'knowing' that acknowledges the *reality of the thing known, as something other than the knower* (hence, 'realism'), while also fully acknowledging that the only access we have to this reality lies along the spiraling path of *appropriate dialogue or conversation between the knower and the thing known* (hence, 'critical')."

In critical realism, Wright notes, the idea of "critical" is passive—it is realism subject to critique, rather than Kant's active meaning of "reason that provides a critique" (35 n. 12). He places it between a naïve realism, where all things are immediately apparent—an approach that led to the church's errors with regard to astronomy that gave the Enlightenment impetus—and a relativism produced by phenomenalism, where all one knows is what one can sense. In my view, critical realism has far more to offer than most postmodern philosophical moves to various forms of nonfoundationalism, where "webs of belief" are affirmed without any clear affirmation that God speaks in a revelatory way that privileges some texts (i.e., the Bible), making their content unlike that of other written works and giving us access to a truth that is more than mere subjective perception.

to one another (source criticism). Inspiration does not preclude the possibility that elements of the gospel story circulated orally before they were recorded. In fact, the point that the account about Jesus was passed on orally is made in Luke 1:1–4 (see esp. v. 2). This consideration also leads us to the issue of forms, or studying the different types of story units within gospel tradition that were passed on with a structure that shows up in its written form (form criticism). Understanding the nature and variety of these Gospel units can make us more sensitive to how the accounts are presented. The inspired text itself manifests the differences one sees among the accounts, raising the possibility of seeing how the accounts are editorially different from one another (tradition history and redaction criticism). The value of pursuing a careful historical study of the text and judiciously using methods that help us answer such questions is that a better and clearer understanding of Scripture can emerge. We continue our study of criticism in the Gospels to see what history and those methods might teach us.

chapter 7

Source Criticism

The decisive evidence for the use of sources in the New Testament lies in the New Testament documents themselves. Not only are there dislocations and apparent duplications in the documents which suggest that the gospels, for example, have undergone a more complex editorial process than is often imagined; but much more important and much less ambiguous evidence is provided by the striking phenomena of agreement between the synoptic gospels in certain passages. The agreement is too close to be explained as the accidental convergence of independent accounts, and the only adequate explanation is either in terms of a common source lying behind the different accounts or in terms of mutual dependence.[1]

This citation gives the basic elements of why students of the Gospels examine the relationship among the Gospels and the sources the evangelists apparently used in writing their Gospels. Though a consensus has emerged in the last century that Mark was the first Gospel written, that consensus has not gone unchallenged, especially by views that place Matthew first.[2] What most today do agree about is that the relationship among the Gospels has major literary roots in sources, in contrast to

---

1. David Wenham, "Source Criticism," in *New Testament Interpretation*, ed. I. H. Marshall (Grand Rapids: Eerdmans, 1977), 139.
2. For a solid study of the issues tied to source criticism, see Robert H. Stein, *Studying the Synoptic Gospels: Origin and Interpretation*, 2d ed. (Grand Rapids: Baker Academic, 2001), 29–169.

some claims that each Gospel was produced independently. This chapter covers the history of this discussion as well as treating the method of source criticism itself.

The Early Church Discussion

In discussing the order of the Gospels, the place to start is the evidence from early church tradition.[3] As we shall see, it is not entirely consistent or straightforward. It is still useful, however, because it tells us what the early church believed about the Gospels and their authors.

The early church tradition is consistent in claiming that Matthew wrote his Gospel in Hebrew for the Jews (Irenaeus, *Against Heresies* 3.1.1). It is also possible that he recorded some sayings of Jesus that others translated (Eusebius, *Eccl. Hist.* 3.39.14–17, where he records the still disputed remarks of Papias; see below). Mark was written to record the preaching of Peter about Jesus (Justin, *Dialogue with Trypho* 106.9–10; Clement of Alexandria, *Commentaries on Some of the Catholic Epistles;* Tertullian, *Treatise against Marcion* 4.5.3; Old Latin Prologue to Mark). Luke recorded the teaching and preaching as it came through Paul (Irenaeus, *Against Heresies* 3.1.1; Tertullian, *Treatise against Marcion* 4.5.3; Muratorian Canon lines 1–4). John, often said to be writing last, composed a Gospel designed to supplement the other three and tell aspects of Jesus' life that the other Gospels did not cover (Irenaeus, *Against Heresies* 2.1.1; Muratorian Canon line 9; Old Latin Prologue, recension 2). The major concern of the fathers was to defend the integrity of the Gospels by connecting each of them to apostolic roots (Tertullian, *Treatise against Marcion* 4.2.1–5). The Anti-Marcionite Prologue to Luke notes that when Luke wrote, Matthew and Mark already existed, a point the prologue says that Luke's preface suggests. This account is paralleled in the Old Latin Prologue. The relevant portion about Luke's composition reads, "For though Gospels had already been written, by Matthew indeed in Judea, and by Mark in Italy, he, spurred by the Holy Spirit, wrote down this Gospel in the regions of Achaia, indicating in the preface that others had been written before his." Eusebius mentions these common views in his *Eccl. Hist.* 5.8.1–5 in summarizing Irenaeus's views. Other summaries appear

---

3. The evidence of church tradition for introductory issues tied to each Gospel was noted earlier in chapter 1.

in 3.24–25 and 6.14.5–7, although the meaning of the second passage is disputed.[4]

Particularly important are the remarks attributed to Papias by Eusebius in 3.39.14–17. The dispute surrounding these key remarks causes questions about church tradition. Papias, through Eusebius, says, "For Matthew composed the *logia* in the Hebraic dialect ('Εβραΐδι διαλέκτῳ τὰ λογία συνετάξατο, *Hebraidi dialektō ta logia synetaxato*); but each recorded them as he was in a position to." It is disputed whether the Gospel of Matthew is meant by the term *logia*. In addition, there is the issue that the biblical version is in Greek, not Hebrew. Some argue that "in Hebrew dialect" means in Hebrew style, so that the reference is to the form, not the language, of the Gospel. However, that other church traditions seem to speak of a Matthew in Hebrew raises questions about reading this as a reference only to style (see citations in the introduction under "Matthew"). On the other hand, other allusions to Papias's use of the term *logia* in the title to a series of books he called *Interpretations of the Lord's Logia* appear to suggest he can use the term with a sense that could refer to a Gospel. Eusebius mentions this work in *Eccl. Hist.* 3.39.1. This book is not extant, so we are unable to assess its content; but it was probably a commentary, in part, on the Gospels, because Papias claims that he checked the teaching in books against the oral tradition (as reported by Eusebius, *Eccl. Hist.* 3.39.4).[5] This, in turn, leaves two options for the saying. (1) Matthew wrote a version of his Gospel originally in He-

4. The second text from Eusebius (6.14.5–7) discusses Clement of Alexandria's view of the Gospels as originally recorded in his *Hypotyposes*, which is now lost to us. According to the common interpretation of this passage, Clement argues that the Gospels with genealogies (i.e., Matthew and Luke) were written before Mark and John. However, this interpretation is not without problems, chief of which is the apparent conflict it creates between Clement's view of the tradition and that of his famous student Origen. Also claiming to appeal to tradition, Origen (as quoted in Eusebius, *Eccl. Hist.* 6.25.4–6) argues for the order Matthew, Mark, Luke, and John. Origen's order is by far the most common in the ancient tradition known to us. Another way to read the Clement passage is to see him as referring to the "public," or official, role of the Gospels of Matthew and Luke rather than to the order in which they were written. For this understanding and a fuller treatment of *Eccl. Hist.* 6.14.5–7, see Stephen C. Carlson, "Clement of Alexandria on the 'Order' of the Gospels," *New Testament Studies* 47 (2001): 118–25.

5. This problem is discussed by Donald Guthrie (*New Testament Introduction*, 4th ed. [Downers Grove, Ill.: InterVarsity, 1990], 44–53), who suggests that Papias may be wrong about this detail concerning Matthew's use of Hebrew. Guthrie's discussion may suggest that Papias's use of *logia* for "Gospel" is more evident than it really is; it is not clear that the Eusebian citation of Papias's view of Mark uses *logia* of that Gospel.

brew, and it soon came into the church in its Greek form. (2) Papias has alluded to some other teaching collection here, like a collection of Jesus' sayings (perhaps Q? see below) that Matthew gathered.

Thus church tradition is consistent in the authors it ties to each Gospel, but this testimony is not without some controversy or inconsistency in other details at its earliest points. Papias is a significant early witness, because he was bishop of Hierapolis and his dates are early (c. A.D. 60–138). Eusebius regards him as one of the most important transmitters of tradition about the apostles.[6] Inconsistencies and obscurities in some details have made some scholars hesitant to draw much from church tradition at this point. At the least, difficulties here must be admitted.

Nevertheless, by the time of Augustine (fifth century; *De Consensu Evangelistarum* [also known as *The Harmony of the Gospels*] 1.1–4; 1.3.6; 1.4.7; 4.10.11), the order of Matthew, Mark, Luke, and John was fairly well received. In 1.4 Augustine writes, "Of the four, Matthew alone is said to have written in the Hebrew language, the others in Greek, and although each of them seems to have retained his own particular literary sequence of writing, nevertheless each of them is found not to have desired to write in ignorance of his predecessor, nor to have omitted what the other is found to have written except by deliberate purpose; but each has added without any superfluity the cooperation of his own work, according to the manner in which he was inspired."[7] Augustine appears here to affirm both inspiration and a recognition that the Gospel writers (at least some of them) may have been aware of some of the others' work. What is omitted is done so deliberately, while what is added

6. This discussion in particular and that of this entire section has been informed by Bernard Orchard and Harold Riley, *The Order of the Synoptics: Why Three Synoptic Gospels?* (Macon, Ga.: Mercer University Press, 1987), 111–221, where the early church evidence through Augustine is cited and discussed. Orchard prefers to see Papias referring to Hebrew style here, but this is a difficult reading to sustain. The uncertainty surrounding Papias also raises questions about how much stock can be put in an argument based on his testimony on Matthew in support of a case for independence, as Robert Thomas and F. David Farnell attempt to do in *The Jesus Crisis* (Grand Rapids: Kregel, 1998), 39–46. If one assumes that Papias is right, then to argue with Papias that Matthew's Hebrew version of the Gospel is the first of the four Gospels is not to have established the timing of the release of the later Greek version used in the Bible. Thomas and Farnell's discussion appears to equate the two, but how do we know the timing between the versions? On the other hand, if Papias is wrong or means something else, like a sayings collection, then his evidence cannot be used for the point Thomas and Farnell try to make.

7. I cite Orchard's translation in *Order of the Synoptics*, 212–13.

is done so without undue superfluity.[8] Here is a major figure of the early church trying to deal with one of the most complex aspects of the Gospels that emerge from the four texts, namely, the combination of similarity and difference among them.

The Rise of the "Synoptic Problem" and the Data

Here is where things stayed until greater attention came to be paid to issues of detailed wording and order of the texts. Also, there arose more consideration of the contents of the various Gospels in terms of omissions and additions. It was this move to consider the internal evidence of the text itself that reopened the discussion of the Synoptic order in the eighteenth and nineteenth centuries. This study became known as the "Synoptic problem" and asks how one accounts for the combination of agreement and diversity in Matthew, Mark, and Luke.[9] The attempt to solve this problem became known as source criticism because the goal was to determine what sources the evangelists had worked with as they produced their Gospels and in what order they worked. The hope of source criticism is that an understanding of the sources an evangelist used will help to explain what he chose to emphasize in his own presentation. To some degree, this can be done whether or not one can definitively answer the question of sources, because we can always compare the texts we have to one another. Even if we are not sure of the Gospels' sequence historically or are uncertain if an evangelist had another Gospel while composing his text, we can still compare the Gospels. Even this kind of comparative criticism can be of value in showing how the Gospels complement one another. If the order is known, however, then one can say even more about what took place.

A look at data will help to explain the Gospels' interrelationship. Two tools enable us to see these internal relationships more clearly. One is a chart of the paragraph relationships among the Gospels. Here a dia-

8. This point is made contra Thomas and Farnell's claim (*Jesus Crisis*, 62–72) that Augustine does not hold to any form of literary dependence. Their interpretation of this text misreads the force of "superfluity" in this context as meaning that to have copied would have been to have added superfluously to the record. Yet the mere fact that the inspired record does repeat the same events, even if done so independently, shows that this is not an argument to be made because mere repetition of key events is not seen to be superfluous at all. Augustine's point is that what is included does not merely result in meaningless repetition.

9. A good discussion of this question in all of its aspects is in Guthrie, *New Testament Introduction*, 136–208.

gram of Synoptic relationships is helpful.[10] Second is a synopsis, which lays parallel or conceptually similar passages next to each other in columns so that the wording can be compared line by line. Many synopses have been published, and there is always discussion about how they are laid out, especially concerning which Gospel (Mark or Matthew) serves as its structural base. Kurt Aland's two synopses, one Greek only and the other a Greek-English diglot, are the most common ones used today.[11] Each one places Mark in the middle but also is laid out in canonical order as one moves on the page from left to right. These tools or ones like them show quickly exactly how the Gospels compare to one another. Discussions about the sources and order of the Gospels attempt to work internally, with the evidence coming from these texts themselves.

Here are some of the raw data. Luke is the longest Gospel, containing about 1,149 verses.[12] Matthew is next at 1,068 verses. Mark is the smallest at 661 verses. The numbers that come next are estimates, because some parts can be variously assessed. Nonetheless, most scholars working with the material think that the following numbers state the situation well. Eighty percent of Mark's verses show up in Matthew to some degree, while 65 percent of them are also in Luke.[13] Allan Barr states the numbers this way: Matthew has 609 of 662 Marcan verses, which is closer to 90 percent. Luke, however, has 357 of Mark's verses and another 95 that may be reflected there. This is well over half of Mark. Barr also notes that the material from Mark that appears in Matthew and Luke is condensed. The 609 Marcan verses that show up in Matthew are represented by 523 verses there, and the 357 Marcan verses in Luke make up 325 of Luke's verses. Only 30 verses of Mark lack a parallel in Matthew or Luke.[14]

---

10. For example, see Allan Barr, *A Diagram of Synoptic Relationships* (Edinburgh: Clark, 1938).

11. The Greek version is *Synopsis Quattuor Evangeliorum*, 13th ed. (Stuttgart: Deutsche Bibelgesellschaft, 1985). It works with the Nestle-Aland 26th edition of the Greek text. This version also includes citations from the fathers about the passages, making it valuable to those who can work with Greek. The diglot version is *Synopsis of the Four Gospels*, 2d ed. (Stuttgart: United Bible Societies, 1975). It contains the RSV.

12. The verse numbers for a Gospel might vary a verse or two in a few locations, depending on some text-critical decisions about whether to include or exclude a verse (e.g., Matt. 23:14; Mark 9:46).

13. For these figures, see Raymond E. Brown, *An Introduction to the New Testament* (New York: Doubleday, 1997), 111–12. See also Frans Neirynck, "Synoptic Problem," in *The New Jerome Biblical Commentary*, ed. Raymond E. Brown et al. (Englewood Cliffs, N.J.: Prentice-Hall, 1990), 587–95.

14. *Diagram*, 1–7.

Number of Verses in Mark, Matthew, and Luke

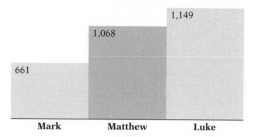

		1,149
	1,068	
661		
Mark	Matthew	Luke

Number of Marcan Verses Paralleling Matthew and Luke

Parallel to Matthew

662 Total Verses
609
Parallels

Parallel to Luke

662 Total Verses
357 Close Parallels
95 More-Distant Parallels

Note: Of Mark's 662 verses, 609 verses parallel Matthew, and 452 verses either parallel Luke or correspond more distantly with Luke. Numbers for this chart come from Allan Barr, *A Diagram of Synoptic Relationships* (Edinburgh: Clark, 1938), 3–5. Barr's reliance on an older edition of the Greek New Testament explains his use of 662 as the total number of verses in Mark, rather than the 661 of current reckoning.

Number of Matthean and Lucan Verses Containing Marcan Material

Matthew

1,068 Total Verses
523 With Marcan Material

Luke

1,149 Total Verses
325 With Marcan Material

Note: Marcan material is found in 523 of Matthew's 1,068 verses and in 325 of Luke's 1,149 verses. Numbers for this chart come from Allan Barr, *A Diagram of Synoptic Relationships* (Edinburgh: Clark, 1938), 3–5.

Word counts also exist. These can be found in a book by Robert Stein,[15] who gets them from Joseph B. Tyson and Thomas R. W. Longstaff.[16] Their numbers are quite high: 97.2 percent of Mark's words have a parallel in Matthew, and 88.4 percent have a parallel in Luke. Those who reject literary dependence question these numbers and supply their own.[17] In other words, a substantial portion of Mark is found in Matthew and Luke. The estimates run from 92 to 96 percent, as various portions of Mark show up in each Gospel. This is one reason many believe there is some literary relationship among the Gospels and that Mark is either first or last in the sequence. About 45 percent of that Marcan total is in both Matthew and Luke.

Second, about 250 verses are said to be shared between Matthew and Luke. Some of these might be challenged as genuine duplicates.[18]

15. *Studying the Synoptic Gospels: Origin and Interpretation*, 2d ed. (Grand Rapids: Baker Academic, 2001), 50–52.

16. *Synoptic Abstract*, Computer Bible 15 (Wooster, Ohio: College of Wooster, 1978), 169–71.

17. See Thomas Edgar, "Source Criticism: The Two-Source Theory," in *Jesus Crisis*, 132–57; and Linnemann, *Is There a Synoptic Problem?* Edgar cites the differences among synopses (and there are differences in how they break up the material) to suggest that they are severely biased. He produces his own statistics. His low-end numbers are important to consider. Thirty-eight percent of Mark agrees with Matthew in form and sequence, a test that goes beyond mere wording. The average agreement in word length is 2.43 words, and Matthew-Mark agreements occur at 1,887 places. Of these, only thirty-eight examples involve ten words or more. This statistic does not note where clusters of agreements reside that are broken only by an incidental word or two. Nor does it treat cases where the same words may be present but in a different syntactical order. Both of these features appear frequently in this common material. For Edgar, Matthew and Mark share 68 percent of the same subject matter, while Luke and Mark share 41 percent. When agreement is tested for exactness, it is 17 percent of the total for Matthew and Mark and 8 percent for Mark and Luke. He acknowledges that even on a strict estimate, 20 percent of pericopes have enough agreement to be possible evidence for dependence. Linnemann argues that in terms of words, 53.51 percent of Mark is not paralleled in Matthew and 63.83 percent is not in Luke. The thing to note is that even the most modest estimates represent significant percentages of the total work. Linnemann's work is a valuable treatment of the dangers of criticism and their origin in skepticism, though her argument seems to be overdrawn in terms of the conclusion that she believes the textual evidence requires. My reasons for this assessment follow below.

18. Edgar ("Source Criticism," 148) argues that eighty-four units of John C. Hawkins's classic defense of these texts (*Horae Synopticae* [Oxford: Clarendon, 1909]), often called "Q," can be reduced to seven. However, a consideration of placement of these texts and their substantial conceptual-lexical overlap shows this to be excessive. Some have reduced the number of verses to two hundred or so for this list. Brown (*Introduction*, 111) speaks of 220 to 235 verses and conveniently charts them on pp. 118–19 so one can see the progression of their sequence and lack of sequence, as the chart lists the passages by Lucan order. See also table 6 in Stein (*Studying the Synoptic Gospels*, 114–15), who looks at twenty-three passage clusters. Barr (*Diagram*, 5) states that 171 of Matthew's verses "closely parallel" with 151 of Luke's, while another 90 "more distantly" correspond to 94 of Luke's. This estimate is the high end. For more about Q, see my "Questions about Q," in *Rethinking the Synoptic Problem*, ed. David Alan Black and David R. Beck (Grand Rapids: Baker Academic, 2001), 41–64.

Still this overlap of material is significant. It means, most likely, that Matthew and Luke worked with each other or they worked with similar material. Matthew has 29 percent unique material, while Luke has 50 percent unique material. Much of the parabolic material and other teachings of Jesus are unique to Luke, while 28 percent of Matthew is in both Mark and Luke, 26 percent of Luke is in both Matthew and Mark, and 47 percent of Mark is in only Matthew.

These overlaps by themselves would prove little. However, the combination of overlap, sequence, and wording is key here, alongside the changes in sequence that exist. They show that at many different points the Gospel writers took the same events and sequenced them differently. The difference was usually for some kind of thematic or topical reason (cf. Mark 2:1–3:6 and how Luke 5:11–6:11 keeps the events together as Mark has them, while Matthew scatters them in Matthew 8–12 among a variety of other events). It is the combination of mixing and matching that produced discussion about the "problem," which is not a problem about the texts but a historical problem of how this situation came to be.

Four Proposed Solutions

These kinds of factors led to consideration of what might explain the phenomena in the text. Four solutions have dominated recent discussion.[19]

1. Some argue for *independence*. They attribute the results to the randomness associated with inspiration about events that were a historical given, so that agreements simply reflect history. In the nineteenth century, well-known scholars such as Westcott and Alford preferred this view.[20] Linnemann has been its most vigorous defender today. Reicke's entire study (*Roots*) has also argued for a more prominent role for this approach.

19. Bo Reicke (*The Roots of the Synoptic Gospels* [Philadelphia: Fortress, 1986], 1–23) summarizes the history of Synoptic criticism in the nineteenth and twentieth centuries. He divides solutions into four types: the utilization hypothesis (literary solutions), proto-Gospel theories (usually either a Hebrew Matthew or an early version of Mark [*Ur-Markus*] standing at the base of the gospel tradition and supplying its basic order of events), the tradition hypothesis (oral tradition/independence), and multiple-source theories. The four I discuss are the tradition view and three variations of the utilization approach, because they are the most prominent options today, although all four classes of explanations Reicke notes are still defended.

20. Henry Alford, *The Greek Testament*, vol. 1, *The Four Gospels* (London: Rivington's, 1863), 2–6; B. F. Westcott, *An Introduction to the Study of the Gospels* (London: Macmillan, 1895).

However, pervasive similarities among the passages seem to be too great to be attributed merely to mutual eyewitness reminiscence, common oral tradition, coincidental agreement of diverse traditions, or a shared use of an *Ur*-Gospel (now lost) in Aramaic or Hebrew. It is here that issues tied to wording and clusters of syntactical order are important. Not only is the event recalled but the details of wording and setting are such that it does not look like something people independently telling the same story would happen to hit upon together (cf. Matt. 3:7–10 = Luke 3:7–9; Matt. 14:3–4 = Mark 6:17–18; Matt. 11:2–19 = Luke 7:18–35; Matt. 9:14–17 = Mark 2:18–22 = Luke 5:33–39; Matt. 11:20–24 = Luke 10:12–15; Matt. 11:25–27 = Luke 10:21–22). In addition, it is quite likely that the teachings of Jesus have been translated from one language into another. All of this agreement after translation makes the likelihood great that what is at work are evangelists sharing the same sources at various points.

2. The *Augustinian hypothesis* argues for what is now the canonical order of *Matthew, Mark, and Luke*, with dependence also coming in that order. It has the weight of the support of church tradition behind it. B. C. Butler and John Wenham are among modern advocates of the view.[21] The major problem, already noted above, is that Mark has a position that makes him appear to be first or last in the sequence. Of all the Gospels, he is either the most used or has incorporated into his work the least amount of independent material. His position as the middle element is harder to correlate to these data.

The choice between the next two options is harder, for each approach has strengths and weaknesses.

3. The *two-Gospel hypothesis* argues that the order of composition is *Matthew, Luke, and then Mark*. Its origins go back to J. J. Griesbach (1745–1812), who set forth his case in 1783, although Henry Owen made a case for it as early as 1764.[22] As discussion of Mark as the first written Gospel was also surfacing, Griesbach argued that Matthew's Gospel, if it came from an apostle, would not have used a Gospel by a nonapostle like Mark. Of course, this ignores the connection of Mark to Peter. Griesbach was not entirely clear about how he saw the relationship between Matthew and Luke. Among modern adherents, the most

21. B. C. Butler, *The Originality of St. Matthew* (Cambridge: Cambridge University Press, 1951); John Wenham, *Redating Matthew, Mark, and Luke: A Fresh Assault on the Synoptic Problem* (London: Hodder & Stoughton, 1991).
22. Johann Jakob Griesbach, *Commentatio qua Marci Evangelium totum e Matthaei et Lucae Commentariis Decerptum esse Monstratur* (Jena, 1787–90) is his most detailed presentation. Henry Owen, *Observations on the Four Gospels* (London, 1764). The bibliographic data for these early works comes from William Farmer, *The Synoptic Problem: A Critical Analysis* (New York: Macmillan, 1964), 7 n. 8.

published work comes from William Farmer, Bernard Orchard, and those who have worked with Farmer to restate the case for this view. Recent adherents posit that Luke used Matthew.

The Griesbach hypothesis can draw on the support of church tradition that Matthew was the first Gospel, and it can claim that there is no need for a "hypothesized" source like Q. (The Q source will be a key element of the next option.) It also can point to places where Matthew and Luke agree with one another against Mark (about five hundred such locations). Thus this approach espouses literary dependence and yet has the simplest source structure of the options, while acknowledging an appropriate placement of Mark as either first or last.[23] In other words, Griesbachians acknowledge that if they are wrong and Matthew was not the first Gospel written, then Mark was the first Gospel written.

But the Griesbach approach also shows weaknesses in its ability to explain internal features that show how the Gospels are related to one another. A major problem is justifying Mark as the last Gospel. One has to explain why Mark as a summarizing Gospel lacks certain things Matthew and Luke possess, passages such as an infancy section and either version of the Sermon on the Mount/Plain. One also has to explain how it is that Mark as the summarizing Gospel is more detailed in those units he does include that overlap with Matthew and Luke. Perhaps more important are the 220 to 235 verses where both Luke and Matthew overlap. Mark lacks this material. How could so much shared material in Mark's base sources be missing? Finally, in the tradition shared by all three (the triple tradition), it is the Marcan version that often raises more questions than Matthew or Luke, giving the feel that ambiguities in Mark have been smoothed out in Matthew and Luke, rather than introduced by Mark into his Matthean and Lucan source material.

4. *Marcan priority* is the most common view today and comes in two subforms: one that includes Q (called the *four-source view*) and one that rejects the presence of Q material (called the *Farrer hypothesis*). Its most frequent expression is the four-source view, which is currently the most widely received among students of the Gospels. The four-source view consists of two closely related claims: Mark is the first Gospel, and Matthew and Luke did not use each other but share a common source for the verses where they overlap. This source

23. Farmer, *Synoptic Problem*; Bernard Orchard and Harold Riley, *The Order of the Synoptics: Why Three Synoptic Gospels?* (Macon, Ga.: Mercer University Press, 1987); David J. Neville, *Arguments from Order in Synoptic Source Criticism: A History and Critique*, New Gospel Studies 7 (Macon, Ga.: Mercer University Press, 1994); Allen J. McNicol, David L. Dungan, and David B. Peabody, eds., *Beyond the Q Impasse—Luke's Use of Matthew: A Demonstration by the Research Team of the International Institute for Gospel Studies* (Valley Forge, Pa.: Trinity Press International, 1996).

has been called Q, which has traditionally been taken to stand for *Quelle*, the German word for "source," although the actual history of this abbreviation is not clear. However, not all those who hold to Marcan priority agree that Q existed; one variation, known as the Farrer hypothesis, accounts for the overlap between Matthew and Luke by saying that Luke used Matthew.[24]

Contents of Q by Topic

Topic	Luke	Matthew
John the Baptist and Jesus	3:7–9	3:7–10
	3:16–17	3:11–12
	4:1–13	4:1–11
	6:20–49	5:3–12, 38–47; 7:12; 5:48; 7:1–2; 15:13–14; 10:24–25; 7:3–5, 15–20; 12:33–35; 7:21–27
	7:1–10	8:5–13
	7:18–35	11:2–11; 21:28–32; 11:16–19
Jesus and His Disciples	9:57–62	8:18–22
	10:2–3	9:37–38; 10:16
	10:8–16	10:15; 11:20–24; 10:40
	10:21–24	11:25–27; 13:16–17
	*11:1–4	6:7–13
	11:9–13	7:7–11
Jesus and His Opponents	11:14–26	12:22–30; *9:32–34; 12:43–45
	11:27–28	no parallel
	11:29–36	12:38–42; 5:15; 6:22–23
	11:42–52	23:23, 6–7, 27, 4, 29, 31, 34–36, 13
	12:2–3	10:26–27

24. The origin of the sigla Q appears to go back to Johannes Weiss in 1890 (see Christopher M. Tuckett, *Q and the History of Early Christianity* [Edinburgh: Clark, 1996], 1 n. 1), although credit is often given to P. Wernle in 1899. Tuckett's book is probably the best recent treatment of themes of Q. See also David Catchpole, *The Quest for Q* (Edinburgh: Clark, 1993), which goes through Q passage by passage and is an attempt to present and assess its contents; and Dale Allison Jr., *The Jesus Tradition in Q* (Harrisburg: Trinity Press International, 1997). The classic study on Q is found in T. W. Manson, *The Sayings of Jesus* (1937; reprint, London: SCM, 1957). Some hold to Mark being the first Gospel without embracing the existence of Q and argue that Luke used Matthew. The Farrer hypothesis was defended by Austin Farrer in "On Dispensing with Q," in *Studies in the Gospels: Essays in Memory of R. H. Lightfoot*, ed. D. E. Nineham (Oxford: Oxford University Press, 1955), 55–86. It is an important minority position within Marcan priority. Those who find the evidence for Marcan priority compelling but see too many problems with the Q hypothesis end up here.

Topic	Luke	Matthew
	12:4–12	10:28–31, 32–33; 12:32
	12:22–34	6:25–33, 19, 21
The Future	12:35–59	25:1–13; 24:43–51; 10:34–36; *16:2–3; 5:25–26
	13:18–21	13:31–33
	13:22–30	7:13–14; 25:10–12; 7:22–23; 8:11–12; *20:16
	13:34–35	23:37–39
	14:15–24	22:1–10
	14:25–27	10:37–38
	14:34–35	5:13
	16:13	6:24
	16:16–18	11:12–13; 5:18, 31–32
	17:22–37	24:26–27, 37–39; 10:39; 24:40–41, 28
	*19:11–27	25:14–30
	*22:24–30	19:27–29
Other	14:1–6	12:11–12
	14:7–12	23:6–12
	17:1–2	18:6–7
	17:3–4	18:15–17, 21–22
	17:5–6	19:19–20
	18:14	23:6–12

*Added by Kloppenborg

Note: The data is adapted from T. W. Manson, *The Sayings of Jesus* (London: SCM, 1959). For a complete list of possible Q texts, some of which are incorporated here, see John S. Kloppenborg, *Q Parallels: Synopsis, Critical Notes, and Concordance* (Sonoma, Calif.: Polebridge, 1988), xxxi–xxxiii. Some texts' presence in Q is disputed. For more on Q, see Robert H. Stein, *Studying the Synoptic Gospels: Origin and Interpretation*, 2d ed. (Grand Rapids: Baker Academic, 2001), 97–123. Stein also offers charts of the proposed contents of Q and a discussion of order (114–17, tables 6–8).

Within the four-source view, the other two sources consist of material unique to Matthew (M) and to Luke (L). Thus the four sources are Mark, Q, M, and L. The classic statement of this full view is B. H. Streeter's *The Four Gospels.*[25]

The roots of this view go back to Gottlob Christian Storr (1746–1805), who was "primarily concerned as a biblical supernaturalist

25. Streeter, *The Four Gospels: A Study of Origins* (London: Macmillan, 1924).

with demonstrating the truth of the New Testament documents."[26]
He expressed a preference for Mark as the first Gospel by arguing
that it was hard to explain why Mark omitted what he did from
Matthew and Luke if he were last. Others, like Gotthold Lessing,
argued for Mark but also posited earlier sources behind the canonical tradition such as a proto-Gospel produced by the Jewish Christian Nazarenes. Thus the case for Marcan priority was argued either working from the evangelist himself or by appealing to an
earlier base Gospel. Another major early figure was Karl Lachmann (1793–1851), who argued in 1835 that the order of the triple
tradition (i.e., when Matthew, Mark, and Luke are parallel) had a
pattern. Matthew and Luke follow each other substantially faithfully in the triple tradition, but in the nontriple tradition, they do
not. In addition, Matthew and Luke never agree in order against
Mark, whereas Matthew and Mark sometimes agree in order
against Luke, just as Luke and Mark sometimes do against Matthew. Thus he argued that Mark was closer to any *Ur*-Gospel than
Matthew or Luke. It is important to note, although many do not
make the distinction, that Lachmann did not argue that Mark was
the first Gospel. Rather Mark reflected an earlier tradition that was
written first, and thus his order of events is the one rooted in the
earliest tradition. This observation did not prove Marcan priority,
but it did limit the options, so that *if* one could show that Matthew
and Luke did not use each other and that Matthew was not written
first, then the case for the priority of the Marcan tradition became
most likely.[27]

26. This description comes from Werner Georg Kümmel, *The New Testament: The
History of the Investigation of Its Problems*, trans. S. McLean Gilmour and Howard C. Kee
(Nashville: Abingdon, 1972), 75. There is a question whether Storr was totally committed
to supernaturalism, as he dismissed the infancy accounts, though he did seek to preserve
scriptural authority as a rationalist; see Hajo Uden Meijboom, *A History and Critique of
the Origin of the Marcan Hypothesis, 1835–1866: A Contemporary Report Rediscovered*,
trans. and ed. John J. Kiwiet, New Gospel Studies 8 (Macon, Ga.; Mercer University
Press, 1993), xvii, 16–17. The importance of Storr's background is that not everyone who
engaged in early criticism was working with totally antisupernaturalist suppositions.

27. Stein, *Studying the Synoptic Gospels*, 74–76. For a summary of seven reasons ad-
duced for this view, see 94–96. Blomberg (*Jesus and the Gospels*, 87–90) lists nine
strengths of this view: Mark's vividness, Mark's rougher grammar and style, the presence
of embarrassing details about the disciples or problematic details that other evangelists
lack, his shortness in total length yet generally greatest detail in the units, the fact that
so much of Mark is in Matthew and Luke, Mark's tendency to be the point of agreement
with the other Gospels, the highest incidence of Aramaic words, lack of explanation (if
written last) for omissions from Matthew and Luke, and finally a claim that the theological patterns of the differences are more readily explained when Mark is placed first.

This leads to the evidence for Luke and Matthew not using each other, despite agreeing in about 220 to 235 verses. Several issues arise here. (1) There is a complete lack of overlap in the infancy accounts and significant differences (primarily omissions) in key discourse material (like the Sermon on the Mount/Plain). (2) A significant number of Matthean additions to the triple tradition do not show up in Luke. Either Luke chose to omit all of this material, or he did not know it. (3) There are numerous cases where the shared material between Matthew and Luke possess distinct contexts. Why would this be if they knew one another? (4) On order, Matthew and Luke never agree against Mark. How can this be if they knew one another? It is these internal factors that lead to the view that agreement of 220 to 235 verses (about 20 percent of each Gospel's content) and a lack of knowledge of one another suggests that a shared tradition did exist between the two.

The origin of this Q discussion dates back to Christian Hermann Weisse (1801–66) in 1838, who spoke of a shared sayings source, as this material is almost exclusively Jesus' sayings. His views had roots in remarks made about Papias's citation in Friedrich Schleiermacher (1768–1834, writing in 1832) and Lachmann (writing in 1835).[28] Other key names in the development of the view are G. Ewald (1848) and H. J. Holtzmann (1863) in Germany, and John Hawkins (1899) and B. H. Streeter (1924) in England. Holtzmann called the source L, for *logia*, an allusion to the nature of the source and the remarks of Papias. Primary arguments are grounded not just in the amount of overlapping material but this material's wording and order.[29] Note that within this material, however, there is enough verbal and order variation that the positing of either a single, fixed written source or the attempt to argue about how Q was put together is too speculative to prove compelling.[30]

This four-source view is not without problems. A major difficulty is Luke's so-called Great Omission; he lacks any use of Mark 6:45–8:26. Proponents claim that these passages contain "doublet" events, which Luke chose to omit rather than repeat. Not all of this material reflects a doublet, however, so this cannot be a comprehensive explanation. Second, there are more than five hundred minor agreements between Matthew and Luke, which are said to be too many for Marcan priority. However, these agreements represent only about 6 percent of the total

---

28. For a work critical of the development of this hypothesis and especially the work of Weisse, see Hans-Herbert Stoldt, *History and Criticism of the Marcan Hypothesis*, trans. and ed. Donald L. Niewyk (Macon, Ga.: Mercer University Press, 1980). It is a translation of a work done in Germany in 1977.

29. Stein, *Studying the Synoptic Gospels*, 112–19.

30. This discussion is the focus of my "Questions about Q."

number of agreements between the gospels (a decidedly minority phenomenon). Third, does the date of Mark in the early to late 60s give enough time for it to be used by Matthew and Luke if they are before A.D. 70, the date of Jerusalem's destruction and a key demarcation in the dating of the Gospels? Those who hold that Matthew and Luke are later are not concerned about this problem, but if Luke is also in the 60s, as seems likely, one must admit that the compositions fall quite close to one another. Next to this must be placed the possibility that Matthew also was written before Luke, further narrowing the chronological separation between each of the three Gospels.

Finally, there is the evidence of the church fathers that Matthew was first. The problem here is that this detail looks to be rooted in a claim of a Hebrew version of Matthew, as the Papias citation showed. However, canonical Matthew is in Greek. What is the relation between the two, if the tradition is correct? How much time passed between the writing of the two, and does that affect the discussion about the canonical Gospels? If the tradition has confused the Hebrew and Greek Gospel, can we rely at all on the tradition? This situation does raise some question about the trustworthiness of this detail or what conclusions can be drawn from it. In addition, it is possible that the explanation may have had an apologetic motive, given that out of Matthew, Mark, and Luke, only Matthew has a direct apostolic connection. Thus the fathers may have assumed that the directly apostolic Gospel came first among those that were so similar. All of this makes the testimony of the fathers more complicated to use as a key argument. At the least, the problem needs to be noted as making the evidence less than clear.

Conclusion

I have surveyed the history of the Synoptic discussion because it has been the source of much debate, including debate among conservatives. One has to admit that much of the case for Marcan (four-source or Farrer) rather than Matthean priority (Augustine, Griesbach) is circumstantial, yet there are also good reasons for holding to it based on strictly internal, textual considerations. These three literary dependence alternatives appear to be more likely than claims of independence.

However, one final point needs emphasizing. The choice among these alternatives is not a matter of orthodoxy. Efforts to suggest otherwise are misguided. The debate is about the solution that makes the best case as a historical matter, considering both the external evidence of church tradition and the internal evidence of the Gospels. Conservative students of the Gospels have held to each of these views without any desire to deny or challenge the inspiration of the text. This is important to note, because some suggest that those who argue for another view are bibliologically misguided.

The debate is not so simple. Even if one opts for the solution that some strongly claim is the "most orthodox," namely independence, one still has to explain the differences among the Gospels as they relate to the question of historical detail. These issues remain regardless of which view is taken, although those advocating independence often sound as if that is not the case. Whichever view is taken, care should be made to note that it is adopted as a *likely* scenario, rather than a certain one. What one can confidently do, regardless of which view is adopted, is carefully note the differences that do exist among the texts and work with those to help see how each Gospel proceeds in ways like and unlike its counterparts. Such merely "comparative criticism" can also be enlightening, even if one speaks with less certainty about what an evangelist added, altered, or omitted with reference to another Gospel.

chapter 8

Form Criticism

When I was a child, there was a special moment when the teacher said, "Once upon a time." I knew it was time to hear a fairy tale. I also could count on the last words bringing joy and something like, "And they lived happily ever after." Such is the nature of form. In a set format, stories or events are told in certain ways, with certain stylistic or programmatic indicators that let the reader know the type of account that is present.[1]

Form is another way to study literary subunits. Form can come in all kinds of shapes and sizes. It can be fictional or nonfictional. For the Gospels, a more complicated question is how the Jesus material was circulated in units and "passed on" as tradition that eventually became written. Since the first century was long before the printing press, telephone, radio, television, and the Internet, how did people tell about Jesus? Such concerns are part of form criticism, which has great value as a literary tool but is of lesser value in making historical judgments, as more-skeptical scholars are prone to use it.[2]

About Ancient Form

Luke 1:2 states that the tradition of Jesus was "passed on" by "eyewitnesses and ministers of the Word" in its earliest stages. This detail serves to remind us that first-century culture was primarily oral, not written, as ours is. That the roots of the Jesus tradition begin with those who ministered with him is important because it indicates that those

1. Darrell L. Bock, "Form Criticism," in *Interpreting the New Testament: Essays on Methods and Issues,* ed. David Alan Black and David S. Dockery (Nashville: Broadman & Holman, 2001), 106.
2. For a more complete look at issues tied to form criticism, see Robert H. Stein, *Studying the Synoptic Gospels: Origin and Interpretation,* 2d ed. (Grand Rapids: Baker Academic, 2001), 173–233.

who reported and formed the earliest traditions of the teaching of Jesus experienced what they passed on.

Nonetheless, a study of the Gospels' internal wording suggests that these accounts tended to be passed on in certain discernible types with a certain structure or "form," which helped to make them memorable. One of the goals of form criticism is to identify and describe these forms and their literary characteristics.[3] The other goal of form criticism has been to assess the historicity of events on the basis of these forms. More will be said about this second goal later.

History of and Debate about the Method

This particular approach to Gospel study emerged in 1919–21 with the work of Karl Schmidt, Martin Dibelius, and Rudolf Bultmann.[4] Key was Bultmann's work *The History of the Synoptic Tradition*, in which he tried to classify the forms of all the Gospel material. He also began to engage in a type of tradition history of the given units to get at their historical development. He argued, probably correctly, that many of the portions in the Jesus tradition were passed on orally in small units—as individual accounts of a miracle, as a pronouncement tied to an event, or as part of a collection of sayings. However, this more tradition-historical use of form criticism was problematic, as it was directed by the application of some suppositions about the development of the tradition and these small units, suppositions that were more assumed than demonstrated.

As a historical discipline, form criticism has for the most part assumed Marcan priority. Moreover, it has argued that the tradition was influenced more by a concern for the life setting (*Sitz im Leben*) of the community to which the tradition was directed than for the setting of the event in Jesus' life. This supposition divided the relationship between history and preaching far too much. Although we recognize that concerns for the audience being addressed did affect what was said to that audience about Jesus and that this explains some differences among the Gospels, it is not demonstrable that in showing concern for the community setting the tie to the historical Jesus was unimportant. Thus, in following this historical direction and emphasizing the community at the expense of the historical roots

3. I have addressed this discipline in much more detail in my "Form Criticism," 106–27.

4. K. L. Schmidt, *Der Rahmen der Geschichte Jesu* (1919; reprint, Darmstadt: Wissenschaftliche Buchgesellschaft, 1969); Martin Dibelius, *From Tradition to Gospel*, trans. Bertram Lee Woolf (New York: Scribner, 1965 printing of 1919 ed.); Rudolf Bultmann, *The History of the Synoptic Tradition*, trans. John Marsh (New York: Harper & Row, 1963 printing of 1921 ed.).

of the tradition, many form critics tried to make the method do more than it was capable of doing. Such criticism of the method came early on as the scholar most responsible for introducing the method to Britain, Vincent Taylor, complained about this misdirected use in *The Formation of the Gospel Tradition*.[5] As a historical matter, the evangelists were viewed as "collectors" of material from the tradition and the communities. Many of the original form critics saw the communities as making additions in such a way that allowed them to address issues Jesus never faced. In this way, these critics argued that teaching was placed into Jesus' mouth that had little or nothing to do with what he actually taught. It is a perspective and an approach like this that spills over into the claims made by the Jesus Seminar, whose members argue that at most only about 20 percent of the teachings attributed to Jesus go back to him.[6]

However, other studies have argued that the roots and method of Jewish tradition would have had a conserving effect on how texts were passed on orally. The work of Birger Gerhardsson, Harold Reisenfeld, Rainer Riesner, and E. Earle Ellis presents the proper context for considering how first-century oral tradition worked.[7]

5. Vincent Taylor, *The Formation of the Gospel Tradition: Eight Lectures* (London: Macmillan, 1933).

6. Robert W. Funk, Roy Hoover, and the Jesus Seminar, *The Five Gospels: The Search for the Authentic Words of Jesus* (New York: Macmillan, 1993), esp. 25–34. I have in mind, here, their red (Jesus said exactly this) and pink (Jesus said something close to this) categories. About another 30 percent represents sayings in the evangelists' words that might have roots in Jesus (gray). This means that almost 50 percent of the sayings have no connection to Jesus (black). The seminar used these colors to indicate the likelihood of a given saying going back to Jesus, as determined by the vote of committee members.

7. For brief summaries of these emphases, see Rainer Riesner, "Jesus as Preacher and Teacher," in *Jesus and the Oral Gospel Tradition*, ed. Henry Wansbrough, JSNTSup 64 (Sheffield: JSOT Press, 1991), 185–210; E. Earle Ellis, "Gospels Criticism: A Perspective on the State of the Art," in *The Gospel and the Gospels*, ed. Peter Stuhlmacher (Grand Rapids: Eerdmans, 1991), 26–52; and esp. idem, "New Directions in Form Criticism," in *Prophecy and Hermeneutic in Early Christianity: New Testament Essays* (Grand Rapids: Eerdmans, 1978), 237–53. Ellis notes important Jewish forms that show up throughout the New Testament, especially those related to arguing from Scripture, and suggests that these help us to appreciate just how grounded in a tradition-sensitive, accuracy-concerned method the early church was. The groundbreaking study by Gerhardsson was *Memory and Manuscript: Oral Tradition and Written Transmission in Rabbinic Judaism and Early Christianity* (Lund: Gleerup, 1961). For another study working in detail with Matthew, see Samuel Byrskog, *Jesus the Only Teacher: Didactic Authority and Transmission in Ancient Israel, Ancient Judaism, and the Matthean Community*, ConBNT 24 (Stockholm: Almqvist & Wiksell, 1994). This study shows how the teaching tradition tied to Jesus remained uniquely focused on his teaching and authority. Even where there is flexibility, it is rooted in a memory of Jesus' teaching. The study's rootedness in Jewish background makes it a better model than efforts to ground the tradition in later models of how oral cultures work. See especially his remarks on pp. 306, 307, 310, 319, 330, 364–65, 397, and 400.

In sum, form criticism has had limited value as a historical tool and has produced misleading results, especially when it has ignored the Jewish context of tradition transmission that Gerhardsson and others have noted. There is little way to verify its early founders' abstract claims for the tendencies of how the oral tradition developed. In fact, some studies examining those claims have shown that the so-called abstract principles of form transmission do not work.[8] When form critics attempt to strip away the secondary accretions in the tradition on the basis of their supposed later expansion and get back to the historical kernel, their work becomes suspect and speculative.

There is positive evidence for the credible roots of the Jesus tradition.[9] Higher-critical study of the Jesus tradition ignores the eyewitness base of that tradition and the importance of memorization in ancient culture. It is in the words of Jesus that the tradition is the most consistent. Variations that do exist do not alter the basic thrust of the teaching (more on this issue is presented in the next chapter). The preaching missions of the Twelve and the seventy-two produced a setting in the life of Jesus for forming a tradition about his teaching to those villages the disciples visited on his behalf. That many of Jesus' teachings do not address issues of major concern to the audiences of the evangelists shows that a lot of what they recorded was passed on in order simply to record Jesus' teaching. The preservation of the Son of Man title in Jesus' teaching, even when it was not used in the churches addressed by the Epistles, shows this tendency. The recording of details of the legal disputes with Jewish leaders, even when such issues of the law were not a matter of intense dispute in the Gentile-dominated communities, shows this tendency as well. Similar in this regard is the retention of difficult sayings material, such as Jesus' seeming claim in the Olivet discourse that he will return soon (Mark 13:26–30).

Although the oral tradition as it shows up in the Gospels reflects differences of wording and gives evidence of some fluidity, it does not require the supposition that sayings were placed wholesale into Jesus' teaching. Such a claim seems to work with the assumption that if only one Gospel writer reports a saying, he must be the source of that saying. This supposition denies the likelihood that the oral tradition was quite complex and that each evangelist would have had access to unique material. In sum, as a historical tool, form criticism cannot get

8. E. P. Sanders, *The Tendencies of the Synoptic Tradition* (Cambridge: Cambridge University Press, 1969).

9. See the discussion in Blomberg, *Jesus and the Gospels*, 84–86, as well as his *Historical Reliability of the Gospels* (Downers Grove, Ill.: InterVarsity, 1987).

us back to the "kernel" form of a saying or help us assess a saying's historical authenticity.

The Forms and Form as a Literary Tool

As a literary tool, however, form criticism can help us understand the material in the Gospels. Identifying the various kinds of material within the tradition, how they work, and what they emphasize can help us understand the teaching. This is the case even when some of the names given to these categories, like "legend" and "myth," begin to cross the literary-historical line and suggest that more than a form description of the unit is taking place. It is here that what is described for literary purposes needs to be distinguished from how we judge the historicity of the content.

A look at the types of forms can help us sense the benefits and limitations of form criticism as well as understand the names that form critics use. As I name these categories, it is important to recognize that mixed forms exist, so a passage may belong to more than one category. Five basic form categories exist, with most having subforms.

1. A common form is the *pronouncement story* (also known as *paradigm* or *apophthegm*). These accounts drive to a punch line, which is the saying that closes out the account. That saying can be a single idea or a combination of ideas, but the point of the account is found in a response by Jesus. Pronouncements come in various types. In a "scholastic" pronouncement, Jesus simply answers a question (Mark 10:17–22). In a "controversy" account, Jesus is challenged or a question is raised about his practice (five of these appear in a row in Mark 2:1–3:6). In a strictly "biographical" account, the point tells us something about what Jesus teaches (Luke 10:38–42).

2. *Miracle stories* have also been called in some sources "tales" or "novellas." Here the name crosses over into suggesting something non-historical. This is why Vincent Taylor rightly preferred the descriptive name "miracle story." They come in six types: exorcisms, healings, epiphanies (appearances like those in the resurrection accounts), rescue miracles (calming of the storm), gift miracles (where something is provided—like the catch of the fish that provides the temple tax), and rule miracles (that show Jesus' authority). In some cases, a text can operate in two of these categories, for the healing of the paralytic is both a healing and a rule miracle, showing Jesus' authority over sin. Most miracles proceed in a fourfold manner, with a description of the setting and problem, the approach to request or seek healing, the act of healing, and the reaction to it. A detailed example of this form is Mark 5:1–

20, where the initial verses describe the seriousness of the condition. In contrast to it is Luke 11:14–23, where all the miracle elements are in one verse, and the rest is the reaction. The distortion of the normal form points to the importance of the commentary about miracles offered in the reaction. It suggests that in this passage Jesus' miraculous ministry as a whole is explained.

3. *Sayings* also encompass a wide variety. They include short maxims (Matt. 12:34b), metaphors (Mark 4:21), parables (Luke 15:11–32), prophetic calls (Matt. 5:3–12), short commands (Matt. 18:10), and extended commands or full discourses (Luke 6:27–49). Apocalyptic predictions appear in the Olivet discourse (Mark 13:1–38). Admonitions are warnings that can appear independently (Matt. 11:20–24) or as part of a parable (Luke 12:42–46). Some are "legal sayings," which set forth a procedure (Matt. 6:14–15). "I sayings" are mission statements about why Jesus has come or what he is doing (Mark 2:17; Luke 4:43). Parables themselves also possess variety. An "example story" tells its point through an exemplary figure (the good Samaritan). A similitude makes a comparison, for example, comparing the kingdom to leaven. These are usually extremely short. A parable is a more complete story, containing various points, usually on the basis of how many characters are present.[10]

4. *Stories about Jesus* are also known as *legends*. For a second time, we can see a name that tends to cross the literary-historical line. The literary point of a legend, or, better, a story about Jesus, is that it is told to exalt the key figure. As a literary account, the story of Jesus as a twelve-year-old shows how wise Jesus is at a young age. It engenders admiration and respect for him.

5. The last category was first noted by one of the pioneers of form criticism, Martin Dibelius. He spoke of *myths,* by which he meant texts that refer explicitly to supernatural figures. Few texts fit this category, and again the name implies a worldview rejecting the reality described. The point of the name is to note, correctly from a literary point of view, the explicit presence of the supernatural. The baptism with the descent of the Spirit, the transfiguration, and the temptations are placed here. It would be better to think of these accounts as *supernatural encounter accounts.*

Just a survey of this list shows that knowing the categories helps one to observe distinctions among the types of units in the Gospels. I grant

---

10. Craig Blomberg (*Interpreting the Parables* [Downers Grove, Ill.: InterVarsity, 1991]) speaks of one-point, two-point, and three-point parables, which generally correspond to the number of central elements in the parable. This works as a good rule of thumb.

that these observations could be made without a study of forms, but the advantage of form criticism is that it leads one to ask the right kinds of questions about the kind of account present and its key elements.

To see how various evangelists work with form in groupings, one can compare Mark 2:1–3:6 with its parallels. Luke basically gives events in a similar sequence. Both present five controversies in a row, almost as if they were a topic of the unit. In both cases the opponents determine to stop Jesus as a result of five confrontations involving the forgiveness of sin, associations with tax collectors and sinners, fasting, and two Sabbath incidents involving "labor" and "healing." In contrast, these five accounts appear in Matthew 9:1–8; 9:9–13; 9:14–17; 12:1–8; and 12:9–14. Thus Matthew has in a broken-up sequence what the other Synoptics place together. He also has the opponents' reaction after the last miracle, but at a literary level the connection is not as tight as in the other Gospels. One evangelist or the pair of them have reordered the events for some reason. Another example of this is the sequence of four miracles in Luke 8:22–56, where the progression works from nature to demons to disease to death, as it does in Mark 4:35–5:43. Jesus' authority is comprehensively seen in this tight sequence. These events are more widely distributed in Matthew (8:23–27; 8:28–34; 9:18–26). Once again some type of choice about sequencing is evident in the differences, regardless of how one sees the order of the Gospels.

Conclusion

The study of form has a mixed history. As a literary tool, it can help us observe the basic structure of many units and offers keys for understanding a unit. However, form criticism has been pressed as a historical tool to make decisions about which traditions are original to Jesus and which are not. Rules made on the basis of form for historical questions have not proven reliable. On the other hand, form criticism can help us spot places where authors may have worked more thematically with the story of Jesus. Clearly, the different evangelists ordered their material differently and felt free to slightly alter the presentation of their content. This leads us naturally into the issue of the editorial work of the evangelists, what is also called redaction.

chapter 9

Redaction Criticism

Redaction criticism is concerned with the manner in which the respective evangelists and their communities edited the written traditions. It is assumed that much can be learned about the evangelists and their communities by carefully observing what traditions were retained, how they were supplemented, how they were reworded, and how they were recontextualized. The evangelists' literary work is assumed to provide important insights into their respective theologies.[1]

Another area of much controversy is redaction criticism, which studies in detail the alterations in wording between parallel Gospel accounts as well as the differences in structure in how each evangelist presents his Gospel.[2] These differences in wording extend down to the speech attributed to various figures reported in the Gospels. Thus this chapter considers not only redaction criticism in general but the debate over *ipsissima verba* (the very words) and the *ipsissima vox* (the very voice) of speakers in the Gospels, especially Jesus.

Origin and History

The differences of wording among the Gospels, plus the likelihood that later evangelists used earlier ones (Mark as the base ac-

---

1. Craig A. Evans, "Source, Form, and Redaction Criticism: The 'Traditional' Methods of Synoptic Interpretation," in *Approaches to New Testament Study*, ed. Stanley E. Porter and David Tombs, JSNTSup 120 (Sheffield: Sheffield Academic Press, 1995), 33.
2. For a more complete look at redaction criticism, see Robert H. Stein, *Studying the Synoptic Gospels: Origin and Interpretation*, 2d ed. (Grand Rapids: Baker Academic, 2001), 237–79.

cording to Marcan prioritists or Matthew according to Matthean prioritists), cause scholars to discuss the "redaction" or editorial work by the evangelists in presenting their work.[3] In contrast to form critics, who see the Gospel writers as collectors of tradition, redaction critics see each evangelist as a theologian in his own right, telling the story of Jesus to reaffirm points in the tradition and to make fresh theological points from it. They study carefully the changes Gospel writers make in presenting their own version of the accounts of Jesus. Redaction highlights the surfacing of these fresh perspectives. However, sometimes redaction critics make too much of a particular difference of wording in the text. Not every change of wording means the rejection of a former way of stating things. The difference may only supplement the older tradition or be an alternate way to state the matter.

Spotting these changes involves noting differences among the Gospels in the individual wording within units. Redaction also looks at the arrangements of the order of events and how that affects the Gospel's presentation and message. What is added, omitted, reworded, or rearranged are all noted with an attempt to explain what theological motives produced the changes. Attention is also given to key repeated terms and themes as well as how passages are linked to one another by "seams" (the narrative links that tie one passage to another or that introduce a passage). Redaction criticism assumes the results of source and form criticism in its work. Most redaction criticism is written from the perspective of Marcan priority, so that Matthew and Luke are seen to alter Mark.

The discipline emerged in the 1950s. One of the anomalies of the approach is that it began with work on Mark, which was viewed as the first Gospel by the man who coined the discipline's term, Willi Marxsen. He was the first to speak of *redaktionsgeschichte*, which translates into English as "history of redaction."[4] His work was the most speculative in form because as a Marcan prioritist he had to posit what tradition Mark worked with and how the evangelist changed it. This quest for absent sources proved speculative and their existence difficult to demonstrate. However, the principle he sought to establish, that the Gospel had a theological coherence

3. See Grant Osborne, "Redaction Criticism," in *Interpreting the New Testament: Essays on Methods and Issues*, ed. David Alan Black and David S. Dockery (Nashville: Broadman & Holman, 2001), 128–49; and Evans, "Source, Form and Redaction Criticism," 33–37.

4. *Mark the Evangelist: Studies on the Redaction History of the Gospel*, trans. James Boyce et al. (Nashville: Abingdon, 1969 translation of 1956 German work).

that could be examined through its details and arrangement, was a helpful methodological approach. This kind of study had been done, but not named, for Matthew and Luke, where potentially one could examine more concretely the source base, if one held that Mark was used by both. Marxsen's study of Mark had precursors in the work of others who claimed that the evangelists were theologians. William Wrede, writing in 1901, argued that Mark had created a "messianic secret" to explain how a nonmessianic ministry of Jesus (as Wrede alleged) came to yield a messianic confession in the church.[5] Wrede argued that Mark had creatively supplied this explanation; Wrede was willing, like many critics, to give the evangelists a creative role in formulating theology while understating the historicity of the tradition. R. H. Lightfoot also attempted to study the theological themes and emphases of Mark.[6] An evangelical, Ned B. Stonehouse, undertook such work as he considered the christological emphases within the Synoptics.[7]

Work on Matthew began in 1948 with Günther Bornkamm's examination of the stilling of the storm passage in Matthew 8:23–27, which differs in tone from its parallel in Mark 4:35–41. For example, Bornkamm argues that Matthew reinterpreted Mark to highlight discipleship. In doing so, Bornkamm also may attribute too much creative freedom to Matthew, but his point about Matthew's distinct emphasis on discipleship and a response of awe to Jesus' power as a basis of discipleship is well taken.[8] Bornkamm continued to write on other aspects of Matthean emphasis.[9]

Luke also became a point of focus of such study, generating a whole series of redactional examinations. Hans Conzelmann was the key fig-

5. *The Messianic Secret*, trans. J. C. G. Greig (Cambridge: Clarke, 1971 translation of 1901 German work). See discussion above in chapter 5.

6. *History and Interpretation in the Gospels* (New York: Harper, 1935).

7. *The Witness of the Synoptic Gospels* (1951; reprint, Grand Rapids: Baker, 1971).

8. My criticism of Bornkamm here addresses a general tendency among critics to pit Gospel perspectives against one another. In this adversarial approach, an evangelist writes to challenge or reject the earlier evangelist's portrayal. This "divide and conquer" approach is not the only or even most plausible option. Rather, one evangelist could write to supplement what another evangelist says by opening up fresh perspectives that the event raised. Significant historical events are often complex, so that different writers can credibly raise distinct points that emerge from the event. Mark highlights the disciples' struggle initially to trust Jesus, while Matthew focuses on the awe, worship, and later reflection on the event that the outcome also produced.

9. See Bornkamm, Gerhard Barth, and H. J. Held, *Tradition and Interpretation in Matthew*, trans. Percy Scott (Philadelphia: Westminster, 1963 translation of 1960 German work).

ure.[10] The value of such seminal studies was not so much the conclusions they drew but the methods they used, which showed a potential for fruitful textual observations. Thus fresh avenues of insight about the work of the individual evangelists opened up because appropriate questions were asked about the individuality and unique emphases of these Gospels. Luke in particular has benefited from this line of inquiry, coming into his own as an appreciated theologian of the early church. Previous to redactional studies, his work tended to get lost in the debate over whether Matthew or Mark was the earliest Gospel.

Assessment of Redaction Criticism

Redactional studies have a few key benefits. The first positive is the pursuit of the story and theology of each Gospel as a whole. It allows each Gospel to make its own presentation of the Jesus account. Second, it allows us to see concretely how the Gospels have been recontextualized. In some of these differences, historical teaching by Jesus is re-presented in a new setting with fresh points of emphasis. Studying how the Gospel writers worked with applying the teaching of Jesus can help us think through how we can apply the text today. It gives us a glimpse of how instruction about and from the life of Jesus took place, both in terms of its parts and its whole. These new emphases often make explicit issues that were implicit in Jesus' original teaching or else express the teaching in a way that is more intelligible to the new audience. Such reasons for the evangelists' making changes are appropriate to show the real force of Jesus' teaching. Examining the rationale for the change helps us better appreciate the evangelist's approach to a given saying.

Nonetheless, redactional criticism does possess weaknesses. First, to the extent that it depends on Marcan priority and the four-source view, it is vulnerable if another view of the Synoptic problem is actually correct. But the approach does not require a particular view of the Synoptic problem. Second, many redaction critics view each change as a skeptical statement on the work of the Gospel that is altered. They often

10. *The Theology of Saint Luke*, trans. Geoffrey Buswell (New York: Harper, 1960 translation of 1954 German work). The German title, *Die Mitte der Zeit* (The middle of time), is a better title for this work, because Conzelmann sought to stress how Luke (and also Acts) presents Jesus as at the center of God's salvation activity, belonging during his ministry to a period all his own. He also argues that Luke, because of the delay of the parousia, devised a salvation-historical way of looking at Jesus to cope with the delay. Though several aspects of Conzelmann's approach have subsequently been challenged and found wanting, the impetus of his study and the reactions to it have led to many profitable insights about Luke and Acts.

view the change as a creation of the evangelist. This is a presupposition rather than an established point. Fresh insights about events may well be based on additional information the evangelist has about the event or represent a credible interpretation of the implications of what Jesus taught. A solitary witness is not automatically a bad witness. Third, redaction critics tend to downplay efforts at harmonization by interpreters too much, rejecting it in principle. Fourth, some redactional analysis is microanalysis. Some alterations are not made for theological reasons but are merely stylistic. Fifth, sometimes, like form critics, redaction critics speculate too much on trying to find the community that has generated the theological emphases. Gospels were written for the church and not necessarily for just one community. Once again, historical conclusions are made from a tool that has only limited capabilities in answering such questions in detail because of the limited nature of the evidence it uses to examine this question.

In considering some examples of redaction, I have already noted the incident of the stilling of the storm, a text that is worth reading in Matthew and in Mark just for their different emphases. One could also point to the temptation accounts of Matthew 4 and Luke 4. They are presented in a distinct order; what Matthew has as the last temptation is second in Luke. Why is this so? A close look at the text shows that the more precise time markers are in Matthew and that Matthew has Satan explicitly dismissed at the end in a way Luke lacks. It seems likely, then, that Luke has shifted the order. He wishes to leave the temptation about the temple and Jerusalem at the end because of the importance that this theme has for him as he develops his account, which highlights a journey to Jerusalem (9:51–19:44) in a way the other Gospels only implicitly mention. Another example would be to compare the placement and sequence of events in Matthew 8–9 with their parallels in Mark 1, 4, 2, and 5 (note the divergence in order) or Luke 5, 7, 4, 9, 8, 5, and 8 (note also this divergence).[11] Here it appears that Matthew has done some topical grouping, as most of the events in his section are miracles. Matthew simply concentrates on this aspect of Jesus' ministry at this point of his Gospel.

The Issue of Differences in Wording in Parallel Sayings

Other redaction questions deal with specific wording, especially in the reported sayings of Gospel participants. These differences also

11. For a chart, check the index to any synopsis or Darrell Bock, "The Words of Jesus in the Gospels: Live, Jive, or Memorex?" in *Jesus under Fire*, ed. Michael J. Wilkins and J. P. Moreland (Grand Rapids: Zondervan, 1995), 84–85.

raise the question of how the words of Jesus are reported. Are they always exact, or does the gist of a saying suffice? This raises the issue of the "very words" (*ipsissima verba*) of speakers versus the report of the "very voice" (*ipsissima vox*) of participants—that is, whether the exact words or only the ideas are being conveyed. There is also the possibility that some dialogue is reported in summarizing or paraphrastic fashion.[12] Such reports need not compromise the integrity or historicity of an account if the intention of the evangelist is appreciated. It is to such examples I now briefly turn. Careful attention to such details in the wording of the Gospels can help us appreciate how the Gospels work.

Sorting out this kind of issue requires that we take a careful look at texts. Numerous examples could be noted. It is important to remember that Jesus is not the only speaker to whom the examples apply. When one sees the differences, one must try to explain them. The examples all involve discussions that appear to be at the same point in the dialogue. In other words, arguing that this is a separate event or the remark is something that happened twice is not as likely given the event's placement and the saying's locale in the unit. Some argue in such cases that it is better to combine all the accounts' dialogues, adding all the dialogue together, so that the historical sequence is more complex than any Gospel indicates and the *verba* in each end up being preserved. Though this may be possible in some cases, it seems cumbersome in others. It leaves an impression of the account that is not reflected in any individual account. In addition, for defendants of the "always *verba*" view to be correct, this must work every time, which seems less likely.

The voice from heaven in Matthew 3:17, Mark 1:11, and Luke 3:22 is a good example. In Mark and Luke, the divine voice says, "*You* are my Son, the beloved; with you I am well pleased." In Matthew, the voice says, "*This is* my Son, the beloved; with you I am well pleased." The difference is not great; in one utterance Jesus is directly addressed, while the other presentation looks more general. The issue of what exactly the voice said remains regardless of what one thinks about the order of the Gospels. The apocryphal *Gospel of the Ebionites* solves the problem by having the voice say both things. This harmonizes the problem, but it is not a particularly compelling solution for this example because the impression in each Gospel is that there was a single, climactic utterance, much like a pronouncement account. Another option is to suggest that Matthew took a direct address to Jesus and paraphrased it to highlight its historical significance, a historical significance the event did have. In other words, Matthew redacted the tradition to stress that

---

12. This question I have studied in greater detail in ibid., 73–99.

here was an event where God marked out and identified his anointed one as *this* one, by what he did. Both renderings are accurate historically and summarize what the content of the utterance was but with slightly different purposes. If this view of redaction is right, then Matthew gives us the *vox*, while Mark and Luke give us the *verba*.[13]

Numerous other examples of this type could be noted, such as Jesus' question and Peter's reply in the confession at Caesarea Philippi (Matt. 16:13, 16 = Mark 8:27, 29 = Luke 9:18, 20). Jesus' reply at his examination by the Jewish leadership is also similar, although some might question whether the Lucan scene is a separate morning trial (Matt. 26:63–64 = Mark 14:61–62; these texts may parallel Luke 22:67–70). At the least, Mark and Matthew report the same dialogue. The point to make is that each reply gives the same gist of what was said. Another example is the parable of the wicked tenants (Matt. 21:33–46 = Mark 12:1–12 = Luke 20:9–19), where differences exist between the details of who among the messengers was killed and when, but the thrust of the story remains the same. These small differences indicate that the way the texts record the details of events can have small differences in them without those differences affecting the general historical impression of the whole tradition. The parallels show that "precision" is not automatically a standard for citation. Sometimes we have the "voice" accurately summarized or interpreted rather than the "exact words" cited. A clear precedent for this type of "citation" can be seen in how the words of the Old Testament are cited in the New. The Hebrew text is often cited in the New Testament, not exactly in its Greek translation, but with slight alterations that paraphrase or explain. Such alterations also appear in the citations of the Greek Old Testament (LXX), which sometimes renders the texts with differing emphases from the Hebrew original.

Such differences among the sayings in the Gospels can often be explained redactionally. For example, Luke 22:69 lacks a reference to the Son of Man returning on the clouds, which is present in Matthew and Mark, because Luke's Gospel stresses the authority Jesus had as a result of exaltation. The point about exaltation could be made without having to mention the issue of a return to judge. Only a study of Luke's emphases throughout his Gospel would help one see why the detail is lacking here.

As the examples show, it is more likely that in some cases we have the "voice" of Jesus summarized rather than a precise quotation. Both types of citation are historical in that both types reflect his teaching.

13. Even if this particular suggestion is not right, then the other option could be to explain why both Mark and Luke (together or independently) made a change from Matthew. We would still be discussing redaction then, although the explanation would differ.

The Gospels themselves appear to give evidence of such variation, a variation also seen in how Scripture is cited within Scripture.

A Sample of Redactional Logic

One final example will show the logic of redactional analysis. The saying in Luke 11:20 = Matthew 12:28 is identical except at one point: "But if I cast out demons *by the Spirit* (Matthew)/*by the finger* (Luke) of God, then the kingdom of God has come upon/to you." The saying looks to be part of the same event, the debate with the leadership over the source of Jesus' power to heal and exorcise. In form, it is part of a passage where the normal miracle story has been turned upside down, as the exorcism takes one verse to tell in its entirety, while the reaction goes on for several verses. Most miracle accounts have the reverse proportion.

But how can one explain this difference? One important point is that Luke loves to discuss the Spirit throughout his Gospel. It is one of his major themes, showing up in numerous texts where the parallels lack such a reference or in passages unique to Luke (cf. Luke 4:14a = Mark 1:14a = Matt. 4:12; the emphasis on the Spirit in the final commission in Luke 24, a passage unique to Luke). Thus, if the original wording of the tradition had "the Spirit" in it, it is hard to explain why Luke would take it out. More likely, then (please note this is not stated with certainty), Luke had the original wording, "the finger of God," which itself alludes to the LXX language of Exodus 8:15 and the power of God during the exodus. Matthew chose to highlight the agent and power through whom Christ worked, making the reference to "the finger" less metaphorical, in the process showing the close connection between Jesus and the Spirit already inherent in the saying. Placing the texts side by side and considering them as a whole, a connection emerges between the presence of God's power and the work of the Spirit through Jesus, indicating the presence of kingdom authority. When we ask and look for redactional issues, such observations become possible.

Conclusion

Redactional study carried out exhaustively is tedious work, going term by term or phrase by phrase. More skeptical critics often make too much of these differences in wording. However, careful attention to such detailed differences frequently leads to greater insight into how a particular writer presented Jesus, as well as to complementary appreciation for what an event meant historically. Thus such study can pay dividends to the student of the Gospels when used with appropriate restraint. This kind of comparison between similar or parallel sayings has led to a consideration of tradition criticism or the study of a unit of tradition across its various uses. It is to this area of study that we now turn; here the discussion focuses on the criteria for authenticity.

chapter 10

Tradition Criticism

A final example that shall be mentioned with regard to the attempt to establish a general attitude towards the question of historicity and our Gospels is to evaluate the process by which the tradition was preserved and passed on. In this method, sometimes called Form Criticism and sometimes Tradition Criticism, various arguments are frequently raised in support of the substantive accuracy of the gospel accounts.[1]

The connection between tradition and historical assessment has been the major task of tradition criticism. Before discussing the criteria used in assessing authenticity, Robert Stein suggests that certain general factors speak for the general trustworthiness of the tradition: (1) the eyewitness base, (2) a center of leadership in Jerusalem that would have caused the traditions to be passed down carefully and accurately, (3) the high view of the New Testament toward these traditions (e.g., 1 Cor. 7:10, 12; 15:1–3), (4) the faithfulness in transmitting the sayings (within the variation noted in chapter 9 above), (5) the unlikelihood of the church creating sayings of Jesus out of nothing on topics that were no longer central to them, and (6) the fact that the ancient culture was more attuned to memory and tradition than our own. This list suggests a presumption in favor of the quality of the tradition as it appears in the New Testament.

The Criteria of Authenticity

One of the most controversial parts of critical study involves the criteria of authenticity associated with tradition criticism, which analyzes the

1. Robert Stein, "The 'Criteria' for Authenticity," in *Gospel Perspectives*, vol. 1, ed. R. T. France and David Wenham (Sheffield: JSOT Press, 1980), 226.

history of a given event or saying in its various uses.[2] Tradition history is the larger part of what redaction criticism considers and has often been linked to the criteria of historical assessment in form criticism. While redaction looks at individual changes, tradition history considers all of them and their sequence. Even nonconservative scholars have heavily debated whether these standards can claim all the authority that many have attached to them. Many critics use the criteria to substantiate whether Jesus said something the Gospels claim he said. The inherent premise, that such a thing needs to be proved, already involves an attitude that approaches the text with skepticism, which is unlikely in light of the six points made in introducing this chapter. Such skepticism is a significant feature of the work of the Jesus Seminar. For most of the seminar members, a text is inauthentic until proven authentic.[3] Knowing the criteria is important because many who approach the text in this skeptical way make extensive use of them. Others use them to try to make the case for or against the authenticity of certain texts and to engage critics in debate about the credibility of passages.[4] Still others argue that the criteria cannot absolutely determine the question but better serve as a type of general guide. This latter approach is a better way to proceed.

The three most prominent criteria we consider first. Then we look at other suggested criteria.[5]

Dissimilarity argues that a saying of Jesus that is unlike what Judaism would argue or is unlike what the early church would argue goes back to Jesus.[6] Such a criterion shows those places where Jesus' teaching is entirely unique. Yet it is decidedly minimalist. It supposes that

2. For this section see ibid., 225–63; Stewart C. Goetz and Craig Blomberg, "The Burden of Proof," *JSNT* 11 (1981): 39–63; Craig A. Evans, "Authenticity Criteria in Life of Jesus Research," *Christian Scholar's Review* 19 (1989): 6–31. For the internal discussion among critics, see Morna Hooker, "On Using the Wrong Tool," *Theology* 75 (1972): 570–81, which treats especially the criterion of dissimilarity; and Robin Barbour, *Tradition-Historical Criticism of the Gospels* (London: SPCK, 1972).

3. While discussing the work of the seminar, one of the major participants in the seminar told me that this was his approach.

4. It is important to clarify what the criteria are able to demonstrate. The three most prominent criteria can show only that Jesus said something very much like what is recorded. Criteria with a linguistic element, like one that looks for Aramaic roots (see below), try to substantiate the exact wording.

5. On this discussion, see Grant Osborne, "Redaction Criticism," in *New Testament Criticism and Interpretation*, ed. David Alan Black and David S. Dockery (Grand Rapids: Zondervan, 1991), 204–7.

6. The principle is most succinctly stated by Ernst Käsemann, "The Problem of the Historical Jesus," in *Essays on New Testament Themes*, trans. W. T. Montague, Studies in Biblical Theology 41 (Naperville, Ill.: Allenson, 1964), 37. In the section explaining the criterion, he discusses the phrase "but I say" (ἐγὼ δὲ λέγω), the Sabbath saying in Mark 2 ("the Sabbath was made for man"), and Mark 3:27 (= Matt. 12:29).

Jesus taught without relationship to his Jewish roots and without affecting his followers. Both are fallacious assumptions about any significant teacher in history, including Jesus.

Multiple attestation argues that a saying that appears in multiple strands of tradition (usually seen as Mk, Q, M, L) or in multiple forms (miracles, maxims, pronouncements, etc.) is likely to be authentic. The logic is that the more levels of tradition that attest an event, the more likely it reached the tradition early. For example, the idea that Jesus ministered to tax collectors and sinners is well attested at various levels of the tradition. But this criterion is often not consistently applied. The Son of Man sayings of Jesus should be substantiated on this basis, yet many critics reject them by breaking them up into subcategories: earthly ministry Son of Man sayings, suffering Son of Man sayings, and apocalyptic Son of Man sayings. By subdividing the sayings, the amount of multiple attestation drops within each category of saying, as each category has less distribution. This method for classifying the sayings may be artificial, given the fact that the Son of Man sayings consistently appear only from Jesus and not in comments by the evangelists. In principle, however, the criterion is a good one for what it can show.

The principle of *coherence* argues that whatever is consistent with what is already shown to be authentic also has a good claim to authenticity. This standard is really a secondary test, and it is only as good as the results the other criteria yield. For example, some might argue that because Jesus spoke of God as his Father, this coheres with him speaking of himself as Son of God.

Other criteria are less commonly used. Nevertheless, they can also be of some value. The criterion of *divergent patterns* argues that a story that is retained in the face of its difficulty is likely to be authentic. For example, texts that are embarrassing to the disciples because of their inadequate responses are more likely to go back to Jesus and are unlikely to have been created by the early church. Sometimes this criterion is called the criterion of *embarrassment*. Jesus saying he does not know the time of the return in Mark 13:32 is another example. The logic of this criterion is clear: the difficult text was preserved because it belonged in the tradition.

The criterion of *unintentional signs of history* argues that particularly vivid details of an eyewitness can demonstrate accurate knowledge of the environment of an event. This contributes to the credibility of a text.[7] This

---

7. A criterion like this one supports my claim that the examination scene of Jesus before the Jewish leadership in Mark 14 is culturally credible because of the Jewish expressions that appear there (e.g., "son of the blessed" and "right hand of power" in Mark 14:61–62). See my *Blasphemy and Exaltation in Judaism and the Final Examination of Jesus*, WUNT 2/106 (Tübingen: Mohr, 1998), 214–20.

might include details about the Palestinian practices as they surface in certain parables.

The criterion of *Aramaic linguistic features* argues that traces of Aramaic syntax or wording underlying a tradition point to the tradition's age and authenticity.[8] Sometimes translating the text from Greek back into Aramaic will reveal Semitic meter, word plays, or other evidence that points to a Semitic context. Two problems with the criterion are that (1) sometimes Septuagintal renderings could indicate such evidence (which would mean it may not have emerged from a Semitic setting), and (2) the presence of Aramaic only gets one back as far as the period of the earliest church, which also expressed itself in Aramaic. So the presence of Aramaic could indicate Jesus or a strand of the early church.

A recent criterion suggested by N. T. Wright is called *double similarity and double dissimilarity*.[9] He argues that texts have a solid claim to authenticity if they are similar to but distinct from Judaism in some respects and if they are similar to the early church in some respects but also distinct at other points. This is an attempt to take a more careful look at dissimilarity and remove its limitations. For example, the evidence for Jesus' messianic claims fits this category. Jesus' messianic claims have roots in Jewish expectation but differ in their emphasis on suffering. They parallel the messianic emphases of the early church only in a seminal form, in that Jesus does not declare this messianic role as openly as the early church did.

Assessment

This range of criteria indicates how people argue when they are attempting to show that a text goes back to Jesus and not merely claim that it does. For conservatives, such an exercise seems like an act that denies a text, but it can be a way to make a case for someone who doubts a text by attempting to give an evidentiary basis for an appeal to accept it.[10] One should remember that failure to meet the criteria does not establish

8. This work goes back to Gustav Dalman, *The Words of Jesus* (Edinburgh: Clark, 1902 translation of 1898 work). He issued a second German edition in 1930. Such work continued in Jeremias, *New Testament Theology* (New York: Scribner, 1971); and Matthew Black, *An Aramaic Approach to the Gospels and Acts*, 3d ed. (Oxford: Clarendon, 1967).

9. Wright, *Jesus and the Victory of God*, 131–33. Wright also correctly stresses that events are as important to understanding Jesus as what he taught.

10. Such argumentation helps someone wrestling through what evidence supports the historicity of a passage other than the presentation of a claim based on dogmatic theology. Such dogmatic claims may not be persuasive in themselves.

a text's inauthenticity, because the criteria cover only a limited amount of assessment factors. The problem with many critics' use of this material is that they claim to prove too much by these criteria. In other words, these criteria serve better as a supplemental argument for authenticity than as criteria that can establish authenticity. The reverse is also true. They are not absolute standards. As Grant Osborne argues, "Demonstrating the reliability of the material is an important step in itself, for it anchors interpreters in history and helps them realize they are not simply studying the ideas of Mark or Matthew (one danger of a redaction-critical approach) but the teachings of Jesus himself."[11]

Tradition history tends to focus on issues of authenticity and redaction. As such, it shares the strengths and weaknesses of redaction criticism noted above.

Conclusion

Source, form, redaction, and tradition criticism represent the methods many scholars use in approaching the Gospel texts. This survey has attempted to show the premises, strengths, and weaknesses of each approach as well as give some examples of how each approach works. Many technical commentaries on the Gospels, as well as studies on the life of Jesus, use these tools, although how they apply these methods is as much a function of each scholar's presuppositions as they are of the inherent method itself. The product of such approaches is rapidly becoming more evident in the public square as well, as recent works and television documentaries use such approaches.[12] Thus to understand how many scholars study the Gospels and why there is such diversity in their approach to the Gospels, it helps to know the methods and presuppositions that have been applied to Gospel studies as well as what those methods can and cannot do.

Such study has led to attempts to discuss the life of Jesus as he was in his original historical setting for his original Jewish audience. But the Gospels themselves are set out as narrative, a historical account with a developed story line. Thus we turn now to the last key method of study, narrative criticism.

11. "Redaction Criticism," in *New Testament Criticism and Interpretation*, ed. Black and Dockery, 207.
12. Note the numerous popular books by members of the Jesus Seminar, the 1998 PBS special titled *From Jesus to Christ*, and the Peter Jennings ABC special *The Search for Jesus* (2000) as attempts to present how the historical Jesus is seen in many religious study departments on university campuses. A response to Jennings has been produced on video by John Ankerberg, *The Search for Jesus Continues* (2001).

chapter 11

Narrative Criticism and Gospel Genre

Literary criticism focuses on the finished form of the text. The objective of literary-critical analysis is not to discover the process through which a text has come into being but to study the text that now exists. . . .

    Literary criticism emphasizes the unity of the text as a whole. Literary analysis does not dissect the text but discerns the connecting threads that hold it together. . . .

    Literary criticism views the text as an end in itself. The immediate goal of a literary study is to understand the narrative.[1]

This chapter considers those elements that go into reading each Gospel as its own narrative account. Here the study concentrates on the text as we have it and on the story as the author presents it. Even though these Gospels are historical works, the methods used to read narrative, whether fictive or nonfictive, apply. To underscore the kind of narrative we possess, the chapter ends with a consideration of the nature of the ancient genre to which the Gospels belong. Then a summary word wraps up this introduction to the study of Jesus.

Narrative Criticism

The study of the Gospels as narrative has come in for renewed attention, especially in the United States, since the late 1970s. Many turned

---

1. Mark Allen Powell, *What Is Narrative Criticism?* Guides to Biblical Scholarship (Minneapolis: Fortress, 1990), 7.

to it in a reaction against historical criticism, arguing that criticism had yielded little of substantive value. Others appreciate the contribution of the historical-critical approach but recognize that narrative criticism is an important supplement to historical study. Key contributors to the narrative approach include Jack Kingsbury, David Rhodes and Donald Michie, Robert Tannehill, Charles Talbert, Alan Culpepper, Joel Green, and Leland Ryken.[2]

The advantages of such a study are that it pays careful attention to each Gospel by insisting that its story be read on its own terms and in light of its own sequence without any outside influence. The limitations of restricting Gospel study to a literary approach is that studying a historical text without attention to its setting and background risks misreading the text, either through one's own cultural expectations or through ignoring important historical factors that contribute to the text.[3]

For this section, I treat the key definitions of technical terms and the elements of what literary critics look for in a narrative. Then I turn attention to the issue of the literary genre of the Gospels. Though the method described is often carried out with fictional material, the literary features of presenting an account apply to both historical and fictitious narrative, so there is value in seeing how authors present their accounts and what to look for in them.[4]

One of the things often lost in studying a Gospel is that it is a *narrative*, presenting a sequenced story. Sometimes we forget to read the Gospels this way because the individual episodes are so familiar to us or because we read them to answer other, often theologically moti-

2. Kingsbury, *Matthew as Story* (Philadelphia: Fortress, 1986); Rhodes and Michie, *Mark as Story* (Philadelphia: Fortress, 1982); Tannehill, *The Narrative Unity of Luke-Acts*, 2 vols. (Philadelphia and Minneapolis: Fortress, 1986, 1990); Talbert, *Reading Luke: A Literary and Theological Commentary on the Third Gospel* (New York: Crossroad, 1982); Culpepper, *Anatomy of the Fourth Gospel* (Philadelphia: Fortress, 1983); Green, *The Gospel of Luke*, NICNT (Grand Rapids: Eerdmans, 1997); Ryken, *How to Read the Bible as Literature* (Grand Rapids: Zondervan, 1984); and idem, *Words of Life: A Literary Introduction to the New Testament* (Grand Rapids: Baker, 1987). The series Literary Currents in Biblical Interpretation, edited by Danna Nolan Fewell and David Miller Gunn for Westminster/John Knox Press, is dedicated to publishing studies using this approach.

3. For an incisive critique in this regard, see Craig A. Evans's assessment of intertextual reading in "Source, Form, and Redaction Criticism," in *Approaches to New Testament Study*, ed. Stanley E. Porter and David Tombs, JSNTSup 120 (Sheffield: Sheffield Academic Press, 1995), 37–45.

4. The following section reflects observations discussed in more detail in Shlomith Rimmon-Kenan, *Narrative Fiction: Contemporary Poetics* (London: Routledge, 1983); Robert Funk, *The Poetics of Biblical Narrative* (Sonoma, Calif.: Polebridge, 1989); and Powell, *What Is Narrative Criticism?* Although the first work is on narrative fiction, the author, an associate professor of English in Israel, makes the point that the observations can apply to nonfictional narrative as well (3).

vated, questions. The evangelist, however, selected those events to present his version of the Jesus story. A narrative cannot and does not tell everything that occurred from every point of view. It is inherently selective, as John 21:25 tells us.

Events in a Gospel break down into story, text, and narration. The *story* designates the narrated events. The *text* is spoken or written discourse that tells the story. The *narration* is the entire complement of literary means used to tell the story. Although the author is responsible for the narration, he is not the same as the narrator, because a narrator can take a point of view in telling the story that need not match the character or perspective of the author. Some works speak of the *implied author* to designate the internal teller of the story. *Narrators* can be in the third person. If the narrator is a character within the account, then this is first-person narration. Narration can switch between events as well, reflecting a perspective told from inside the events or outside them. In the Gospels, there is usually little difference in theological perspective between the evangelist and the internal narration.

The story of events revolves around two types of issues: *time* and *causality*. Within the issue of narrative time and sequence is *plot*. Plot summarizes the movement of the story to a goal. That goal is often thwarted by an obstacle, a problem, or a set of challenges. The essence of the narrative is to resolve the tension between the goal and the obstacle(s). Plot can be evaluated at a paragraph level, in light of a whole section of material, or in light of an entire given work. Of course, in the Gospels, one of the major plot elements is the interplay between Jesus and his opponents as he attempts to proclaim the kingdom and bring people to response. Another key plot element is to explain how Jesus could be the chosen one when he was rejected and sent to his death.

Causality can be noted explicitly (as when the Jews plot to kill Jesus after he rebukes them in a series of controversies in Mark 2:1–3:6). But it is most commonly implied by the sequence of events. The juxtaposition of events can suggest a linkage. Causality can be determined as the story is revealed by explanatory connectives that tie units together, by the account's details that point to a connection, by narrative asides, or by reflection on the whole toward the end of the account.

Getting to causality often involves interaction with both the events in the text and the comments made about them. *Discourse* (narrative comment about or description of the events, as opposed to dialogue) often serves to reveal a state of mind about a point in the plot or deals with the proper response to a situation posed within the plot. These take the form of various kinds of narrative comments on the action. For example, the notes of joy expressed in the hymnic material in Luke 1–

2 move the plot along and raise the themes of joy, expectation, and fulfillment early on in Luke's account.

The analysis of events also involves distinct categories. Events can be considered as *actions* or *states*. Jesus' speaking and healing involve actions, but the lame man lying on a mat in need of healing is a state. The interplay between actions and states, along with the events that alter these circumstances, are important to plot development.

Events can also be broken down into *kernels* or *catalysts*, depending on how they relate the action. Kernels are events that open up alternative ways of action. Catalysts move the action along but not in the way that makes for a choice. Jesus' question, "Is it right to heal on the Sabbath?" is a kernel because it calls for a choice—to accept or reject Sabbath healing (Luke 6:9). The choice is raised within the narrative for the characters, but it also calls for a response by the reader to reflect on the choice called for from the characters. Thus kernel events have a way of drawing the reader into the narrative by forcing a reaction to or judgment about what is being presented. In contrast, Jesus' getting into a boat to teach by the sea is a catalyst—there is no choice called for by participants (Luke 5:1–3). In a paragraph, there are many microevents, some of which call for response (kernels), while others simply accompany the description of what happens and move the narrative forward (catalysts).

The presentation of time in a narrative is also of importance. Note that time in a story does not equal real time. Time can be *accelerated* (made to move quickly, e.g., in teaching summaries) or *decelerated* (slowed to tell an event in great detail, e.g., in many miracles, parables, and discourses). When deceleration occurs, the events take on greater importance. For example, when the compassion of the good Samaritan is developed with six verbal descriptions of how he helped the man by the road, the parable draws attention to the details of the Samaritan's compassionate care, highlighting each step of his example. An author can accelerate a story by *ellipsis*, leaving out information. All these details, whether included or excluded, affect the story's pace.

Time can be handled in a manner that juxtaposes two or more settings. The narrator or characters in the account can jump through time, either by *foreshadowing* an event, hinting at its later arrival or nature, or by outright *prediction*, which looks more explicitly to what will occur. For example, Simeon's remark in Luke 2:34–35 about the baby Jesus being sent for the rise and fall of many in Israel foreshadows that a major element of the narrative will be the choice Jesus forces upon those in the nation. Some will decide for him and others against him. The additional note about Jesus' work revealing the state of many hearts also makes clear whose side Luke is on as he tells that story. This implies that the reader should also consider what side he or she is on. The less explicit the nature of a reference to the future, the more drama and intrigue accompany the account, because it raises the question of what exactly is meant or how something will come to pass. If predictions are stated with enough vagueness, only their subsequent realization will fill in the additional explicit detail of how the prediction is fulfilled. Subsequent passages also might show whether the prediction contains a pattern (or typology) of events and what their real sequence is. Fitting in here is a complicated passage like the Olivet discourse with its fused reference to the destruction of the Jerusalem temple in A.D. 70 and to the end, whenever it comes (Matt. 24–25; Mark 13; Luke 21).

The presentation of time can go backward as well, in *flashback* and *retrospect*. An example of a flashback is the two men on the Emmaus road reviewing their discussion with Jesus in Luke 24. When this occurs, it points to a key event. Flashback highlights the importance of the event because it retells the event, usually from a fresh perspective, making it more than a mere review. Events can also occur *singularly* (one time but possibly descriptive of a kind of event—e.g., a Gospel may have only one account of a certain type of healing, yet Jesus probably performed more than one healing of that type, as the healing summaries make clear), *repetitively* (telling multiple times what happened once—like Paul's conversion, Acts 9:1–19; 22:1–21; 26:9–23), *iteratively* (telling one or more times what happened over and over—any summary of Jesus' teaching, such as meal scenes or the multiple Sabbath controversies in Luke), or *representatively* (a synagogue speech like Luke 4:16–30 as a sample of Jesus' preaching, or a cluster of similar events—the Sabbath controversies in Luke or the meal scenes happen so repetitively that it is clear they "represent" a key component of Jesus' regular ministry). In cases where events are retold, it is important to see how the various versions of the event are alike and unlike one another, because the author can develop his understanding of the event in those omissions, additions, or alterations. An author can also choose to group material together under topics, ignoring time sequence in the process by becoming *anthological* (the five controversies of Mark 2:1– 3:6; the cluster of miracles in Matt. 8–9).[5]

Characters are often a powerful means by which the story and its plot are carried forward. How often do you remember a character an actor played rather than anything about the actor as a person? Many

---

5. Such a move is not ahistorical; it simply presents the history with a different intention, to summarize by grouping like things together.

identify Charlton Heston with Moses as a result of his work in the movie *The Ten Commandments* or Harrison Ford as Han Solo because of his appearance in *Star Wars*. This illustrates the power of characterization. As with events, a text is selective in what it reveals about a given person in a story. *Round* characters are multidimensional and are developed so that their personalities have a depth of portrayal. *Flat* characters only serve as background with no development. Some round characters are described by the *functions* or *roles* they have: hero, villain, donor, helper, sought-for person, dispatcher, supporter, opponent, observer, or messenger. These are but a few of the possibilities. A simpler classification used by some literary critics is: sender, object, receiver, helper, opponent, or subject.

The nature of characters is determined by (1) how they are described or named by the narrator, (2) what they do, (3) what they contemplate doing, (4) how others in the story characterize them, (5) what they say and how they say it, (6) physical description, and (7) the environment or mood set by their presence (their social class, their geographical location, or their use of space). An example of the use of space to characterize is the Levite and priest "passing on the other side" in the parable of the good Samaritan. Similarly, Luke's description of the older brother at the end of the parable of the prodigal son ("outside" the party and choosing to be there, Luke 15:28) makes a literary point about where the brother's choices have left him. The scene creates a kernel choice for him and the reader when the father urges at the end of the account that accepting the prodigal was the correct move. What will the older brother do? What should I do? This text is open-ended, because the older brother's choice is never revealed. Its open ending adds to the need to contemplate what the reader thinks about the choice and judgment the father has made. A similar "literary" close is the ambiguous conclusion of Mark 16:8. Here the fearful women are silent on hearing of Jesus' resurrection. There is no announcement of an empty tomb. But Mark's point may well be: Jesus is raised; what will you the reader do with it when the claim confronts you? Characterization need not be constant; a good character in one scene can turn out to be bad in another. Peter fails badly at the denials during Jesus' trials but is heroic in the way he preaches Jesus and responds to the Sanhedrin in Acts 2–4.

In Scripture, characters are often intended to describe a representative type of person. In other words, the reader is to consider the kind of person portrayed and how the Scripture evaluates that character's thought or action. Determining the point of representation can often be a key bridge to application. For example, the women of Luke 8:1–3 show how one should materially support the ministry of the church.

The events in a narrative are told from certain points of view. *Focalization* denotes the perspective from which the story is presented. *External focalization* presents the story through the words of a third-person narrator outside the events. *Internal focalization* tells the story from within the events. Focalization can shift as the story is told.

Another way to look at narration is in terms of space or angle of the perspective taken. An *omniscient narrator* may be said to have a "bird's-eye" point of view, seeing events "from above" with a full understanding of what is taking place. This can also be called panoramic or simultaneous point of view, seeing all things at once. In one sense, the prologue to John takes on such a perspective, as the evangelist begins the story of Jesus with what was happening since the creation. That introduction frames the whole Gospel around the recognition that Jesus is the "Word become flesh." A *limited observer* is one who usually describes events from within the account and does not know everything that is happening. Perspective can also involve time. When the disciples struggle to understand Jesus' announcement of his coming death, the perspective is limited and internal. *Panchronic* narration understands events in terms of the past, present, and sometimes future. This approach usually appears at the start and end of stories. On the other hand, *synchronic* narration lives in the time frame of the event. Some narrators go to great detail to set the stage of a story, while others reveal very little, allowing the story to tell itself and its significance. Contrast how Matthew notes Old Testament fulfillment explicitly in Matthew 1–4, while Luke has citations in the characters' speech with little or no language of fulfillment in his own narrative comments. On this point, the two evangelists handle the details of how to present the Old Testament in opposite ways in terms of narrative style; yet it is crucial to appreciate that both writers are noting fulfillment by what they describe. For example, Peter's speech in Acts 2 does not use much fulfillment language after saying "this is that" about the Joel 2 citation. Nevertheless, predictions and descriptions about the Father's promise of the Spirit set up the speech, so that by the time we read about the outpouring of the Spirit, the event is seen as one that fulfills promise (Luke 3:15–17; 24:49; Acts 1:5; 2:16–18, 32–36; 11:15–18). Depending on the narrator or character, a speaker can be viewed as *reliable* (e.g., when Jesus speaks), *unreliable* (e.g., when Satan speaks), or *confused* (e.g., the disciples often in Mark).

Events can be presented in various ways. There is a key distinction (which can also apply to preaching) between *showing* and *telling*.

Showing simply presents directly the events and conversations in an event. It is like a dramatic sermon or narration in character. There is little or no commentary, just the sequence of events and dialogue. In telling, an event is mediated or described through an outside narrator, the way we often present narrative in the pulpit. For example, Luke shows scriptural fulfillment by presenting his characters as speaking in scriptural terms, while Matthew tells about fulfillment by actually citing texts as a narrator. Such description, when applied to dialogue, can run from summary of contents, to indirect discourse (language summarized in the mouth of the character), to direct discourse (citation of the character directly).

All of these observations and categories help us see what the narrative is doing and how the story is developing. They can make us more sensitive readers, giving us insight into what the story is and how it works. The concern for literary reading also makes us aware of another important distinction to which we must be sensitive. It is the difference between a literary presentation of an event within a particular Gospel and the historical assessment of what is presented in light of the fact that we have Synoptic versions of Jesus' life. The historical assessment must make connections or correlations between different Gospels that a literary reading ignores. Our study of Jesus' life can often move back and forth between literary and historical concerns.

For example, in Mark 1:16–20 and Matthew 4:18–22 is the calling of four disciples. Here is the point when Jesus asked the four to follow him and "fish for people." Luke does not record this event. Rather, he gives an account of a miraculous catch in Luke 5:4–11, where Jesus promised the four with him that they would "fish for people."[6] From a literary standpoint, this is Luke's calling of the disciples, equivalent in function to Mark and Matthew's other story. However, historically, given that all these events describe things Jesus did concerning his disciples, the Lucan event should be seen as a later confirmation of the call, made more dramatic by the repetition of the original commissioning phrase. The point is that the reader would not come to this judgment about sequence unless he or she was working with more than one account. It is this kind of harmonization that critics dislike, but there is a place for it when a sequence between events can be traced in the additional event(s) that one account gives alongside another Gospel. It is this type of synthesis in making judgments about the Gospels that

6. Some scholars reject the historical character of the Lucan version because it contains a miracle and because it has the same punch line as the Matthean-Marcan account. Assuming that this kind of saying had one setting at most in Jesus' life, they opt for the less dramatic version.

can make describing the historical significance of events complex and multilayered. This is because both the historical character of an account and its literary placement teach us about Jesus. Supplemental events that other Gospels discuss teach us even more about Jesus and the initial event when a connection can be made. This is also why the question of the historical Jesus involves more than simply recounting the contents of any single Gospel portrait and more than simply adding up the sum of the various accounts. In some cases, judgments have to be made about the sequence and relationship of accounts among the Gospels. One can say that this is *reading the text horizontally*, that is, across the various accounts. In contrast, when one stays within a given evangelist's account, one is *reading vertically*, that is, merely scrolling through the account in sequence.

The Gospel Genre in Its Ancient Setting

One final topic belongs under literary considerations. It is the issue of the genre of gospel. What specific type of literature is a gospel? How would an ancient reader have classified it? How should a modern reader approach it? For most of the nineteenth and twentieth centuries, it was popular to argue that the gospel genre was a creation of the early church and had no precedent.[7] Above all, a gospel could not be considered biographical. This important distinction seemed to move the Gospels one step farther away from being historically oriented documents. The charge was often made that they were too theological or biased in their approach to be historical. However, recent work has shown that the Gospels read much like ancient Greco-Roman biographies and that the issue of bias does not preclude a discussion of historicity.[8] The modern illustration has often been used of how Jews have sought to preserve the truth of the reality of the Holocaust, to prevent later generations from claiming that it did not take place. They certainly have a perspective they are trying to preserve and defend, but it

7. The best recent treatment of this genre question, including a history of the debate, is Richard Burridge, *What Are the Gospels?* (Cambridge: Cambridge University Press, 1992). An important collection of essays exploring the significance of this genre classification is Bauckham, ed., *The Gospels for All Christians* (Grand Rapids: Eerdmans, 1998).

8. Burridge's results are summarized for a popular audience in *Four Gospels, One Jesus?* (Grand Rapids: Eerdmans, 1994), 5–8. On the philosophical questions involved in such judgments, see Brice L. Martin, "Reflections on Historical Criticism and Self-Understanding," in *Self-Definition and Self-Discovery in Early Christianity: A Study in Changing Horizons—Essays in Appreciation of Ben F. Meyer from Former Students*, ed. David J. Hawkin and Tom Robinson (Lewiston, N.Y.: Edwin Mellen, 1990), 55–77.

is important to the credibility of how they wish history to be remembered that they do it carefully. A similar concern for truth is present in the Gospels.

When we encounter a gospel, we are reading a literary form that the ancient world recognized as biographical. To call the Gospels ancient biography is not to say they are like modern biographies. The Gospels lack the modern biography's tendency to psychologize the inward motivations of the figure, to describe his or her physical features, to relate the exact details of the chronological sequence of the subject's life, or to detail the personality. Ancient biography gives us the portrait of a key figure by examining key events of which he or she was a major part as well as giving us glimpses of the hero's thinking. They tend to present a fundamental chronological outline of key periods starting either with the birth or the arrival on the public scene. Some ancient biographies engage in flashback from the hero's death, although none of the Gospels does this. Deeds tend to come with some sense of order, but teachings can be grouped together with less concern for chronological details. Such biographies often concentrate on the controversies surrounding the key figure, especially the events that lead to a dramatic death, if that is part of the history. It is this kind of work that we read as we turn our attention to the Gospel accounts as they present to us, as history, the life of Jesus. The accounts are steeped in the promises of Scripture and are presented as important, even sacred accounts. This dual focus on the Scripture of the past and on the sacredness of the Jesus story itself is why my companion volume on the life and ministry of Jesus is called *Jesus according to Scripture.*

Conclusion

The careful study of Jesus includes two key elements that are represented in the Gospel texts. First, one must pay attention to the history that preceded Jesus and that fueled Jewish expectations. We have sources that give us a solid glimpse at this world, even though our sources are not exhaustive. This was the burden of the introduction and part 1. Second, we need to pay attention to how our Gospels came to us, how they are put together, and how they can be read with care. The various methods discussed in part 2 have had a controversial pedigree, often rooted in an intense skepticism about Scripture. Nonetheless, the questions the methods often raise help us to pay more careful attention to the text and to give the text an opportunity to present its case, provided those methods are applied with a worldview that does not excessively prejudge what God can and cannot do. This book comes to its completion with the hope that students have a better sense of what is going on in the reading of the Gospels today—and that there is certainly more than one way to read these texts, a way, perhaps, that is far less skeptical than one often hears about on university campuses, in religion courses, or in the media. There is much to be said for Jesus at a historical level as one studies the Gospels as ancient literary texts. The thrust of that unique story can be told with confidence that the Gospels are a solid source of information. Viewing the Gospels with respect and using these methods judiciously, as well as placing Jesus in his Jewish context, will enrich one's study of Jesus and the Gospels. The investment is worth the effort, for here is not only a story that has affected world history but a story that claims to reveal how God has acted on behalf of humanity. For those in search of a way in which humanity has been helped and can be engaged by God, it is a story worth reflection and embrace. Here is yet another reason to consider reading *Jesus according to Scripture.*

My survey of the methods scholars use to study the Gospels has sketched the variety of ways in which the Gospels are assessed. The history of Gospel studies is a checkered one, often revealing as much about the scholar doing the study as the text being studied. Much of this history is filled with skepticism about the Gospels, because presuppositions limiting God's activity dominated the approach. However, that is not the only way to approach the historical study of these texts. Nor does affirming divine activity in the life of Jesus and in the generation of the Gospel texts solve all our problems in determining and discussing what Jesus did and said and what he was about. Inspiration also does not mean that the study of the Gospels makes questions about historical development and relationship irrelevant to pursue. History is not one-dimensional, and determining how various trustworthy sources fit together is not always a straightforward exercise. History is a complex entity, even when one is working with good sources. For a figure as important and complex as Jesus, this is especially so. This is why I have discussed the ways in which we can benefit from the judicious use of these various methods.

We enter the study of the Gospel texts with a sense of confidence about what they can tell us about Jesus, while honestly facing the difficulties of what such a careful study poses at various points. It is important to understand the complexity of the judgments all of us make in these difficult, often hotly debated areas. But I think a case can be made for Scripture while working with these methods of study. A summation of my position echoes E. Earle Ellis:

> There are few if any historical or literary grounds to suppose that the Gospel traditions created events in Jesus' life or, indeed, that they mixed

to any great degree oracles from the exalted Jesus into the Gospel traditions. If a proper historical method is followed, proper presuppositions
observed and the practices of first-century Palestinian Judaism considered, the Gospels of the New Testament will be found to be a reliable presentation and faithful portrait of the teachings and acts of the pre-resur-
rection mission of Jesus.[9]

It is precisely because the sources are reliable that we can pursue the
question of the life of Jesus and think about Jesus according to Scripture. In doing so, however, we must face the fact that how these various
accounts should be woven together into a coherent whole is a complex
matter, even for those who respect the biblical text.

9. Ellis, "The Synoptic Gospels and History," in *Authenticating the Activities of Jesus,*
ed. Bruce D. Chilton and Craig A. Evans (Leiden: Brill, 1999), 57.

Selected Bibliography

The following bibliography is confined to key commentaries and general studies on Jesus. Important works on each of the critical methods and historical-cultural issues raised in the book are cited in full on first mention in the relevant chapters.

Matthew

Blomberg, Craig L. *Matthew*. New American Commentary. Nashville: Broadman, 1992.

Carson, D. A. "Matthew." In *The Expositor's Bible Commentary*, ed. Frank E. Gaebelein, vol. 8, pp. 1–599. Grand Rapids: Zondervan, 1984.

Davies, W. D., and Dale Allison. *Matthew*. International Critical Commentary. 3 vols. Edinburgh: Clark, 1988–97.

Hagner, Donald. *Matthew*. Word Biblical Commentary. Dallas: Word, 1993–95.

Keener, Craig. *A Commentary on the Gospel of Matthew*. Grand Rapids: Eerdmans, 1999.

Mark

Cranfield, C. E. B. *The Gospel according to St. Mark*. Cambridge Greek Testament Commentary. Cambridge: Cambridge University Press, 1959.

Evans, Craig A. *Mark 8:27–16:8*. Word Biblical Commentary. Dallas: Word, 2001.

France, R. T. *Commentary on Mark*. New International Greek Testament Commentary. Grand Rapids: Eerdmans, 2002.

Guelich, Robert. *Mark 1:1–8:26*. Word Biblical Commentary. Dallas: Word, 1989.

Gundry, Robert. *Mark: A Commentary on His Apology for the Cross*. Grand Rapids: Eerdmans, 1992.

Hooker, Morna D. *The Gospel according to Saint Mark*. Black's New Testament Commentaries. Peabody, Mass.: Hendrickson, 1991.

Lane, William. *The Gospel according to Mark*. New International Commentary on the New Testament. Grand Rapids: Eerdmans, 1973.

Marcus, Joel. *Mark 1–8*. Anchor Bible. New York: Doubleday, 2000.

Witherington, Ben, III. *The Gospel of Mark: A Socio-Rhetorical Commentary*. Grand Rapids: Eerdmans, 2001.

Luke

Bock, Darrell L. *Luke 1:1–24:53*. 2 vols. Baker Exegetical Commentary on the New Testament. Grand Rapids: Baker, 1994–96.

Fitzmyer, Joseph A. *The Gospel according to Luke*. 2 vols. Anchor Bible. Garden City, N.Y.: Doubleday, 1981–85.

Green, Joel B. *The Gospel of Luke*. New International Commentary on the New Testament. Grand Rapids: Eerdmans, 1997.

Marshall, I. Howard. *Commentary on Luke*. New International Greek Testament Commentary. Grand Rapids: Eerdmans, 1978.

Nolland, John. *Luke*. 3 vols. Word Biblical Commentary. Dallas: Word, 1989–93.

Stein, Robert H. *Luke*. New American Commentary. Nashville: Broadman and Holman, 1992.

John

Barrett, C. K. *The Gospel according to St. John*. 2d ed. London: SPCK, 1978.

Brown, Raymond E. *The Gospel according to John*. 2 vols. Anchor Bible. Garden City, N.Y.: Doubleday, 1966–70.

Carson, D. A. *The Gospel according to John*. Pillar New Testament Commentary. Grand Rapids: Eerdmans, 1991.

Morris, Leon. *The Gospel according to John*. Rev. ed. New International Commentary on the New Testament. Grand Rapids: Eerdmans, 1995.

Third-Quest General Studies and Articles on Jesus

Allison, Dale C. *Jesus of Nazareth: Millenarian Prophet.* Minneapolis: Fortress, 1998.

Blomberg, Craig. *Jesus and the Gospels.* Nashville: Broadman and Holman, 1997.

Bock, Darrell L. *Blasphemy and Exaltation in Judaism and the Jewish Examination of Jesus.* Wissenschaftliche Untersuchungen zum Neuen Testament 2/106. Tübingen: Mohr, 1998.

Bockmuehl, Marcus. *This Jesus: Martyr, Lord, Messiah.* Edinburgh: Clark, 1994.

Casey, P. M. *From Jewish Prophet to Gentile God: The Origins and Development of New Testament Christology.* Louisville: Westminster/John Knox, 1991.

Chilton, Bruce. *Rabbi Jesus: An Intimate Biography.* New York: Doubleday, 2000.

Dunn, James D. G. "Messianic Ideas and Their Influence on the Jesus of History." In *The Messiah,* ed. James Charlesworth, 365–81. Minneapolis: Augsburg Fortress, 1992.

Ellis, E. Earle. "New Directions in Form Criticism." In *Prophecy and Hermeneutic in Early Christianity,* 237–53. Tübingen: Mohr, 1978.

Evans, Craig A. *Jesus and His Contemporaries: Comparative Studies.* Leiden: Brill, 1995.

Fredriksen, Paula. *From Jesus to Christ: The Origins of the New Testament Images of Jesus.* New Haven: Yale University Press, 1988.

———. *Jesus of Nazareth, King of the Jews: A Jewish Life and the Emergence of Christianity.* New York: Knopf, 1999.

Hengel, Martin. *Studies in Early Christology.* Edinburgh: Clark, 1995.

Jonge, Marinus de. *Jesus, the Servant-Messiah.* New Haven: Yale University Press, 1991.

Kinman, Brent. "The A-triumphal Entry (Luke 19:28–48): Historical Backgrounds, Theological Motifs, and the Purpose of Luke." Th.D. diss., University of Cambridge, 1993.

McKnight, Scot. *A New Vision for Israel: The Teaching of Jesus in National Context.* Grand Rapids: Eerdmans, 1999.

Meier, John P. *A Marginal Jew: Rethinking the Historical Jesus.* 3 vols. New York: Doubleday, 1991–2001.

Osborne, Grant. *The Resurrection Narratives: A Redactional Study.* Grand Rapids: Baker, 1984.

Sanders, E. P. *Jesus and Judaism.* Philadelphia: Fortress, 1985.

Stein, Robert H. *The Method and Message of Jesus' Teachings.* Rev. ed. Louisville: Westminster/John Knox, 1994.

Stuhlmacher, Peter. *Jesus of Nazareth–Christ of Faith.* Peabody, Mass.:

Hendrickson, 1993.

Theissen, Gerd, and Annette Metz. *The Historical Jesus: A Comprehensive Guide*. Minneapolis: Fortress, 1998.

Vermes, Geza. *Jesus the Jew: A Historian's Reading of the Gospels*. 2d ed. New York: Macmillan, 1983.

Webb, Robert L. *John the Baptizer and Prophet: A Socio-Historical Study*. Sheffield: Sheffield Academic Press, 1991.

Witherington, Ben, III. *The Christology of Jesus*. Philadelphia: Fortress, 1990.

Wright, N. T. *Jesus and the Victory of God*. Minneapolis: Fortress, 1996.

Second-Quest Works

Although the preceding list is limited to third-quest volumes, two second-quest volumes should be noted.

Bornkamm, Günther. *Jesus of Nazareth*. New York: Harper and Row, 1960.

Crossan, John Dominic. *The Historical Jesus: The Life of a Mediterranean Jewish Peasant*. New York: HarperSanFrancisco, 1991.

Subject Index

Scripture Index

Darrell L. Bock (Ph.D., University of Aberdeen) is research professor of New Testament studies at Dallas Theological Seminary. In addition to many articles and scholarly monographs, he has written a two-volume commentary on the Gospel of Luke for the Baker Exegetical Commentary on the New Testament.